A VERY Special 90210 BOOK

93 ABSOLUTELY ESSENTIAL EPISODES FROM TV'S MOST NOTORIOUS ZIP CODE

TARA ARIANO & SARAH D. BUNTING
ILLUSTRATIONS BY JULIE KANE

ABRAMS IMAGE, NEW YORK

For Luke Perry

Editor: Samantha Weiner
Designer: Julie Kane
Production Manager: Rachael Marks

Library of Congress Control Number: 2020931297

ISBN: 978-1-4197-4746-5
eISBN: 978-1-64700-010-3

Printed and bound in China
10 9 8 7 6 5 4 3 2

Abrams Image books are available at special discounts when purchased in quantity for premiums and promotions as well as fundraising or educational use. Special editions can also be created to specification. For details, contact specialsales@abramsbooks.com or the address below.

Abrams Image® is a registered trademark of Harry N. Abrams, Inc.

195 Broadway
New York, NY 10007
ABRAMS   abramsbooks.com

Character Comi

Meet the Gang

BRANDON WALSH

The first character we meet in the pilot, Brandon (Jason Priestley) is the show's moral center. As a recent transplant from Minneapolis—according to the writing, the middle of nowhere, at least compared to Beverly Hills—Brandon is sometimes shocked by the social and sexual mores of his new city, but seldom does his self-esteem suffer. (Even a DUI only rattles him for about 15 minutes.) Sporty, confident, cute enough to get cast, briefly, on a show-within-a-show teen drama, Brandon's sports-editor aspirations and job at local diner the Peach Pit put him at the center of a lot of "issues plots." And by that, we mean he only has to have heard about an issue five minutes prior in order to feel empowered to bray about it self-righteously. Brandon may hope his rigidly gelled hair and sideburns make him look taller; they do not.

BRENDA WALSH

Brandon's twin sister, Brenda (Shannen Doherty), is (of course) also newly arrived in Beverly Hills from Minneapolis. Though both twins are anxious about fitting in with their bewilderingly glamorous new classmates—inasmuch as that's possible when such accessories as cellular phones and portable computers are definitely out of their financial reach—Brenda is more open in her attempts at social climbing, and more distressed by her mall-chain wardrobe and embarrassingly attentive parents. Brenda's innate talent for personal drama lends itself to an interest in the performing arts, and it's to her credit that she sticks with it despite the extremely real risk of getting shunned by her peers for being dorky enough to care about something. She's also supposed to be great at math? We're not sure we buy it.

KELLY TAYLOR

Kelly (Jennie Garth) is the quintessential L.A. girl, with all that implies: she's blonde; she's spoiled; she's jaded from living—in an '80s modern mansion with *lots* of glass bricks—through her mother's many divorces. Kelly's also *described* as being boy-crazy much more often than she's actually portrayed going on dates, never mind macking on anyone. Kelly *did* formerly date Steve, before the events of the series, for which reason their social interactions in the early seasons can be somewhat tense. Then again, Kelly starts out as West Beverly's reigning bitch queen; most of her social interactions tend to be unpleasant.

DYLAN MCKAY

If you felt like something was missing in the two-hour series premiere, you aren't alone: Dylan (Luke Perry) arrives in the second-aired episode . . . but then, randomly, is entirely absent from several others in the show's first season, presumably because they didn't air in the same order they were shot. Anyway: as the show's female lead, Brenda needed a love interest, and clearly neither David nor Steve was a believable prospect. "The Green Room," Dylan's debut episode, pretty much exists just to define him as a character—rich, cool, defender of nerdy freshmen—and even though his contact with Brenda is extremely minimal, we absolutely buy that someone with her romantic proclivities would find him irresistible.

ANDREA ZUCKERMAN

Not *every* student at West Beverly High School is a rich jerk! Andrea (Gabrielle Carteris), star student and editor of the *West Beverly Blaze*, actually lives in Van Nuys—the *Valley!!!*—and has registered using her grandmother's in-district address. This scandalous secret, which Brandon accidentally discovers in the series premiere, is what initially bonds the two of them; soon, though, most of their plotlines revolve around Andrea's unrequited crush on Brandon and the producers' inconsistent portrayal of how aware Brandon is of her feelings.

STEVE SANDERS

Steve (Ian Ziering) is Kelly's Los Angeleno counterpart in boy form: also blond, also spoiled. Steve one-ups her by having two showbiz professionals for parents—an actress mother and a producer father, both of whom we'll meet later on in the series run. Steve's function, particularly in the very early going, is to take the wrong position on an issue (cheating, racism) so that Brandon can be seen chafing against it and thus proving himself Steve's superior.

DONNA MARTIN

No character undergoes a bigger evolution from the series premiere than Donna (Tori Spelling). Initially, she's presented as Kelly's vapid shadow, who also enjoys such illicit activities as scamming on guys and throwing boozy parties when her parents are out of town, yet rarely gets more than ten lines of dialogue per episode. It takes until the first season's almost over for producers to give Donna a unique character trait: she has a learning disability! Her Catholicism and commitment to remain celibate until marriage come later still. (As it were.)

DAVID SILVER

In the early going, *Beverly Hills, 90210* thought it should devote some airtime to plots involving younger kids, and that's where freshman David Silver (Brian Austin Green) comes in. Desperately enamored of Kelly, he spends much of the first season trying to get close to her and the rest of The Gang. Sometimes David's striving is farcical, but other times it's downright creepy (spying on Brenda's slumber party) or cynical (using his grandparents for their Palm Springs real estate but treating them rudely in front of the cool kids). His DJ/musician/hip-hop dancer persona is still evolving, but the fondness for XXXXXXL shirts is, alas, there from the start.

Other Characters

SCOTT SCANLON

Every Bratman needs his Robin, and Scott Scanlon (Douglas Emerson) is David's. Scott is a guileless bully magnet, but while he's a supportive wingman for David's attempted incursions into the in-crowd, he's not nearly as interested in currying their favor or pretending he's something he's not. Scott's *presence* doesn't do much to distinguish him (uh . . . spoiler?); he's primarily a sounding board for David's social-climbing schemes.

CINDY & JIM WALSH

Cindy (Carol Potter), a stay-at-home mom who never really does make friends of her own outside of Anna the housekeeper, is a warm and supportive maternal presence—to other kids too. When less "traditional" family situations fall apart, there's always a spot at the Casa Walsh kitchen island, and a snack or casserole presided over by Cindy. Jim (James Eckhouse), the accountant whose job brought them to L.A. (and threatens to send them home again), is a hirsute, decent dad who likes keyboards and giant bathrobes. His attitude toward his daughter—or, really, her sex life—is a retrograde cliché, particularly compared to how Jim often seems to crave his son's approval and make allowances for his brattiness.

JACKIE TAYLOR

Kelly's mom, Jackie Taylor (Ann Gillespie), is an oft-divorced former model who initially presents as the "cool mom"—gossipy, into the kids' fashion, full of compliments for her daughter's friends. But after a breakup pushes her off the wagon, Jackie has a coked-up meltdown at a mother-daughter fashion show. Scared straight by how ashamed Kelly is of her (and how Cindy has to step in on the mothering front), Jackie goes to rehab. She comes out a genuine cool mom, though she never loses her taste for door-knocker earrings and garish Hermès-knockoff shirts, bless her.

MRS. YVONNE TEASLEY

Denise Dowse was originally cast in what would have been a one-off role—playing a college professor conducting a twin study in which Brandon and Brenda participate in "The 17 Year Itch"—but returned later in the first season as Yvonne Teasley, West Beverly's guidance counselor. One of a tiny handful of recurring characters who aren't white, Mrs. Teasley is warm and patient, always giving her privileged, ridiculous charges the benefit of the doubt despite their almost never deserving it.

NAT BUSSICHIO

After a brief stint at a tony restaurant specializing in delicious cumin, Brandon takes a job at a diner to the old-Hollywood stars, the Peach Pit. The owner, Nat Bussichio (Joe E. Tata), inherited the joint from his father, Sal, and makes a lot of Italian-dad jokes and references to Humphrey Bogart. The Pit is known for its pies, officially, and probably unofficially for Nat's tendency to minister to his adolescent customers' emotional travails with free food, so it becomes the *de facto* hangout for the gang. Nat comes to think of Brandon like a son, and over time becomes as maddeningly deferential to Brandon's blustery opinions as Brandon's actual father, while not insisting that Brandon wear an undershirt to serve food.

HENRY & ADELE SILVER

Due to exigencies of the plot, we meet David's paternal grandparents, Adele and Henry (Erica Yohn and Al Ruscio) well before either of his parents shows up: when spring break arrives, David attempts to move into The Gang by volunteering his grandparents' Palm Springs house as a party location. Since Kelly et al. are accustomed to getting what they want, they think nothing of this boon, and Henry and Adele are so happy to get to spend time with David that they eagerly play host—a little too eagerly for his taste, embarrassing him in front of the popular kids he's dying to impress. In the end, David learns a lesson about kindness, or not taking advantage of people, or something. The elder Silvers then remain offscreen for the next six seasons, until Henry dies (also offscreen), leaving David $250,000 and catalyzing a period of wild spending that coincides with a bipolar diagnosis.

And So It Begins:
The Series Premiere

We don't need to explain why the series premiere is here—but "Class of Beverly Hills" is also significant for the elements we *don't* recognize, the things that have been filtered from our memories after ten long seasons, from characters to sets to central premises that evolved or got discarded along the way.

But let's start with the original, deeply earnest logline that defined the premiere, and most of the first season: well-meaning teen twins from Minneapolis must find their way in Beverly Hills, a world very different from the one they've left. (And yes, *we* know Minneapolis is not the Mayberry the show usually makes it out to be.) We open on Brandon (Jason Priestley), then Brenda Walsh (Shannen Doherty) on their first day at the notoriously competitive West Beverly High, with Brandon and his pilot mullet expositioning about their situation while Brenda frantically tries to find something "music video" enough to wear (relatable!). Parents Jim (James Eckhouse) and Cindy (Carol Potter) locate us in L.A. with a gridlock reference, then remind us that, with two non-famous parents still married to each other and the non-luxury clunker they're obliged to drive to school, the Walsh twins have a struggle ahead of them to reconcile their family's staid traditional blah blah with this new sea of glitz glamor blah. It's a fish-out-of-water pitch, in other words, that let creator Darren Star and his writing team showcase mainstream values while giving viewers a peek into America's toniest Zip code.

From the jump, *Beverly Hills, 90210* is determined to cast the rich kids and their priorities as out of whack, but: "great" news! Brenda's in with the in crowd almost immediately—albeit accidentally, and only because Kelly Taylor (Jennie Garth) saves Brenda a seat to protect *herself* from nerd cooties. This is our intro to Kelly, recent rhinoplasty recipient, and she's *mostly* friendly and fun . . . for now. Kelly comes with a cat pack of fellow mean-ish girls, one of whom is Donna Martin (Tori Spelling), who has only a few lines but is still country miles from the saintly dumbbell we come to know later in the series.

Brandon's also making friends, ish: Steve Sanders (Ian Ziering) is already pretty much fully realized character-wise as a fratty bubelatty. Brandon's also trying to catch on as a sports writer for the *West Beverly Blaze*, but the single student in Spanish II who seems to have passed Spanish I, Andrea Zuckerman (Gabrielle Carteris), is the editor-in-chief. Andrea, also already completely herself in the pilot, gives Brandon her variation on the Bechdel test vis-à-vis writing assignments (he fails) and clenches up when he asks her for a date-night restaurant rec . . . but not for a date.

Our twin-tagonists learn, in the inaugural episode, that sexual politics among Angeleno adolescents is a fraught business, especially when you're pretending NOT to be an adolescent. That's the tack Brenda decides to take when, somehow allowed to go out clubbing with the Kelly clique, only *Brenda's* Kelly-doctored fake ID convinces the bouncer (Djimon Hounsou!) that she's of age. She finds herself alone and getting creeped on by lawyer Jason (*Grease 2*'s Maxwell Caulfield!). As obvious as her fugazi license should have been to security, it should be even *more* obvious to Jason that Brenda is a child. She is overly enthusiastic about Jason, who is 25; then very flinchy when he tries to shift gears from kissing—in front of his floor-to-ceiling bubble-wall . . . feature?—to taking their clothes off. Brenda's backstory about her entire sorority transferring from Minnesota State is punctuated with so many cringes and thinky faces, even Little Jason should know something's off.

But he doesn't, and the parts of Brenda's journey that don't involve Shannen Doherty mugging while drinking Ocean Spray "wine" do feel realistic, like when she, Kelly, and the Kelly-ettes hunker around a pay phone to listen to Jason's voice on his answering machine. Jason's harassive "c'mon, one drink, I'm a nice guy" and imperious "expect to spend the night" patter is off-putting to us *now*, but at least one of us would have put that aside for a guy who looked like Caulfield. (That one is Sarah. Don't get up, she'll fire herself.)

But this was 1990, when casual sex had lethal consequences, so Brenda decides to come clean, expecting that if Jason really loves her (oh, Bren), he won't mind that she's a lying high-school virgin. (We're paraphrasing.) Oops: Jason minds so much that a waiter wordlessly flees before he gets to hear the best line of the episode, Jason glowering at Brenda, "I should sue your parents . . . Yes." (He doesn't.) Brenda weeps in Cindy's arms and learns a Very Important Lesson about pretending to be something she's not.

Brandon has problems of his own. Stranded at the school year's first rager, he strikes up a conversation with a sexy stranger—who turns out to be the host, Marianne Moore (Leslie Bega). "Party girl" is Bev Niner code for "slut," and that's Marianne's "rep" at school, but she's mostly just lonely and bored. She takes a shine to Brandon, though, and throws herself at him in the hot tub on their first date, which prompts Brandon to wonder, hasn't anyone told her to play hard to get? It's an all-too-accurate depiction of high-school sexual politics at the time. Marianne is offended by Brandon's citation of them anyway, yay! . . . Because she thinks that means he isn't attracted to her, booooo.

After another date, Marianne sends Brandon roses in Spanish class. Brandon's classmates infer that Brandon is an icon in bed, and he's questioned during laps in P.E. class as to what exactly he did with Marianne. Brandon coyly says that what he and Marianne did, his classmates "couldn't handle." Based on the other dudes' scandalized reactions, that translates to "butt stuff," and this information winds up on the school's radio station . . . which has a "Wild Thang" report that consists of a list of *minor children who attend the school* who are Doing It with each other.

Anyway, when Marianne hears herself and Brandon on the "Wild Thang" report (. . . sigh), she's furious, but what puts a stop to this toxic slut-shaming is *Brandon*, who comes on the show to rescue Marianne's reputation (barf) and reinforce his own role as the show's moral center (double barf), using his patented baby voice of performative regret (barf hat trick!).

So, Brenda learns to be herself; Brandon learns . . . actually, probably nothing; and *we* learn that these crazy kids will probably be just fine if they can only hold on to those good ol' midwestern values . . . and their looks.

"I just don't believe in winning through intimidation. Unless, of course, I'm doing the intimidating."

Meet the Beverly Hills Bad Boy Whose Forehead, for a "Boy," Is Unusually Corrugated

SEASON 1 | EPISODE 2
THE GREEN ROOM

Producers, having figured out they were missing a guy to make Brenda horny, decided to introduce a whole new main character.

Brandon has stopped by his "Tech" class (what) when a couple of West Beverly toughs start menacing Scott Scanlon (Douglas Emerson). Brandon risks his non-existent social capital by impotently saying "Hey *hey* hey GUYS" in a voice slightly louder than his normal speaking bray. The bullies are rightly ignoring Brandon and threatening to delete Scott's work when suddenly, a figure speaks up that no one had noticed despite his perch between a buzzing Van de Graaff generator and a Jacob's ladder. (Who teaches this class, Victor Frankenstein?) This haunted loner in a white T-shirt and black mechanic's jacket is Dylan McKay (Luke Perry), who has so much charisma that he runs off Scott's antagonists by threatening physical violence, even though they both have several inches and about 50 pounds on him. This is the first episode since Brandon, our alleged hero, tried to social-climb by implying that he'd fucked Marianne, so it's refreshing that *this* crush object is so contemptuous of clichéd high-school behavior.

Alas, the writers are trying so hard to establish that Dylan is a different kind of boy from the ones we've met thus far that they end up making him the kind of pretentious goober most girls don't encounter until college, which is probably not what they were going for. He parks in front of a club to complain about how boring it is. He drives around with Byron's collected works on the passenger seat, declaiming, "'Mad, bad, and dangerous to know.' That was him, and that's me." He pretends to break into a hotel room to impress his surfer buddies rather than imperil his calculated "authenticity" by admitting that he's rich. Brandon haughtily refuses . . .

WHAT MEANS "Braying"?

Before anyone thought to get this book in front of your eyes, your coauthors were cohosts of a podcast, *Again With This*, in which we discuss each episode of *Beverly Hills, 90210* in granular detail and support our reactions by playing clips from the show. We hadn't gotten too far into the first season before we had to find the right word to describe the tone and quality of Brandon Walsh's speaking voice. All these years later, we still feel we nailed it: "braying."

Admittedly, it's harder to make this case in print. But if you've watched any episode of *Beverly Hills, 90210* in which Brandon appears, you probably know what we're talking about. Brandon is presented to us as the show's conscience: fighting for justice, sticking up for little guys, shaming the powerful into doing the right thing. Sometimes he does, and in those instances, it's appropriate for his voice not only to get much louder but also for it to take on a strident, sneering tone, and even for him to bare his teeth as he lectures, and rants, and probably spits.

It's not merely "yelling"; that doesn't capture how nasal he gets. "Bellowing" is close, in terms of volume and force, but doesn't adequately connote his attitude of superiority. "Roaring" is too powerful; "screaming" is too shrill. When we want to encompass all the nuances of how it sounds when Brandon is furious with, or appalled by, or even merely irritated at anyone—literally anyone, from near-total strangers to members of his own family—there is but one word that will do.

And that word is "braying."

(The fact that it's associated with jackasses doesn't hurt.)

lawfully acquired room service, but Brenda still has FOMO the next day because even she knows the legends: "I heard he got this girl in Paris pregnant."

There's also a teen message plot: one of Dylan's surfer friends is Sarah (Heather McAdam), whom he and his bros call "Betty," shortened from the dismissive "Surf Betty"; she drinks too much and lets the more boorish guys mock her because she has low self-esteem. (She's from the Valley.) She surfs drunk and gets rescued by Brandon and Brenda, and the word "hero" is bandied about, excessively. But Sarah's travails are less important than Dylan's: we leave him fruitlessly calling France to try to reach either of his parents. Note for the continuity-heads: the writers hadn't yet decided Dylan's parents, Jack (Josh Taylor) and Iris (Stephanie Beacham), were long divorced, because Dylan's side of the call makes it clear they're together on this trip.

Other than her heroics (ugh) on Sarah's behalf, Brenda is with the girls, desperately envious of Kelly and her sheaf of credit cards. They attend a beach party together where Kelly, cold because she's showing off the expensive bustier Brandon accurately says makes her look "like a reject from a Megadeth video," is a pill even before she and Donna ditch the Walsh kids. Anyone who was ever in high school knows: to abandon those depending on a ride from you is to break *a sacred trust*; not even Season 1 Kelly can help being chastened by Brenda's justified ice-out.

Brandon ties it all up with his first editorial for the *Blaze*, which he forces Brenda to read aloud, *to him*. Instead of writing on the topic Andrea had assigned— "From the Midwest to West Beverly: A Transfer Student Speaks"—it obliquely refers to the lessons he's learned from Sarah's near-death experience and Dylan's posturing; basically, looks can be deceiving, and anyone who's interested only in surfaces shouldn't bother trying to be his friend. "Brandon, it's beautiful," Brenda breathes. It's really not.

"You just won't know until you do it."

Crazy Sheryl Visits from Minneapolis and Relieves Brandon of His Virginity

SEASON 1 | EPISODE 4
THE FIRST TIME

Brandon's serious girlfriend from back in Minnesota, Sheryl (Paula Irvine), comes for a surprise visit.

They broke up before the Walshes moved, because Brandon "doesn't do" long-distance relationships, so presumably that's why he's never mentioned her even tangentially before, but whatever—after a lot of awkward STUFF when the family's around, Brandon entreats Sheryl to come to his room after everyone's fallen asleep. We endure a lot of whispery making-out and every possible angle on Jason Priestley's tongue, plus numerous cutaways to the master bedroom where Cindy is freaking shit that it's happening on her watch, and then Brandon and Sheryl Do It.

The next morning, Brandon's celebratory oo-bop-sha-bam music wakes up the household, and if his family didn't already suspect that he'd gotten it in the night before, the fact that he's freshly squeezed orange juice should confirm it. (Brenda steps over from her worthless B-plot to make the most of the rare punchline on this show that lands: "He even strained the pulp!")

Alas, Sheryl's more into the status-conscious, star-fuckish aspects of Beverly Hills—and specifically more into Dylan's sweet vintage car and parentless hotel living—than Brandon would like. After a mix-up at the door of a private nightclub, Brandon cock-walks in to find Sheryl and Dylan slow-dancing, a bad (by which we mean "weird/out of character") look for Dylan. (Ditto the reference Sheryl makes to herself and Dylan having had "a couple" of bright-blue cocktails; Dylan's in AA.) Paternalistic braying (at Sheryl) and fisticuffs (well, one, on Dylan's face) ensue, along with the revelation that, while Brandon lost *his* virginity the night before, Sheryl had already lost *hers* to someone else—information that causes Brandon's face to not just fall but collapse straight down on itself like a controlled demolition. Oh, and: it turns out Sheryl isn't "visiting." She's run away from home.

Why Sheryl would run toward an ex who guilt-trips her for making him "wait and wait" to have sex is explained, to a degree, when Sheryl says that the whole Walsh family made her feel safe and loved and let her escape a tumultuous home sitch. But that then raises questions as to what, exactly, Sheryl ran away *from*. The episode is rahhther elliptical on that point, referring to vague "problems" with her stepfather that, combined with her drinking and other acting out, have always suggested to us that the "problem" was Stepdad touching her. Brandon's response to Sheryl's issues is to brood in a single streetlight beam in his room about how it affects *him*, and sigh, "The only thing I really want to say right now is goodbye." Make a note, teenage girls: guys don't like chicks with problems!

It's definitely for the best that, for once, *Beverly Hills, 90210* avoids taking a stand on an issue it's nowhere near qualified to comment on, opting to send Sheryl back to Minneapolis—but not before obliging her to announce within ear-shot of Brenda that Brandon is "a wonderful lover." Duly fluffed, Brandon toddles outside to play basketball with Jim, who is ickily proud that his boy is now a voting citizen in these Bone-ited States. (To whichever writer had Jim ask if Sheryl caught her flight on time with the line "Sheryl get off okay?": no.)

Sheryl? We never see her again. It's also the last we see of the allegedly "gorgeous" algebra teacher (he isn't) who has Bren and the other girls swooning until his wife's henpecking deflates their lady boners.

However, Brandon's weird blocking with his jeans pockets is here to stay.

"You rich white boys, you get the world handed to you, no strings attached, and you honestly think that's how it is for everyone."

Brandon Gets in a Black Kid's Face for Being a Ringer

SEASON 1 | EPISODE 5
ONE ON ONE

Let's leave aside the fact that Brandon is about a foot too short to have a shot (as it were) at making the varsity basketball team. . . . Wait, actually, let's not, since the episode makes a point of having two separate characters ask Brandon if he isn't "a little short" for hoops, although we also have to admit that, for his height, Jason Priestley is in fact a half-decent low-post passer.

But it's not Brandon's wee stature that's going to keep him off the squad, nor the pressure he's under to live up to Jim's fabled championship-game buzzer-beater during *his* high-school b-ball days. It's that West Beverly is allegedly importing ringers from outside the district. G . . . asp?

Of course, that Brandon first hears this allegation from Steve—employed here, as he so often is in the first season, as the bigoted foil to Brandon's naïve crusader—should automatically render it unreliable intel, but one suspected ringer in particular is battling with Brandon for the last spot on the varsity team. His name is James Townsend (Tico Wells), and he's a hot prospect . . . with no transcripts on file with the fig-leaf program the district uses to funnel good players West Beverly's way, and no placement tests either! Horrors!

Brandon dumps the job of writing this exposé for the *Blaze* and its many parental readers on Andrea, citing conflict of interest, but she sets aside her own out-of-district conflict (much more on that later!) to research the story. When Andrea uncovers James's missing academic records, Brandon is *more* than happy to tag back in and scream in James's face about the unfairness of it all. James proceeds to get an A-plus from *us* for hollering right back at Brandon with the facts, namely that his father works for the city library, thus assuring James a spot at *any* school in the Beverly Hills system—not that he even wants to go to West Bev, since he was uprooted mid-semester (and since his new school is peopled by chucklefucks like Steve who root for the Celtics because of all the white dudes on the team, but that part is silent).

Wells, as James, really gets into full-snarl fact-checking Brandon's assumptions, and we always enjoy seeing Brandon's privilege read for absolute hazmat filth by a person of color. We're not big fans of what inevitably follows: Brandon lamely apologizes slash claims it's "not about race," then is forgiven, and even given a respectful nickname, "Minnesota," by a previous antagonist, ugh.

We never see James again; would that we could say the same about Brenda's asinine B-plot, which becomes an unfunny runner going forward. It's her third go-round in driver's ed, and the third time is not a charm, for her or us. A storyline in which a Walsh almost fender-bends someone she suspects is Henry Winkler should be a corker; it isn't. But it's worth noting that it's Kelly's ability to manipulate Brenda's social insecurity by singsonging that Brenda's her "best friend" that sets in motion the whole "Mondale runs out of gas, then is towed" disaster.

Jackie's All Coked Up at the Fashion Show

It's not the first "Beverly Hills kids have problems too" episode in the show's run, but it's one of the most memorable: even as Jackie (Ann Gillespie), Kelly's mom, is charming Brenda with her friend-mom permissiveness and love of fashion, she's melting down, self-medicating with vodka after a breakup, then making a coked-up ass of herself emceeing the annual mother-daughter fashion show.

The fashion show sequence is still legitimately cringey on the order of Jackson Maine lurching up onstage at the Grammys in *A Star Is Born*: you know what's coming, yet you still find your shoulders up around your ears.

That's mostly down to Ann (now Reverend Ann!) Gillespie's performance as Jackie; her rendition of the downward spiral isn't quite verité, but it's pretty nuanced for this show. And when she gets a chance to do something besides talk about clothes or cute guys, Jennie Garth shines as an exhausted, mortified Kelly. Honorable mention too to Carol Potter—the "daughter of a 'square,' reliable mom is an ingrate until her friend's cool mom fucks up" storyline was done so much better in *My So-Called Life*'s "Other People's Mothers" a few years later that Brenda's journey to appreciating Cindy hardly rates, but Potter's exquisite hurt upon realizing that Brenda didn't even *tell* her about the fashion show is well done.

And can we talk about Potter's bangin' figure in that red sequined number? The mom-wear of the time was *really* unfair to her. (We'd also like to talk about the extremely weird layout of Jackie's bedroom, which appears to have been built on a set that already had a kitchen in it. Her bed is shoved up against what looks like a '60s telex? And then there's a microwave on the other side? Look, now that we've seen it's *possible* to nuke ourselves some popcorn without getting out of the queen-size, we're not against it. It's just odd.)

Meanwhile, David's video-yearbook stalking has sunk to the level of a felony in several states, as he tails Kelly through the halls, then creeps into the fashion-show dressing room while nearly shorting out the camera with drool. Someone should have thrown this *Dorky's Revenge* horseshit, and David, into a volcano, though he redeems himself *very* slightly at the end when he turns the videotape of Jackie's disintegration over to Kelly so that she can destroy it. (Only one physical copy of a video: the past was so quaint.)

Elsewhere in the episode, Andrea takes another bashful baby step toward becoming a full-fledged member of The Gang when Brandon presumptuously invites her to walk with his mom and sister in the show; Donna's nonregulation mother is a different actress, and the character has a different name from the one we'll come to know later; and while there is Jim electronic-keyboard STUFF, we shan't dignify it.

"He just gets to me. He always gets to me!"

Jim Makes Dylan Irresistible to Brenda by Forbidding Her from Seeing Him

SEASON 1 | EPISODE 10
ISN'T IT ROMANTIC?

Not until Dylan slides out from under a car, artfully covered in grease, and eyes up her short-jorted legs does Brenda suspect he could actually see her as *a woman*.

Her own loins are set a-throb when she barges into the bathroom yelling at Brandon, only to discover the shower is occupied by Dylan, who has no compunction about standing *real* close to the transparent shower curtain. Dylan invites her to join him and Brandon for *Animal Crackers* (*eye roll*), and Brenda manages to stay cool, probably because she doesn't think it's a date. But she starts tensing up when Kelly says Dylan's "a man of action" who "doesn't waste his time on just anybody." When Dylan invites Brenda, without Brandon, to another showing at the Marx Brothers film fest, Jim tells Cindy he doesn't want Brenda dating Dylan because his father, Jack, is "an unethical bastard, and that's putting it politely."

As Brenda discovers when Dylan brings her back to his new hotel suite to find it already filled with Jack and a bunch of his henchmen, Jack (played here by Terence Ford, the first of three actors to portray the character) is a stressed-out rage beast (to put it impolitely). He and Dylan have a screaming fight, and Dylan storms out, Brenda helplessly trailing behind. Dylan rebuffs Brenda's efforts to reframe the situation while she cries and begs him to stop yelling at her;

fortunately, her reflexes are in good working order, because when he smashes a flowerpot on the sidewalk, she *hauls ass* away from him. He catches up and enfolds her in his duster (ugh), crooning apologies, and since Brenda likes Dylan but *loves* drama, it works.

The next day, they're already insufferably couple-y, and perhaps because Brandon is justly grossed out, he doesn't defend Dylan when Jim forbids Brenda from seeing him. Brenda exits the conversation in the most '90s way possible: "Thanks for dinner. It's been real." She then heads to see Kelly, who states that Brenda *will* still go out with Dylan Friday and stay at Kelly's that night. Since Kelly knows Dylan, she suspects that sex will occur. Brenda nervously says she's more interested in the romance, but Kelly briskly tells her contraception isn't optional: "Basic rule #1: never rely on the guy." "You sound so clinical," Brenda gasps. "Dear, clinical is 'What time shall we schedule the procedure?'" Kelly replies, awesomely. Brandon is also pretty sure Dylan's going to fuck and run, and pulls him aside at school to bray that Brenda's a virgin. No one needs to have worried: stood up outside the interminable Marx Brothers festival, Brenda cries.

Somehow Brenda manages what neither of us could have with our own mothers, being allowed to skip school due to heartbreak, and is pouting alone when Dylan shows up to apologize: he had to help his dad pack so that Jack could flee the country ahead of an indictment on securities fraud. "You are so warm," Dylan eventually purrs, and they're making out when Brenda hears Jim's car. Jim catches Dylan as Brenda tries to sneak him out the back door, and a fiery argument ensues regarding Jim's policing of Brenda's sex life as opposed to Brandon's. "It is different with girls," Jim sputters. "It just is!" Oof.

Brenda has finally received permission to see Dylan, and Brandon has also made peace with him, when everyone gathers to hear a sex talk from guest speaker Stacy Sloan (Kathy Molter). Anyone expecting a saucy Dr. Ruth–style lecture is disappointed when Stacy announces, 40 seconds into her sub-three-minute speech, that she has AIDS. Steve, who had tried to hit on her, is moved; Brenda interrogates Dylan on his history of unprotected sex and extracts a promise that he'll get tested, even as she worries that she's overthinking. "Brenda," says Dylan, "I love it that you think." Swoon?

"Don't you get tired of always trying so hard to do the right thing?"

Brandon Gets a DUI

SEASON 1 | EPISODE 11
B.Y.O.B.

. . . Didn't remember Brandon got busted for drunk driving back in the first season, did you? That's probably how *Beverly Hills, 90210* wanted it, because a DUI hardly fit with the golden-boy image the show had already begun carefully cultivating for him.

The ep opens with Donna 1.0—the Donna who, it was implied, drank and made out with dudes on the reg—taking advantage of her parents' vacay to throw a "strictly A-list" party. When Dylan chooses surfing Baja over attending a high-school alcohol-poisoning-fest, Brenda's social insecurity whinges at Brandon until he agrees to go with her.

It's not really Brandon's scene, possibly because it's not terribly realistic—granted, we didn't grow up in the Zip, but in our experience, underage drinkers aren't trying to fuck around with frozen foof like the Mucho Mahvelous [*sic*] Mango Margaritas Steve's whipping up. More likely, it's because, as Donna's prep-school trick notes, Brandon is a "buzzkill." Still, it's deeply uncool of Steve to pretend he's making Bran a virgin marg, then spike it.

But it's even *less* cool of Brandon to drive himself and Brenda home—and then, when Cindy thinks she smells booze on Brenda's breath, to let their parents assume that only Brenda was drinking. That's the senior Walshes for you, though: Brandon's the responsible one, while Brenda's overdramatic and easily influenced, so not only would he *never* drink, *he's* the one they leave in charge when they go to Palm Springs for the weekend. He's less than a minute older than she is!

Brenda does wheedle The Responsible One into "allowing" a small gathering in their parents' absence, but since you've watched television before, you know that of course half the school district shows up (including David and Scott, the latter of whom gets off a good line about the kids who ignore him at school ignoring him at the party as well). Brenda and Brandon have agreed not to drink, but when some of the friends of friends bring tequila, Brandon's down to partake (and to *dance!*), leaving Brenda (and a gallant Dylan) to parry the cops while Brandon macks on a disgusted Andrea.

Then the booze runs out, and Steve *also* drives drunk to go get more; Brandon is dispatched on a separate errand to stock up on snacks, but while Steve gets away with it (we assume), Brandon crashes into a pickup and is taken to jail.

Brenda calls Jim and Cindy to break the news—saving them from the unwanted attentions of a Texan couple at their resort trying to get them to "swing," and us from another who-cares C-minus plot about the parents—and then we cut to fucking Brandon *agonistes* in a darkened cell, squinting miserably into a single beam of light that caresses the two cosmetic smudges on his face. Wait: are we supposed to feel *sorry* for this little squeef?

. . . We are. We're supposed to feel bad for him when he blares at his parents that Brenda wasn't drinking. We're supposed to feel bad for him when he loses his license *for three weeks*. We're supposed to feel bad for him when he lies to Jim about how and when he got drunk, and when he brays at Brenda for calling him on it, and when he bitches to Dylan about his parents' disappointment. Dylan hears him out, then brings him to an Alcoholics Anonymous meeting to point out that some people have real problems, because Dylan too is a friend of Bill W. Brandon makes concern brows for 20 minutes.

Kudos to Dylan for pulling an interactive "well, actually" on Brandon there; kudos also to the WBH administration for shitcanning the "Wild Thang" report, although apparently they've replaced it with . . . David Silver.

"I used to be fat, and now I'm thin. And I'm a bitch."

The Slumber Party

SEASON 1 | EPISODE 13
SLUMBER PARTY

What makes "Slumber Party" such a classic? Maybe it's because the show is the most recognizably *itself* it's been up to this point in its run.

Many of the elements we consider "canonical" Brenda-era *90210* are present, and many of them seem to crop up for the first time here: that "The Gang" as we understand it has cohered into the core group at last (on the girls' side, anyway), with Andrea a real part of the group; that Donna is written the way we remember her, guileless and daffy, versus the cynical party girl we've seen previously; that Brenda and Kelly are already getting into it over Dylan. And it's all thanks to hall-of-fame one-off TV bitch Amanda.

A senior and a friend of Kelly's (never mentioned before or since), Amanda (Michele Abrams) is reluctantly attending the "evening of female bonding" at Casa Walsh along with the regulars. Brenda et al. insist repeatedly that it's not a "slumber party," which would be babyish, but between the Ouija board, the dance party, and the 10,000-calorie download, it looks like a slumber party to us. Amanda tries to tempt Kelly into going to a frat party with her instead, unsuccessfully, and when it's finally too late (because fraternities . . . close at 11?), Amanda decides to make everyone as miserable as she is with a game of Skeletons in the Closet.

Despite the characters' resistance, the game gets dark in a hurry. Kelly shares that Ross Weber had bad sex with her (that's the generous assessment; whether Kelly *really* consented is murky), then ghosted her. Her tears have barely dried before Andrea is getting grilled, first on the pronunciation of her name, then on whether she wants to bone Brandon. When Donna has nothing of interest to confess to, Brenda gets crazy eyes and tries to meet Amanda's challenge by admitting she kissed her Minnesota bestie's boyfriend. (Whose name is Jim Townsend, a name the show basically *just* used for accused basketball ringer James Townsend in "One on One.")

Then Kelly admits to trying to "get a date with" Dylan after he and Bren started dating. (For you "Kellan soulmate" truthers out there, Kelly claims Dylan was flirting with her "all last year," before the Walshes moved to town.) They argue, everyone's over it, and the party's about to break up when Brenda softens and says she's glad Kelly told her about Ross. Apologies and hugs all around—except for Amanda, who rolls her eyes and heads for the door, as we admit we also might have if Andrea had called us "gossipy" and not meant it as a compliment.

But Amanda's left her purse, which only TV characters ever do, and when Donna spills the contents, we see Amanda's got a bunch of loose diet pills in there. Kelly confronts her about prizing thinness over a non-methy personality. (Remember this in a couple of seasons when Kelly almost Dexa-dies.) Amanda, looking hunted, can still get it up to deliver one of the great kiss-off lines in history: "I used to be fat. And now I'm thin. And, I'm a bitch."

Amanda is about to sweep on out of there with her glorious '90s mane of curls and her odd Hepburn-y accent, but Brenda urges her to stay and be real and silly with the others. Amanda snuggles on the couch and asks for a whole box of cookies. This outcome is not credible, healthy, or in character, and yet it's *so* satisfying for some reason! The only thing that could make this episode better: if the girls *had* called the cops on David and Scott for taking pictures of them in their PJs.

This is also the episode in which Brandon and Steve—well, Little Brandon and Little Steve, really—get short-conned out of Steve's 'Vette by two scantily clad "bebs." Brandon yells at Steve, Steve cries, and it serves them both right, but of course the car is returned and nobody learns anything.

Brandon Solves Racism, Ethical Labor Practices

SEASON 1 | EPISODE 14
EAST SIDE STORY

Brandon comes home to find his parents in intense conversation with their housekeeper, Anna (Luisa Leschin), and a couple of other grown-ups. He thinks Anna's about to get fired, but as usual, he has no idea what he's talking about: they're discussing Anna's niece, Karla (Karla Montana), who needs to use the Walshes' address to get out of a bad situation at her own school by attending West Beverly.

The senior Walshes make sure this plan is okay with their children before proceeding—a mistake, since it reinforces Brandon's notion that *he* is Casa Walsh's decider-in-chief, but the kids are fine with it. Brandon's even finer with it when he meets Karla at school and sees that she's hot. She's also Latinx, so of course Brandon has to condescend that West Bev might be "a little more competitive than [she's] used to"—only to get utterly shown up by Karla in all three of the classes they share.

This leads, somehow, to Brandon and Karla snottily talking past each other in the hallway over his assumptions about "minority" scholarships, then to a series of mutually defensive conversational skirmishes about undocumented workers, the sights of East L.A., and Brandon's blinding privilege—all accompanied by "The Castanets of Doom" from *The Big Album of Racist Music Cues, Vol. II*.

Despite Brandon's gum-chomping, looming into Karla's personal space, and disastrous dancing—and despite the neon I HAVE A SECRET sign flashing right above Karla's head—the two begin to fall for each other. Things fall *apart* just as quickly, though, at the party the Walshes are contrivedly hosting for beach-fashion king (?) Chick Schneider (Mark Lonow). Anna is catering the party, and Karla pitches in to help, touching off a cascade of Brandon tantrums ("Brant-rums"?) when he (1) gets weirded out that his Latinx love interest is waiting on him; (2) lures Karla upstairs to "help him bring down some chairs," then gets mad when she doesn't think his predatorily interrupting her when she's working is cute; (3) ruins a group photo of The Gang in Schneider's designs by fuming; and (4) mortifies Jim by squalling at *his father's client* about exploited workers at the Schneider plant in Mexicali. A reminder: Brandon, having *already forgotten* about the unfair labor practices facing Latinx workers that had him quitting a snooty eatery in "Every Dream Has Its Price (Tag)," has *re*-learned precisely *one thing* about this issue *two days* before the party, but feels qualified to blare about living wages—which, for all he knows, Schneider actually does pay his workers. Whereas our parents would have drop-kicked us into next week for acting this sort of fool in front of company, Jim settles for bellowing at Brandon to apologize. Everyone at the party is awked out, especially Brenda and Kelly, who fear Brandon has jeopardized their "trendoid" Schneider freebies.

Brandon does apologize, although to our annoyance this shit-eating happens offscreen. He then sets out to get to the bottom of what Karla's *really* doing at West Beverly, and tracks her down at a family picnic. We'd have climbed a nearby tree to get away from his presumptions, but Karla kindly explains what we'd all guessed from the jump: she isn't Anna's niece; she was in Witness Protection, but now that the baddie who threatened her has pled guilty, she can go back to her family up north and never see Brandon again.

. . . Buuut the episode is still short, so we have to endure more of David's vain attempts to get MC Hammer to play the West Beverly prom, and Debbie Gibson hanging up on him. Nineties much?

"This is so poetically unjust. I mean, he gets to miss school and everything and he doesn't even like *the show!"*

Brandon Craps Out as an Actor While Brenda Creates an Indelible Character

SEASON 1 | EPISODE 16
FAME IS WHERE YOU FIND IT

Brandon's rollerblading around a park, passing a ball with a hockey stick to . . . no one, when somehow this athleticism draws the attention of a crew shooting teen TV drama *Keep It Together*, which finds its cast suddenly short one "surfer dude"; Brandon gets the gig.

In makeup, he meets series star Lydia Leeds (Marcy Kaplan), whom he doesn't recognize because while *KIT* is one of Brenda's favorites, Brandon hasn't watched in years: "It used to be one of those squeaky-clean shows where, by some miracle, every problem got solved just in time for the last commercial." EERILY FAMILIAR.

Brandon nails his line—"Hey, babe! Lookin' good. Real good, babe"—and since producers are in a contract dispute with *KIT* star Sean, chemistry with "the princess" gets Brandon invited to appear in a second episode. Envious Brenda only gets more annoyed when Brandon asks her to cover his Peach Pit shifts so that he can do it. She agrees, but bitches to Kelly and Donna, proving her assertion that she's "the one with all the talent" by busting out a bad Cockney accent, an okay Valley Girl accent, and a barely comprehensible "New York tough guy" accent. Perhaps neither of the twins got *any* of "the talent"? Brandon may be a gifted kisser: that's mostly what his next scene with Lydia entails, and she doesn't mind doing a dozen takes.

Lydia invites Brandon out to a club *on a school night*, which Brandon finesses by promising not to fall behind in his classes. When Lydia shows up while Brandon's still primping, Brenda small-talks that she played Juliet in seventh grade: "Not that what you do when you're twelve years old really matters that much!" "When I was twelve years old, I got my second *TV Guide* cover and my first Golden Globe Award," gloats Lydia. OKAY, BITCH!

Brenda really could have used the boost of some *positive* energy to propel her into her first serving shift: waiting tables is hard, and Brenda sucks at it. Meanwhile, Lydia's at the club, gossiping about her frenemies (including, as "Mackenzie," Melissa Rivers!). Lydia and Brandon are dancing when Lydia sees Sean (Josh Henderson); Brandon does not, so he has no idea when Lydia starts making out with him that it's for Sean's benefit. On set the next day, Brandon learns the big kiss has been cut, and that Sean is there, contract resolved. Lydia joins Sean in mocking Brandon when Sean's character throws a glass's worth of water in his face, then a pitcher's worth; soon Brandon is sneezing too much to be able to deliver a truthful moment, lashing out at everyone. It only belatedly occurs to Brandon that he could be replaced by any dork off the street since *that is how he got the job himself.*

Back at the Peach Pit, Brenda has found fulfillment by creating an over-the-top waitress character named Laverne (pr. "Lavoyne"), costumed in an embellished hairnet, cat-eye glasses, and a pink vintage uniform. In Brenda's Brooklyn (?) accent, sassy Laverne ingratiates herself to patrons by using classic diner lingo and leading a lip-sync to "It's My Party." A crowd hangs around for the show, filling Brenda's uniform pockets with tips.

Shown up at *all* his jobs, Brandon pouts off to the park, where Lydia finds him to apologize. He's a bitch about it at first, but forgives her when she calls him "the natural from Minnesota who knows how to kiss" and promises producers are going to test-market his character to recur. At the viewing party for his *Keep It Together* episode, however, Brandon learns at the same time as all his loved ones that he's been cut out entirely. Afterward, he mopily offers to let Brenda keep his Peach Pit job since she's so much better at it, but she doesn't care to make more money, having saved enough for . . . acting classes.

"Basically our motto is, if you'll sit through it, we'll do just about anything up here."

Brenda Tries Comedy While Brandon Tries Politics, with Similar Results

SEASON 1 | EPISODE 17
STAND (UP) AND DELIVER

Andrea's latest notion to raise Brandon's profile is for him to run for junior class president, and she doesn't agree with him that his recent arrival is an impediment: "No one knows you well enough to hate you!" (Beg to differ.)

Brandon demurs, but in the time it takes Dylan to explain Luke Perry's absence from the rest of the episode by telling Brenda he's going to see his fugitive father in Mexico, Brandon's changed his mind. Kelly immediately gets horny for the "power" Brandon may theoretically enjoy one day. When she and Donna go pick up Brenda later, Brandon's already speeching: Kelly purrs that she's never even voted, and Brandon drones, "It's important to try to change things." Like what, how much school spirit the gym mural needs? Brenda is wounded by Kelly's neglect and sneaks upstairs to CRY before the girls go to The Fallout Club, where MC Sky (the late Carrie Hamilton), supine on a velvet couch, monologues about her childhood. Though neither blonde is feeling it, Brenda is rapt. When Kelly interrupts the next performer, (alleged) comic Jack (Tom McTigue), by calling out for whipped cream on her cappuccino, he roasts her as a "typical California girl . . . into the important things, like clothes, makeup—*way* too much makeup!" Kelly can't take it, but Brenda defends her honor, heckling Jack. Getting the better of him is electrifying, as Brenda tells her parents the day after: "These performance-oriented coffeehouses are really happening!" They're too busy making campaign materials to listen, and aren't the only ones who're enthusiastically organizing for Brandon: Kelly shows up to announce that she's going to be his campaign manager. Andrea, Brandon's *former* campaign manager, arrives just in time to hear, and takes Brandon aside to admit she told him to run because she was too scared to do it herself, and lose. Brandon's sure there's enough work for Kelly and Andrea to share, because he's an idiot.

Brenda ditches them to hang with Sky and learns she dropped out of school at 16. Brenda's inspired to ask a non–Mrs. Teasley for a high school equivalency test, but needs her parents' signatures, which of *course* they won't give; they state that Brenda will grow out of her dreams, just like they did their own. This only convinces Brenda of her own integrity; she won't sell out like they did.

Speaking of sellouts: Brandon is following Kelly's advice, glad-handing fellow students—"Brandon Walsh. Damn glad to meet ya," barf. Kelly induces David to produce Brandon's campaign video; it features *clips from the show* that *we know David was not present to tape*, from Brandon boogie-boarding in "The Green Room" to shooting baskets in "One on One." Horrified by the content-free ad, Andrea quits.

Meanwhile, Brenda's house-sitting for Sky, borrowing her clothes, and offending Kelly: "Hippie Witch is out." "It's not Hippie Witch, it's *Twin Peaks*, and it's very in." Alas, Brenda gets a glimpse at Sky's real life when she comes home to repo men. Brenda then realizes that the gas and phone are out—just in time for Brandon's pre-election party to descend on Sky's apartment; only when the power fails do the guests disperse.

The day of the debate, Brandon wonders, "Maybe I should talk about some of the community programs I want to set up." "Let's wait 'til you're in office to make that stuff happen," Kelly hand-waves. "First you have to win." Then Brandon has his first interaction with his opponent, Michael (Scott Fults), dorky veteran of many failed campaigns, who's pretty sure Brandon, due to his popularity, will crush the vote. Fortunately, the debate is short. Brandon's going to bring in "rock bands" every week; when Michael gently asks how, since it's clear Brandon knows nothing about releases, permits, or insurance, Brandon withdraws his candidacy on the spot to support Michael. Everyone is proud, because the noblest thing a privileged, handsome white man can do, if he knows he's about to lose, is *quit*.

Back at her empty apartment, Sky admits she's broke. "But you've got a job!" gasps Brenda, who has no idea how much worse things will soon be for high school dropouts trying to make it as artists. For now, Brenda can bequeath her equivalency form to Sky and try her own luck as an artist from a cushion of comfort, performing a "comedy" set that highlights Shannen Doherty's lack of comic timing. Brenda realizes she's ready to be a kid a little longer, but also utters the painfully naïve line, "I think I found me right up here." Maybe she should have found Lavoyne.

"Whose face is it on the ball? Who're you trying to clobber?"

Chandler Bing Might Menendez His Dad

SEASON 1 | EPISODE 19
APRIL IS THE CRUELEST MONTH

The *Blaze* is blurring the line between newspaper and hyperlocal fanzine with the "Senior Spotlight" series, and Brandon thinks he has a shot at profiling a real superstar: WBH's prominent student/tennis phenom Roger Azarian (Matthew Perry!).

When we meet Roger, it's evidently not the first time Brandon has pitched him, as he tries to dismiss Brandon after tennis practice: "I told you: no interviews." (Okay, J.D. Salinger.) But he caves almost immediately, and brings Brandon home to the sprawling Tudor manse he shares with his self-made millionaire father, George (Nicolas Coster). The house is filled with antique guns, in an unlocked cabinet, and also with Roger's resentments about his father's oppressive expectations and attempts to advance Roger's interests via nepotism. So starved is Roger for real friendship as opposed to remote adulation that he lets Brandon read his unproduced screenplay, which turns out to be about a guy who lives in a house like Roger's, has an overbearing dad like Roger's, is almost *named* Roger (his screenplay avatar is, lazily, called Robert), and has patricidal ambitions . . . like Roger?

The episode's *Little Archie* take on a noir thriller—the potential murder weapon was formerly owned by Dashiell Hammett, GOOD LORD—culminates in Brandon following all the screenplay's clues not to George's corpse, but to Roger, day-drinking in the pool house (but taking breaks between each pour to hit the fridge for ice, as you do) while trying to work up the nerve to turn Dashiell Hammett's gun on himself. Brandon, naturally, talks him out of it. (No one, evidently, was on hand to talk Perry out of making every one of his acting choices AS BIG AS POSSIBLE.) At the hospital the next day, George promises Brandon, this little puke he's met *twice*, that he and Roger are both getting help, and Brandon—having given away Dodgers tickets Roger pressed on him earlier—settles in to be a friend to Roger by watching the game with him on a minuscule 1991-size portable TV. Possibly not as moving a gesture as it might have been had Brandon arrived before we hear the fully non–Vin Scully announcer call the bottom of the ninth. Roger doesn't get the chance to suggest that Brandon work on his timing or consideration because we never see him again.

What we *do* see again is SAT stress, when The Gangsters all repeat their junior year and hope no one notices. But this is their first time receiving and comparing SAT scores. The Minnesota Twins tie with 1190—630 Math/560 Verbal for Brenda, the opposite for Brandon—meaning they'll have no problem getting accepted at UCLA or the University of Minnesota, as Cindy suggests to a contemptuous Brenda. Not bragging about her scores? Donna, who's cagey as hell about them, then blows off class to smoke with the bad kids, then blows off school entirely to go shopping. Donna finally confesses that she's been acting out due to despair over her future: given her 300 Math and 320 Verbal, her mother (offscreen) has advised, "I better find a rich guy to marry me, 'cause I'm too stupid to take care of myself." This *19th* episode of the series is the first to give Donna anything to do—and that "anything" is primarily to make her keep saying what an idiot she is, which is . . . pretty funny, actually. But then Mrs. Teasley makes her first appearance (Denise Dowse, getting recycled after having already shown up in "The 17 Year Itch" as a college professor doing a twin study) to assure Donna that she's not stupid; she's got a learning disability, just not one the writers felt like researching or naming. As future episodes, of course, would prove, Donna is both learning disabled AND stupid, but for now it's a happy ending.

"How many girls get to have sex for the first time with someone they love?"

The One Where Brenda and Dylan Do Sex

SEASON 1 | EPISODE 21
SPRING DANCE

Can you believe it's taken until the season's penultimate episode for the series to get to a *dance*?

Andrea screws up all her courage to ask Brandon if he's going. As we have already heard *ad nauseam*, he *doesn't* dance, and is happy to come over to her place that night to hang out instead. We learn afterward, however, that Andrea had already planned this "casual" conversation, offscreen, with Brenda, who's disappointed both that Andrea couldn't maneuver Brandon into asking her, and that *she* did not ask *him*.

Along with several other girls, Kelly is named a Spring Princess—first step to becoming Spring Queen! Bored by every other eligible bachelor in the region, she asks Brandon, and is promising to make it worth his while when Steve struts in, ready to throw an invitation to Kelly since Darla Diller (Sharon Case) just rejected him (his Corvette). He barely conceals his heartbreak at seeing Kelly move on, but she points Steve at the equally dateless Donna; Brandon suggests they all go as friends. At school the next day, Kelly's running down all the dance accoutrements she expects Brandon to pay for when Andrea bounces up to see when he's coming over, and learns he actually *is* going to the dance after all. "Don't we make a great couple?" chirps Kelly. More heartbreak!

After school, Brenda and Kelly separately choose the same dress, which is somehow chic enough for Kelly *and* cheap enough for Brenda. As soon as she sees it's within Brenda's range, Kelly rejects it as a tacky, cheap knockoff. A polite fight ensues in which Brenda graciously tells Kelly to get it, to which Kelly sniffs, "I wouldn't wear it." BUT GUESS WHAT: come Spring Dance night, they *both* are!

No sooner has everyone departed the limo than Dylan shows Brenda the key to their room; the night's only two songs in when he starts negotiating their exit. Brenda's concerned that she'll disappoint him, but Dylan promises, "We're not going to be judging each other up there, we're going to be *enjoying* each other." EW.

Kelly proves true Steve's assessment that "she's used to getting what she wants" when she and Brandon make out during a slow dance. He's just finished telling her, post-kiss, that he thinks of her as a sister when a drunk Steve, having seen Kelly putting the moves on Brandon, staggers up to complain that they're *not* all there as friends. Brandon follows him into the bowels of the hotel, where we learn Steve's problem is (1) it's his birthday; (2) he only found out six months ago that he's adopted; (3) no one but Kelly knows that he is; (4) she hasn't acknowledged his birthday tonight. Meanwhile, Kelly wins Spring Queen, but departs her throne when Brandon tells her about the pouty birthday boy. Steve won't accept her apology, and ugly words are flung.

At home, Andrea gets to the bloody climax of *Prom Nightmare* and decides she doesn't want to be left out; puts on her mother's one and only "evening gown" (white lace column with yoga ball–size puffed sleeves? Sure!); gets in a cab (?); and gets to the dance two songs before it ends.

Brenda and Dylan, of course, miss all of this, due to fucking.

Festivities wind up with a dance contest, the winners of which will get to dance the night's final dance with the Spring Queen and King, a certain Brad Phillips who gets no lines. Knowing this, David has bet Scott $20 he'll dance with Kelly before the night is over and easily wins the contest. And peace is made: Brandon gives Andrea a pity dance; Kelly can't keep up her bitchy attitude once she figures out Brenda's just lost her virginity; Kelly and Steve apologize to each other; Steve *also* apologizes to Donna for being a shitty date; Donna apologizes to

Steve for buying a dress with a "stupid," unmanageable hoop skirt. No one in The Gang apologizes for taking up half the floor with a corny seven-way group dance, which is why all their classmates probably hate them.

"But honey, we were just starting to get used to it here."

Before the Walshes Move Back to Minneapolis, Sex Is on Everyone's Agenda

SEASON 1 | EPISODE 22
HOME AGAIN

Jim is concerned that a lunch invitation from some head honcho at his firm means he's about to get canned—but the news turns out to be good, ish: he's actually getting a promotion, but it will require the family to move back to Minneapolis.

He thinks this is a boon—"We've all griped about it here"—and thus proposes a vote on the matter, a democratic plan that we're sure none of our four parents would have ever allowed when we were high school juniors because *we were children and thus did not get a say.* Jim is then shocked to lose the vote 3–1; not even Cindy wants to leave, and *her* only friend is Anna the housekeeper. Jim's call to refuse the offer only convinces his boss he's playing hardball: when he doubles Jim's salary, Jim rejects democracy on the spot.

The kids react realistically to this as the tragedy it would be to people their age, Brenda yawing from worries that returning to Minneapolis will make them look like punks who couldn't hack L.A. to panic about the future for her and Dylan, who tries to convince her that he definitely will *not* resume getting French girls pregnant the second she's out of the state. Bitter, Steve starts preemptively icing Brandon out. But Andrea sees an opening (er, as it were), asking Brandon out for what he thinks is "like a business thing." He's right, in the sense that it's about her lady business: she offers to have sex with him before he skips town. Brandon is dubious until Brenda informs him that she and Dylan have been rounding home for a while, whereupon he suddenly changes his mind, and they schedule Andrea's defloration at the Peach Pit on a Sunday, when it will be closed because its owner, Brandon's boss, Nat (Joe E. Tata), is an amazing businessman.

It's probably just as well neither of them thought to hit up their emancipated minor friend for the use of his parent-free Craftsman cottage, because we then cut over there for Brenda's tearful postcoital breakup. Brandon does the same (minus the tears) with Steve on the beach the next day, so that at least they can part on friendly terms.

Brandon jets from there to his date with Andrea, but we never do discover whether he intended to bone her on the counter, booth seat, or floor, because Andrea—having sought sex advice from Kelly in an offscreen conversation—accidentally got their assignation coopted as a surprise Bon Voyage party. Jim looks on as David videotapes various Gangsters' dopey farewell testimonials, then volunteers to give a speech literally no one wanted to announce that, actually, they're staying—impetuously making a decision that affects the whole family without discussing it with *his wife* for the second time in a single episode. In the cheers that follow, Brandon asks Andrea if she would have actually climbed onto his wee knob (we're paraphrasing); she tells him he'll never know. Elsewhere, Dylan has scarcely finished fist-pumping his joy at the good news that Brenda and Brandon aren't moving when Brenda tells him, "I'm late." "What are you late for?" asks this legendary cocksman. Perhaps he only understands *"Mes règles sont en retard."*

SEASON Two

Comings

HENRY THOMAS

When Brandon decides that buying a hot vintage Mustang to replace his old beater Mondale is more important than honoring his commitments to his boss, he gets poor Nat to agree to give him a fucking sabbatical so that he can spend the summer working at the private Beverly Hills Beach Club and earn fat tips from all the swells. Brandon's manager at the club is Henry (James Pickens Jr.), a brisk and efficient armed forces veteran. Like all authority figures, Henry is forced to act as though Brandon is special. But no one minds seeing him stroll around the club, with perfect posture, in crisp white slacks (and we're not saying he goes commando but we have never seen an underwear line AND BELIEVE US, WE HAVE LOOKED). The strictness with which Henry enforces his rule that no one interrupt his soaps is an example for us all.

CHRIS SUITER

Various members of the gang elect to take a summer-school drama course early in Season 2, and while this makes intuitive sense for Brenda, it's a little off-brand for Andrea, David, and Donna. Perfectly *on*-brand for the *show* is their teacher, Chris Suiter (Michael St. Gerard): he's a "cool" teacher (read: has poor boundaries)

whose bad choices include laughing hysterically at Donna and David doing an unfunny-at-best gender-flipped *Romeo & Juliet* scene and dating Andrea, *a minor child in his class.* Yeah, she looks 30, but that isn't the point. St. Gerard's uncanny resemblance to Elvis Presley (whom he'd played in three previous productions) does little to distract from the fact that, for a guy playing an acting teacher, he's a C-minus actor. (Like Douglas Emerson, St. Gerard quit the biz to give back, and became a pastor.)

KYLE CONNERS

Diminutive alleged football "star" Kyle (David Lascher) is the object of Kelly's summer thirst in his first episode, and after her attempts to hurl herself at him miss every time, he's obliged to reveal that he thinks he might be gay. Kyle also figures in Brandon's exposé on track-team steroid use, but while Kyle himself reappears, his teaching-moment sexual orientation is not mentioned again.

MEL SILVER

An oral surgeon whom his social-climbing son is willing to pretend is a hotshot producer of the same name, Mel (Matthew Laurance—"not the *Not Necessarily the News* Laurance; the other one")—is something of a human

MacGuffin at first: he's dating Kelly's mom, Jackie, and the prospect of David and Kelly becoming step-siblings who share a roof is delightful to David, but horrifying to Kelly. When Jackie falls pregnant unexpectedly, Mel "does the right thing" and proposes, albeit with a fugazi ring and while Jackie is in a dentist's chair at his office . . . and it's just about the last good choice he makes in his time on the show (cheating on Jackie . . . cheating on Jackie again . . . giving the kids booze . . . not firing David into the sun for kiting checks).

EMILY VALENTINE

She's lived all over and is used to being "the new kid"—so you'd think recent Bay Area transfer Emily (Christine Elise, soon to become Jason Priestley's long-term girlfriend) would get a better lay of the land (as it were) before jumping into The Gang dating pool with both feet. Sadly for her, Emily's ignorance of intra-Gang romantic subplots means her punky NorCal energy is decidedly not welcomed by Andrea, who has to pretend she doesn't care that Brandon is taking Emily out instead of her; or Brenda, who doesn't bother pretending she doesn't care that Dylan is *also* taking Emily out, and empties both

barrels into Emily's rep. A détente is achieved among the girls—mostly thanks to Emily driving Brenda and Dylan back together, where they belong—and Emily falls hard for Brandon. The results are potentially fatal—not just for Brandon, whom she doses with drugs; or for the rest of The Gang, whose homecoming float she almost torches after Brandon rejects her; but also for viewers, who must endure some hideously awkward scenes during Emily's initial arc . . . and some hideously awkward '90s hair later on.

IRIS MCKAY

Though Dylan's abandonment issues and his conception of himself as an orphan are formative to his personality, he does, in fact, have two living parents; they're just not great at parenting. Iris (Stephanie Beacham) fled her marriage to a shady finance guy to go discover herself in a tree house on Maui. When she does come to town for the first time to deal with the effects her ex-husband's arrest (on charges of tax evasion) have had on their son, she's as big a New Age cartoon as we have been led to believe: she takes Cindy out to a "mind gym"; she deals tarot cards; she ascribes people's motives to their zodiac signs. She also had the integrity to save her entire divorce settlement for Dylan's use, and the wisdom to put it in a trust managed by Jim, so while Dylan may be annoyed by her in the way that all teens are annoyed by their parents, maybe he could suck it up for the five days a year they're in each other's company and try not to disdain her so openly.

GRANDMA ROSE ZUCKERMAN

Andrea's out-of-district registration at West Beverly would not be possible if not for the in-district residence of her grandmother, Rose Zuckerman (a role originated by Lainie Kazan, and taken over for appearances in Seasons 4 and 5 by Bess Meisler). When Brandon thoughtlessly enters a *Blaze* article of Andrea's for a journalism award, the scrutiny risks exposing the truth about Andrea's residency. Grandma Rose later becomes the first person in Andrea's life to clock that she's pregnant, and is supportive of her (shotgun) marriage to a Catholic. Progress!

PAM SCANLON

Scott Scanlon's mother Pam is, thanks to a performance by the great Jenny O'Hara, one of the most realistic and realized characters on *Beverly Hills, 90210* . . . but she is *awful*. Controlling, clueless, passive-aggressive, it's Mrs. Scanlon who hectors David into putting together the birthday party at which Scott loses his life (uh, spoiler), based on a friendship that hasn't been close for some time. Her grief at Scott's death is unmanageable and cringey; it, and her failure to comprehend that a

relative is abusing her daughter Sue later in the series, feel uneasily true.

SAMANTHA SANDERS

Back in the day, Samantha Sanders (Christine Belford) played the matriarch on *Hartley House*, a saccharine family sitcom that, in the *Brady Bunch* mold, has gained immortal status in syndication. By the time we meet her, she's a working actress who, if she had the chance, might like to recapture some of her early success; she's also mother to Steve, consistently the most trifling-ass character in the show's opening-credits cast, though we don't think that's her fault. In between career moves—dinner theater; a straight play in Toronto; an attempt to revive *Hartley House*— Samantha dates the father of one of Steve's girlfriends (. . . but we'll get to the Arnolds), eventually settling down with a younger woman.

DEIDRE

Other than babysitting and turning a gig covering Brandon's shifts at the Peach Pit into the backdrop for some kind of performance art, Brenda basically never has a job—something that your hardworking former teen minimum-wage-earning coauthors find irritating. But in Season 2, Brenda improbably gets hired as a seasonal staffer at a high-end Beverly Hills boutique, under the management of Deidre (Rebecca Staab). Perhaps the reason Brenda goes on to reject paid employment is the trauma of having Deidre for a boss: in their first episode together, Deidre rudely chases from the store a bedraggled Santa Claus that we viewers know is *actually the true St. Nick!* Deidre, you grinch! Deidre then goes on to use the recession as an excuse for snaking all of Brenda's commissions—until, that is, Brenda enlists Cindy to dress up as a society lady (including a satin turban, obviously), waste Deidre's whole afternoon pretending to shop, stick her with a parking ticket, and swan out. Later-era Brenda would get a multipage quitting screed to deliver, but getting secret revenge on Deidre with an assist from Cindy is fun and, truly, a victimless crime.

TONY MILLER

A brawny flat-topped blond who seems to serve as a Jock No. 3–type seat-filler, Tony (Michael Cudlitz, the show's construction coordinator for several of the early seasons) is often a forbidding presence: he looms threateningly at Brandon during the steroids storyline, and in the direction of Shaw's football players during the disputed dance in Season 3. But all along, he's cherished a crush on Brenda, and by the time the prom rolls around, he's Gang-adjacent enough that Brenda's willing to accept his invitation—but just as willing to shoot down any dreams he might have of using those Math Club condoms with her.

JOHN GRIFFIN

The *Blaze* is usually just the setting for power struggles/one-way romantic yearning for Brandon and Andrea. But in Season 2, we actually see a little more of its staff—not just when Emily transparently volunteers to come on as a writer in order to spend more time with Brandon, but also when Andrea decides to publish content revolving around the subject of sex. AIDS is on everyone's minds, the PTA is up in arms about whether the school should distribute condoms to students, and Managing Editor John Griffin (Andy Hirsch) would *really* like Andrea to read a personal essay submission from someone who feels like he's the last living virgin in America! Spoiler alert: it's John himself. Andrea's not really interested, but it's nice for her to learn that there are multiple boys other than Brandon who might want to kiss on her.

FELICE MARTIN

All hail Felice (Katherine Cannon), socially conservative hypocrite socialite and deliciously formidable battle-axe. When we first meet her (not "Nancy," Donna's mother in Season 1, played by Jordana Capra), she's going toe-to-toe with Andrea over condom distribution at West Beverly, and she's utterly committed to Donna remaining a virgin until marriage. But Felice's "family values" are flexible— like, "cheats on her husband under the same hotel roof as Color Me Badd" flexible. Like, "when her husband cheated on *her* with *her sister*, went along with the lie that the ensuing child was 'just' Donna's cousin for over two decades" flexible. (Also malleable are her ideas on wardrobe; she wants a dress code at West Beverly, but is seldom fazed by her daughter's more revealing outfits.) Felice's attitude toward David often aligns with ours (i.e., that he's useless) but is also flexible depending on the suitability of Donna's other prospective partners at any given time, and she's willing either to pay them to go away (Ray) or to overlook their rapey tendencies (Season 5's Griffin Stone), depending on the net worth of *their* families. Felice softens somewhat in later seasons, but Cannon's relish in playing this redoubtable pill never wanes.

JAKE HANSON

We all know that Dylan has had a fascinating life and crossed paths with all kinds of people whose circumstances would scandalize his classmates. One of those is Jake Hanson (Grant Show), the guy who taught Dylan how to surf, how to ride motorcycles, and how to pick up girls. When he chances to run into Dylan in Season 2's penultimate episode, we learn that after having worked various blue-collar jobs all around the country, Jake's back in town living around Melrose (ooh!) and looking for handyman gigs. What do you know, Jackie's about to marry Mel and needs some work done at the house! Jake is putting together a wedding gazebo when Kelly—who's had a stank attitude about the nuptials for weeks—gets an eyeful of him and decides life might be worth living after all. Jake and Kelly's flirtation never really gets past first base: he's horny enough to want

to kiss her, but savvy enough to know she's underage. But it *does* open up a door—a back door, if you will—into the show's first spinoff, all about Jake and his many colorful neighbors in an apartment complex called Melrose Place.

Goings

SCOTT SCANLON

Probably originally intended as an ongoing main character whose plotlines, with David, would parallel those of the older main cast à la original *Degrassi*, Scott didn't survive the second season. He started that school year with an already reduced role—and pointed mentions of his new interest in country-western culture, particularly guns. That keenness didn't translate to a facility with twirling them; showing off his "gunslinging" to David in his father's study, Scott accidentally shoots himself in the stomach and dies. At least he went out just having dirty-danced with the popular girls . . . which partially makes up for the time capsule filled with self-absorbed tchotchkes The Gang buries in a narcissistic attempt to memorialize him.

Premarital Sex Has Consequences That May or May Not Include Pregnancy!!!

After the gang gets into beachwear to gambol through the new opening credits, it's the last day of their first junior year.

Kelly's got big plans to spend her summer tanning in the mornings and playing volleyball in the afternoons, while Brenda and Donna will be taking a drama class at summer school. Then Brenda reveals to her friends that she's getting a jump on the syllabus with some extracurricular drama of her own: she's *late*. In the midst of a PSA about the fallibility of contraception, Donna gets to debut her new character attribute, reminding Kelly and Brenda that the only 100 percent certain form of birth control is abstinence, then return to her *old* character attribute (stupidity) when Brenda's home test is supposed to be either red or blue but comes out green: "Well, maybe that means twins or something." Maybe Donna should be in summer school to try to pass Sex Ed.

On the eve of her appointment with Kelly's gynecologist, Brenda tells Dylan that they may soon meet Dylan Jr. or Brendina. He's predictably stressed by the news, but even given where their sexual relationship may end up, Brenda and Dylan both agree that "it" was great, suggesting an immediate retcon that they only had sex during the Spring Dance even though we saw them both in Dylan's bed in literally the last episode. Why, once they'd started, would they *stop* having sex? DYLAN LIVES ALONE. Anyway, the next day Brenda gets her period before the gynecologist can even examine her. In his relief, Dylan wonders if, since Brenda's there anyway, maybe the doctor can just put her on the Pill. Shockingly, Brenda not only didn't already ask this herself but bites Dylan's head off for suggesting it. And their problems aren't over, because Brenda sucks at covering her tracks: Cindy finds the empty pregnancy-test box in the trash. Jim and Cindy force her to admit that she wasn't just taking it as a science experiment and has, in fact, Done Sex—terrible timing, given that Dylan is on his way over. But Jim and Cindy would probably be more chill about the whole thing if they knew Brenda already planned to dump Dylan for . . . reasons? (The reason was that when the show portrayed Brenda enjoying sex, conservative parents went nuts and the show caved and wrote this nonsense about her being scared about liking Dylan too much, or something.)

Once Brandon makes it clear to Andrea that, since he's staying in town, sex is off the table, he can start focusing on the vintage Mustang he's much hornier for. Since business at the Peach Pit goes down in the summer (???), Steve points Brandon toward the geographically confusing Beverly Hills Beach Club. (Beverly Hills is landlocked and all California beaches are state parks, but go off, show.) Despite his previous experience as a lifeguard in Minnesota, Brandon is too small, slow, and generally unqualified to rescue anyone from the ocean. But when club manager Henry (the great James Pickens Jr.) learns that Brandon waits tables, he offers him a job as a cabana boy, starting immediately. Instead of just getting Nat to put him on nights for two weeks and working both jobs, as your authors did in their youth, Brandon decides to screw Nat over—and while this is extremely trifling, if Nat has been running this place his whole life and still made a schedule with only himself and a high school student on it, he's not blameless. When the 50th person in his life tells Brandon he owes Nat more than four hours' notice before taking this sabbatical, Brandon finally agrees with them and tells Henry he has so much integrity that he will have to delay his start as Henry's new cabana boy by two weeks. "Mr. Walsh, you better be worth waiting for," grumbles Henry. Darling Henry, you sweet summer child. He absolutely *isn't*!

"I can't have him living in our house!"

A Concussed Dylan Stays with the Walshes, and Kyle Is Gay

SEASON 2 | EPISODE 3
SUMMER STORM

Dylan's father, Jack, gets arrested—possibly for identity fraud?

This is, after all, neither the actor who played McKay *père* in the flowerpot-smashing episode wherein we met him; nor is it Josh Taylor, the third and final Dylan's dad we all remember. Dylan's mother, Iris, buys Dylan a ticket to Hawaii, but he's got no use for her woo-woo ministrations and elects instead for self-destructive surfing during the titular summer storm, to the utter horror of the soundtrack synthesizer. For his broody trouble, Dylan winds up in a local ER, where his emergency contacts,

Cindy and Brenda, find him. They take him home, since it's that or leave him in a hospital where the extras have backward maxi-pads taped over their eye injuries.

It's the kind thing to do (and Dylan's main antagonist at Casa Walsh, Jim, is conveniently out of town on business), but Brenda is outraged that her mother hasn't taken her and Dylan's breakup into account. Cindy points out that Dylan is Brandon's friend too, which should incense Brenda even further, as once again Brandon's feelings are privileged over hers, but she settles for snottily refusing to bring Dylan a tray of food. The inherent drama of the situation exerts its pull on her soon enough, though, and much agonized kissing and pained "what are we to each other"–ing ensues, culminating in Brenda wailing that the writers need to keep them apart for a few more episodes until the Parents Television Council finds some other show to pick o— er, that she needs "this time" to figure out what she wants.

As always, Brenda wants positive reinforcement for being a *literal* drama queen—and she gets it, despite her C-minus in-class performance of an Ophelia monologue from *Hamlet*. Thus buoyed, she's far more nurturing to Dylan when she gets home, bringing him a blanket, his book . . . and her bod. Their umpteenth conflicted make-out sesh goes south when Jim conveniently returns home and immediately starts bellowing about Dylan "taking advantage" of Brenda, then reams Cindy for sending the fox an engraved invitation to the henhouse. (We're paraphrasing.) Never one to turn down some dramz either, Dylan peaces out to the beach club, leaving a note on Brenda's nightstand marked "Read Me." Because Brenda of all people would see a letter addressed to her next to her alarm clock and shrug, "None of my business"?

As Dylan hides out in his family's old cabana at the beach club and sobs through a moist flashback to happier summer days with Dad, Brenda reacts to Jim's dishwasher-loading nitpicks by bursting into tears: Jim drove Dylan away! They have to help him, he can't just walk around in that hideous sleeveless Baja hoodie and sleep on the beach! Part of that may have been silent! A stricken Jim says Brenda's growing up too fast, but agrees to extend an olive branch, and the tense paternal-proxy relationship that ebbs and flows between Jim and Dylan over the next few seasons writes another chapter. It's a glimmer of something interesting that James Eckhouse and Luke Perry always acted well, but which the writing could never *quite* get a consistent handle on.

Elsewhere, the writing struggles with current argot, as a storyline in which Kelly hurls herself at pint-size football star Kyle (David Lascher) features locutions like "making it" (only in the '70s) and "I feel like a fool!" (only on TV). Why does Kelly feel like a fool? Because her flirty skinny-dipping got a nauseated reaction from Kyle commensurate with witnessing a shark attack. Kyle is struggling with his sexuality, you see—and Kelly's cool about his hesitant semi-demi-coming-out, once it's clear it doesn't mean she *personally* is ugly or whatever. Regrettably, she's also cool about Steve's creepy (and underdressed—wear a *whole* tank top, bro!) attempts to insert himself into the situation by haranguing Kyle about not having Done It with Kelly. Okay, perhaps "resigned to" is more accurate, but still.

The less said about David and Donna's "brilliant" drag *Romeo & Juliet* bit—and the overlaughing response from Mr. Suiter (Michael St. Gerard, as bad an actor as his character is an acting teacher)—the better.

"I just have one question . . . Are we having fun yet?"

The Gang, with an Assist from Torrential Rain, Ruin Two Strangers' Honeymoon

> ### SEASON 2 | EPISODE 7
> CAMPING TRIP

The Gang—which now includes Andrea and David—apparently need a vacation from their summer vacation, so they're going camping!

Initially, Dylan was going to skip it to spend time with his still-offscreen mother, but she's informed him that his "planetary alignment is in severe disarray," so she's going to the desert and he's not invited. Brandon convinces Dylan to come camping, and since Steve is being anal about minimizing everyone's luggage in the van, Dylan's going to have to (1) borrow clothes from Brandon that (2) Brenda has to find room for in the bag she and Brandon are sharing. Brandon's jeans are going to be short but otherwise roomy on Dylan's slim pins, but that's not the worst calamity to befall the squad: torrential rains strand them at a rustic cabin resort, where they're all forced to share the last leaky-roofed unit and commence bickering at one another. Only Brandon is able to maintain his good mood, until he wants to change out of his soaking-wet sneakers and finds out that Brenda neglected to re-pack his hiking boots. She defends herself by saying she wouldn't have taken them out of the bag if she didn't have to make room for Dylan's clothes, which sends Dylan into a mope about being a "cosmic jinx." If his goal is to make Brenda reconsider dumping him, this unsexy whining is a weird strategy.

Also posted up at the resort are Neil (Peter Marc Jacobson, at the time Fran Drescher's husband!) and Allison (Gina LaMond), who keep having their wedding night interrupted by these annoying teens, making conversation at the vending machine and stopping by for dry firewood. But then the kids, with nothing better to do, are having a roundtable discussion about the meaning of life (literally) when Allison—scored with a tuba playing a droopy comic version of the "Wedding March" recessional—weepily asks to crash with them because Neil is "a stupid idiot." Turns out they're *both* stupid idiots, who got married without discussing whether they wanted children, only now Allison is pregnant and convinced that Neil's blanket declaration of childlessness-by-choice, made in ignorance of said pregnancy, means they're doomed. While Neil becomes the last to know and tries to absorb the news, Brenda and Dylan repair to the newlyweds' cabin to argue some more about their own relationship. Dylan is pouting when Neil and Allison return, all smiles and vague promises to figure things out; this only enrages Dylan further, and he basically orders Neil to get all the way on board with father-hood, immediately: "I know what it's like to grow up being constantly reminded that you are a mistake, and if you're not prepared to love that baby or give it up, you might as well have an abortion right now." WHOA, BRO. TOO FAR. Leaving Brenda to make apologies for him, Dylan staggers off to take a *long* pull off a tiny airplane bottle of booze . . .

. . . and Brandon, chipper again, finds Dylan the next morning surrounded by—oh no!—*two* tiny airplane liquor bottles. He bucks Dylan up enough to agree to a hike, where the episode's most noteworthy event occurs: Brandon, in his squishy tennis shoes, slips off a cliff; Jason Priestley's very obvious stunt double dangles off a rock face, zero inches above a foothold, between close-up shots of Brandon with a slightly banged-up face and completely immobile hair, until Dylan finally pulls Brandon to safety. Brandon is relieved that he didn't die; Dylan recovers his composure to go apologize to Neil and Allison, who generously tell him he gave them a lot to think about—presumably that parenthood actually isn't worth it if it means your child might grow up to be an insufferable prat like Dylan.

Every Boy Alive Loves Emily Valentine, and Brenda Can't Take It

SEASON 2 | EPISODE 8
WILDFIRE

Another first day of school has come around and brought with it a new transfer: Emily Valentine (Christine Elise)!

She has bleached-blonde hair with *intentional* dark roots! She drives a motorcycle, not that we can recall ever seeing it again after this! She's *late* on her *very first day*! Despite having spent the whole summer whining about Brenda's refusal to take him back, Dylan is instantly attracted to Emily—so enraptured that he exits his car by walking on the upholstery and hopping over the side, apparently forgetting how doors work—and makes a date to show her some of L.A.'s high points and disprove some of her Marin County prejudices. Emily then goes inside and meets her locker neighbor Brandon, who also finds her compelling. Finally, Emily finishes encountering everyone who's anyone in . . . the can, where Kelly, Brenda, and Donna are brainstorming ideas for an "Addicted to Love" song parody to perform at (sigh) Hello Day; "Addicted to Sex" and "Addicted to School" are rejected, but Emily—from inside a stall—pitches "Addicted to Clothes" and gets an invite to join their act.

Emily's over at the Walsh house working on it when Dylan phones for Brandon, and she notes that she just met a Dylan with a Porsche speedster and a "cute little scar in his right eyebrow." For some reason her new friends all just look pointedly at each other instead of telling Emily about Brenda and Dylan's past relationship and thus avoiding a lot of heartache later. Maybe if they had, when Dylan brings her to the Mulholland Drive overlook and tells her he's not looking for anything heavy, Emily might have done something other than reply, "Who said anything about heavy?" and make out with him.

Meanwhile, Brandon dimes out Dylan to Brenda, telling her he brought Emily to the Peach Pit. Brenda claims, "I am not going to be a jealous person," but then (1) phones Kelly and claims "Emily made the first move" with Dylan; (2) gets her girl squad to join her in calling Emily "slut" for getting flirted at by Steve; (3) accuses Dylan of taking Emily on their *one date* because he somehow knew Emily would sleep with him; (4) throws Emily's disclosure about going on the Pill due to two older sisters' implied unplanned pregnancies in Emily's face; (5) ruins a barbecue by reaming Emily out for . . . dating Brenda's ex, which no one told Emily about until after the date. And look, we love that Brenda's bitchiness is starting to come into full flower, but she is *so* over the top given Emily's ignorance of Brenda and Dylan's history—it's not like *she* watched Season 1!—and the fact that Brenda's full-on soap villainess attack (Emily: "This isn't Beverly Hills, it's Knots Landing") doesn't earn so much as an impotent "Brenda!" from either of her parents is actually kind of shocking.

Motivated by a need to get Emily onstage for their Hello Day performance, Brenda manages to apologize (badly), in the course of which Emily tells her not only that she didn't sleep with Dylan, but also that she's a virgin! The act is saved, with Emily singing "Breaking Up Is Hard to Do" instead of "Addicted to Clothes" and joining Cindy in recommending that Brenda reunite with Dylan, which she finally does, THANK GOD.

Douglas Emerson having been busted down to "guest star" status, Scott returns from his summer in Oklahoma a changed dork: now he wears a giant Stetson, presses country CDs on David, and tries to rescue an awkward friend date by shooting his new .22. Scott apologizes the next day, and as he's wandering off, David calls after him: "Cool it with the guns, will ya?" "Okay," Scott grins. And he probably will! Forever!!!

"This is very hip, Brandon. Very hip."

Hillcrest Drive's First Black Family Moves In, and Everyone Handles It Badly

SEASON 2 | EPISODE 9
ASHES TO ASHES

Andrea is excited finally to fill a staff photographer vacancy at the *Blaze* with new applicant Robinson Ashe III (Eugene Byrd), but when she sends Brandon to meet him, Brandon is shocked to learn that the person weighed down by this legacy is not the beefy Scandinavian in Tech class but the African American pipsqueak behind him.

Robby's family, flush with microwave popcorn riches, is newly arrived on the Walshes' street from Inglewood, just in time for the Neighborhood Watch's panic about several area break-ins, which Mrs. Ashe (Tina Lifford) tells Block Captain Cindy they heard about: "In fact, my husband thinks it's a good thing all these break-ins started *before* we moved in." To Cindy's look of horror, Mrs. Ashe must quickly add that she was joking.

Brandon's just dropped Robby at the house when he gets into a minor fender-bender, literally running into Robby's sister Sherice (Vivica A. Fox!), who's pulling her car in as he's backing out of the driveway. Sherice is just as pugnacious as Brandon, which is why both teens are aghast when each of their dads insists on paying for the damage—Jim because, as he carefully avoids saying, he doesn't want to look racist, and Mr. Ashe (Richard "Shaft" Roundtree!) because he knows Sherice is a terrible driver, and is also generally mad at her for still sort of dating Devo (Billy "Sly" Williams), from their old neighborhood. Sherice also still attends her old high school, reportedly telling Brandon, "I wouldn't go to West Beverly if it was the last hellhole in the galaxy. Too many cashed-up snobs." Where is the lie? Because of her own situation, stealing education from the Beverly Hills school district instead of rotting in the Valley, Andrea wants Brandon to . . . do a story for the *Blaze* about why Sherice *doesn't* go there? It's just a flimsy pretext to put Brandon in Sherice's path for interracial flirting, Emily having been mysteriously sidelined, and also to get Brandon to lose Robby's trust by making him trade on their friendship, and *also* to keep making Jason Priestley do his moderately racist impression of Sherice's manner and accent.

Meanwhile, Devo decides to brave Mr. Ashe's disapproval and put some effort into his relationship with Sherice by surprising her with flowers and frozen yogurt. But between busybody Mrs. Cooper's complaints about Mr. Kaplan's noisy dogs and the Walshes' security system's constant false alarms, the Security Patrol ends up trying to pin the rash of break-ins on Devo. Instead of being outraged about Devo's false arrest and physical assault—by representatives of an organization with zero oversight, probably staffed by people too incompetent and racist to make it onto the LAPD, an organization itself not exactly known for its civil rights leaders—the Ashes try to distance themselves from Devo. Brandon, smelling a cover-up by the Security Patrol, refuses to drop it, even taking the perilous journey to *South-Central* to ambush Devo at work and try to convince him to tell his story. It falls to Devo to bring up Rodney King and inform Brandon how tragically unremarkable Devo's experience actually is: "The amazing thing wasn't what happened with Rodney, because, see, that happens every day down here. The amazing thing was the whole thing got peeped out by somebody's home video camera." This episode aired September 19, 1991, so . . . stand by for more as that story developed, sigh.

Eventually, Brenda shows up with Sherice and Robby. Brandon and Robby pose with the tamales that have brought them back together, and poor Dylan is forced to compliment Brandon's story about it: "'It's when we stop looking at the human race as individuals we, as a generation, are in trouble.' Eloquently put." Good thing he's repeating 11th-grade English along with all his other 11th-grade classes, as is everyone else. And since that's a wrap on the Ashes, we'd better shut our mouths.

"I can still do a lot of things."

Cousin Bobby Uses a Wheelchair, and Everyone Is Super-Weird About It

SEASON 2 | EPISODE 11
LEADING FROM THE HEART

Brandon and Brenda's "beloved" cousin, Bobby (Gordon Currie), is about to visit the Walshes; he's considering a transfer to UCLA.

This information is imparted with many significant glances among the Walshes, with the senior Walshes doomsaying about the "ramifications" of Cousin Bobby coming to live with them. Is Cousin Bobby coming to Los Angeles to . . . die? Is Cousin Bobby . . . a rhinoceros? The episode postpones the reveal long enough to give Kelly time to enthuse over pictures of Cousin Bobby she's seen on the Walshes' mantel, and for Brenda to warn her not to commit to a crush narrative before she's met the guy, because: Cousin Bobby uses a wheelchair, and it's time for everyone to learn some important lessons about that.

Cousin Bobby himself could stand to learn a couple of interpersonal/wardrobe lessons, like burning the horrendous Loverboy headband he's wearing, and not commenting on how his *first cousin* has turned into a "real woman." He might also want to work on developing an interest in women his own age; Brenda glowers to Kelly at one point that Brenda's friend, who Bobby was dating, dumped him "right after the accident," which is bad . . . until you consider that Bobby, who is at least 21 in this episode, would have been an 18-year-old dating a 14-year-old at the time, which is *very* bad. One wonders if the "accident" wasn't actually Brenda's friend's father shooting Cousin Bobby in the groin. Either way, he's learned nothing, as he immediately starts flirting with Kelly and she flirts back. Although Kelly's awkward about things Cousin Bobby can and can't "do," like joining her on the couch when it was he who suggested it, they have cute chemistry—a fact of major concern to the twins, who cock-block Cousin Bobby with interminable "hilarious" stories of their youth (Brandon), then creepily eavesdrop on Kelly and CB from the stairs (Brenda).

Cousin Bobby ignores everyone's concern brows to suggest a group horseback outing, which goes fine (failed attempts at humor involving Brandon's feisty mount notwithstanding), and he's then invited to a party with The Gang, which goes less well. The fiesta house has more stairs than San Simeon, and it's an uncomfortable moment, made more so by the stinkface Cousin Bobby pulls—although the guys in The Gang overcompensating with nonsense like "Party starter, comin' through!" as they carry the wheelchair up the staircase make us grimace too. The unfun continues inside, where Cousin Bobby's confronted with yet more stairs; a dry party . . . except for his shirt, which is soon drenched with a clumsy girl's drink; and Tal, the host (Gabriel Macht from *Suits!*), asking Kelly to dance. Instead of no-thanks-ing him to hang out with Cousin Bobby, Kelly takes forever to accept—and asks Cousin Bobby to hold her purse. Girl, he's not a side table. Fed up, Cousin Bobby rips her for treating him like a "novelty," and when Brandon appears, saying he's been "looking everywhere" for Cousin Bobby—like, he's surrounded by stairs; what, he Spider-Manned himself to the ceiling?—Cousin Bobby asks to leave. Brenda assumes the worst and screams at Kelly for breaking Bobby's heart, while at home, Brandon opens a heart-to-heart in his usual respectful way: by braying at his cousin to explain himself. A Casio is sad as Bobby tries to communicate his challenges, before the moment is ruined with an inadvertently hilarious account of Cousin Bobby's fateful encounter with a ski-slope tree. Several dozen constipated faces later, Brandon and Cousin Bobby decide not to ask for another take, ending the scene on a goofy "love you man" exchange that Jason Priestley punctuates by *patting his heart*.

The next morning, Kelly drops by (as does the boom mic) to wrap it up, rightly pointing out that they've known each other for two days, so it's not fair of Cousin Bobby to ask her for a lifetime commitment. Good point, especially since we never see or hear about Cousin Bobby after Brenda drives him to the airport (though Currie does return as a drug dealer later in the series).

. . . And yes, you read that right: Brenda finally gets her license, with an assist from cringey Asian stereotypes and a racist music cue. Cindy actually throws a congrats party around this achievement; we throw a Bon Voyage party for the departure of this so-called "character beat" and the STUFF it has "inspired."

"I was trying to avoid a gas chamber, not trying to sneak into some school district."

Andrea's at Risk of Getting Outed as Lying Valley Scum, and Her Grandma Rose Refuses to Help Sell Her Cover Story

SEASON 2 | EPISODE 12
DOWN AND OUT (OF DISTRICT)
IN BEVERLY HILLS

Learning that Brandon submitted Andrea's famous "cafeteria exposé" for a high-school journalism award, you might think, "Wow, he actually did something thoughtful for once in his stupid life"—but no, it's actually extremely thought*less*, in that drawing attention to Andrea may reveal the truth about where she lives, which is in the Valley and *not* at her grandmother's address within the West Beverly High catchment.

When Andrea wins, she tries to intercept Grandma Rose (Lainie Kazan!) to align their stories before a reporter (improbably) arrives to profile her. Perhaps he hears through the door as Grandma Rose informs Andrea, "If he asks me a direct question, I'm sorry if you're going to be expelled, but I am not going to lie," because he is surprisingly curious about things like Andrea's style of decor and whether the couch she allegedly sleeps on folds out. After he's left, Andrea—wounded by Grandma Rose's refusal to corroborate Andrea's claims—pouts that she isn't, as Grandma Rose puts it, just going to all this trouble "for the privilege of cavorting with rich kids," which, fair. (The ruse is really about the superior resources at WBH, but still—good burn and definitely a side benefit of Andrea's grift.) Andrea then notes, "When you were my age, you assumed a different identity," which, *unfair*, in that Grandma Rose did so not to attend a high school with a superior biology lab but in order to *avoid being killed in the Holocaust*. It's not that we can't imagine a teen character on this show saying something this ignorant, but it's wildly out of character for Andrea.

Grandma Rose ends up being so unconvincing that the reporter dimes Andrea out to Mrs. Teasley, who is forced to initiate an inquiry about Andrea's residency. Kelly, in a rare moment of altruism, volunteers to make over Grandma Rose's living room

Season Two   51 to give the impression that a teenager lives there. Things are trending up, except that every time Andrea mentions her mother, Grandma Rose shuts down. (When Andrea actually speaks *to* her mother, on the phone, Grandma Rose starts vacuuming right beside her to drown her mother out.) Grandma Rose's animosity toward Andrea's mother is not, she insists, because the younger Mrs. Zuckerman isn't Jewish; it's that Andrea's mother reportedly doesn't respect Grandma Rose, but we really only hear about a lack of attentiveness on her part when Grandma Rose broke her leg? So all the plaintive violin music on the score is an ethnic misdirect and this rift is just about typical mother-in-law grievances? Whatever: Andrea doesn't want to be in the middle anymore and storms off on the eve of the home visit, making her peace with her imminent expulsion. In her absence, though, Grandma Rose nails the interview, and Andrea takes advantage of her tender mood to force a phone conversation between Grandma Rose and her daughter-in-law—whose name, we learn, is *Beverly???* We don't know for sure if that Boomer-ish name was put into the script as a placeholder because someone read it on a poster for *this show*, but it's hard not to think so.

In the B-plot, Steve has a completely random Peach Pit meet-cute with Christine (Jennifer Runyon), a *Hartley House* superfan who gets very comfortable very quickly spending Steve's money and living the luxurious lifestyle of the son of a washed-up sitcom star. Steve isn't trying to hear first Kelly and then Brenda as they warn him that Christine is an extremely unsubtle gold-digger, but he can't ignore them entirely, finally setting up a sting operation in a jewelry store: he invites her to guess what he picked out for her, then presents her with an inexpensive-looking bracelet. When she can't hide her disappointment, he also tricks her into admitting that she knew who he was when they met. Steve rekindles his platonic friendship with Kelly, having sent Christine on her way—and let's hope she's learned the lessons from her fumbles with Steve to be a more effective sugar baby in the future.

DeadScott . . . Becomes

It's not the most famous episode in *Beverly Hills, 90210*'s firmament, but it's in the top three for sure: the one in which Scott Scanlon accidentally and fatally shoots himself in the stomach. (Weird choice for a show that isn't called *Antietam, 1862* to have the kid die of a gutshot.)

Everyone remembers Scott's death. What you may not remember is how titanically uncomfortable the episode is about clueless parents, longtime teenage friends growing apart, and unrequited love among the *Blaze* editorial board, until Scott mercifully . . . changes the subject.

And it is *so uncomfortable*. After an interminable opener involving a time capsule buried by the West Bev Class of 1941, we're reminded that David's relationship with his childhood bestie, Scott, has been deteriorating for some time—with, for the writing on *this* show, remarkably careful setup. But nobody informed Mrs. Scanlon, Scott's mom, who appears at school to accost David about helping her plan Scott's birthday party. Thanks to her commitment in the role, character actor Jenny O'Hara's obit is likely to contain a reference to her work here: she is a passive-aggressive and unreasonable terror, starting with her insistence that David round up a bunch of "friends" on 48 hours' notice. Scott has no friends except David, and even he only brings the total to like one-third of a friend, but David feels bad and is also probably scared of Mrs. Scanlon, so he tries to get The Gang to come. Nobody wants any part of it, predictably, though Donna agrees to try to convince them.

Come party time, Mrs. Scanlon's ragging on David for not coming through on the guest list while one of her 14 million other kids is sitting there popping balloons like a dick. Like, she's got bigger problems than David, including the gun-safety PSA her husband, Conrad (Greg Finley, and never has Wardrobe outfitted a man more daddishly), is delivering to some random cousin before Scott can get home to hear it. Donna does get most of The Gang to show up, but Brandon and Emily's lateness ruins the surprise, and none of them remembers to bring Scott a gift. But Scott is *thrilled* that the popular kids are there. Well, until he overhears David's frustrated rant to Donna about Mrs. Scanlon not realizing he *saved* the party, at which time a woodcut of Scott's face goes into the dictionary next to "hangdog."

Guiltily, David organizes a dance contest to resurrect the admittedly lame party; Brenda and Kelly even dirty-dance on Scott. Because it's dancing, though, Brandon has absented himself and Emily to some kid's room to make out—and when Mrs. Scanlon busts them and ejects them from the party, the rest of The Gang is happy to take its cue. David loyally stays. ("I promised his cousin I'd teach her how to freak," he sighs. Hee!) His reward? Getting scolded *again* by Mrs. Scanlon, this time for not having matches to light the cake; following Scott into Conrad's study, where instead of fetching his dad's lighter, Scott is twirling his dad's handgun like Mild Bill Cody; and witnessing Scott shoot himself.

Cut to a hastily assembled memorial at school, and Dylan not remembering who Scott is despite having saved him from bullies in Dylan's debut scene. But at least Dylan isn't making Scott's death about himself, unlike Brandon, who grumbles to Dylan that his new relationship with Emily's going great, except "this whole death thing" has thrown their timing off; Emily, who can't *wait* to mention to Andrea that she shouldn't "cover the funeral" because she and Bran were caught frenching on some little Scanlon's big-boy bed; and Andrea, who's in full clench mode about "Bremily" already *and* treating Scott's funeral like a news event on par with the death of a president.

But they're all coping better than David. He snarls at well-meaning questions about how he's holding up, yells at Mrs. Scanlon, and can't make himself go along with the hypocritical interest in DeadScott that nobody, including himself, had in AliveScott. It's not a great look when, on a hot mic, he rips on Brandon and the *Blaze*'s proposed "four-page insert"—and himself: "I can't even walk through the hall without somebody in my face trying to cheer me up like they're my new best friend. Well, what about my *old* best friend? It doesn't matter what you write about him in the paper, Brandon. It doesn't matter what you say about somebody once they're gone. What matters is how you treat them when they're still here." This rant is actually a pretty good performance from Brian Austin Green, and as a bonus, it's embarrassing for Brandon.

It also releases the necessary pressure, as David brings Mrs. Scanlon a "man-on-the-street" interview video of Scott; apologizes to Donna; and presides over a guerrilla time capsule dedicated to his friend . . . a nice idea that The Gang ruins by throwing a bunch of random crap in there that's all about themselves. (Board wax? Really, Dylwig?) And so we bid farewell to Scott, a casualty (as it were) of the changing priorities of the show, and the underwhelming acting of Douglas Emerson: he got one more role after this, then joined the Air Force, and we thank him for his service. May we all go forth and teach cousins to freak in his memory.

THE SCOTT SCANLON
MEMORIAL REPORT CARD

At the end of "The Next 50 Years," The Gang gathers on the West Beverly High campus in the dead of night to bury a Scott Scanlon memorial time capsule. The time capsule is a callback to a 1941 version unearthed with great ceremony earlier in the episode; an on-ramp to self-absorbed theatrics from our teenage heroes; and a misbegotten idea from the jump. Why do Brandon and Steve dig a grave-size hole for a small trunk? Why don't they do it at the *edge* of the quad instead of right in the middle, where it's sure to be spotted—and probably dug up—immediately? And did none of these dummies think to suggest an air- and watertight container, if the idea is to leave it down there for 50 years?

We know these quibbles miss the point of the grand gesture . . . but that's another, larger issue we have with the Scott Scanlon Memorial Time Capsule, to wit: few of the "gestures" included in it are grand, if "relevant to Scott or his interests" is the metric. In fact, some of the celebrants don't bring a "gesture" at all. Like, that hole has to have taken two hours to dig. You could have run down to the bodega in that time and bought a rose to throw in, *Emily Valentine*. Scott may have been an extraneous character who died so that the writers could make a point about gun violence, but he still deserved better than a quarter-assed remembrance the show should have thought through even if actual teenagers might not have. And since he's not around to judge, we'll have to do it for him.

CONTINUED

IN ORDER OF THEIR (SO-CALLED) CONTRIBUTIONS TO THE SSMTC, THE LETTER GRADE EACH OF THOSE PRESENT RECEIVED ON THIS ASSIGNMENT:

THE GROUP: Books, CDs, and magazines. Standard yearbook-y fodder for such a thing, meant to locate the discoverer in the cultural timeline; no objection. GRADE: B

ANDREA: The *Blaze* editor contributes two copies of their Scott memorial issue, one on recycled paper; the other, on "floppy disk, will undoubtedly be considered a primitive artifact in 50 years." Pretty sure it took only five minutes to throw together, but otherwise Andrea's on point, adding material that is actually *about Scott*. GRADE: A

STEVE: Helped dig the hole, but contributes his Corvette keychain as his "comment on today's technology." Huh? Thing is, it *would* be a subtle shout-out to the fact that, in the pilot, it's David who wrecks Steve's 'Vette, but Scott's hat that's left at the crime scene . . . if the writers remembered that that happened, which they evidently do not. GRADE: D

DONNA: A bolt of Lycra-Spandex. Her rationale is that nylons were a signifier of the 1940s, and the analogous clothing/fabric in the '90s is Lycra, but it has nothing to do with Scott. Also: a whole bolt? Where'd she even get it? GRADE: C+

BRENDA: "A very cool T-shirt in honor of the great Minnesota Twins, for very obvious reasons, I think!" Well, we'd love her to share them with us, because otherwise, it looks like Brenda is eulogizing a *Lakers fan* she barely knew with a shirt aggrandizing . . . herself. The shirt *is* nice as these things go, and she brought *something*, so we won't fail her outright. GRADE: C–

DYLAN: Surfboard wax, to symbolize the cyclical nature of time and eternity via the waves . . . or something. Impersonal, and there are better ways to embody the concept. GRADE: B–

BRANDON AND EMILY: Brandon helps dig, and maybe is copresenting the shirt with Brenda. Emily brings nothing. GRADE: D+

KELLY: Does not dig; does not bring anything. Should throw that shed-size jean jacket she's wearing into this or any other hole, however. GRADE: F

DAVID: David asked Mrs. Scanlon for Scott's prized cowboy hat, so extra credit for making Scott's mom happy in addition to adding one of the few items that isn't about the contributor instead of about Scott. Also furnishes sparklers to light at the end of the committal, because Scott loved the Fourth of July. Well done, for once. GRADE: A+

Emily Valentine Roofies Brandon with Fake Ecstasy

SEASON 2 | EPISODE 15
U4EA

How protective was *Beverly Hills, 90210* of Brandon's golden-boy image? When it came time for its putative protagonist to learn a Very Important Lesson about driving under the influence, it got the storyline rolling by having Steve spike his "virgin" margarita . . . and when it came time for Bran to learn a Very Important Lesson about doing drugs, the writers had *Emily* spike Brandon's drink. All of the hard-won lessons, none of the personal responsibility!

Of course, the strategy backfires by encouraging Brandon's customary self-righteousness, but we'll get to that. First, let's talk about how Brandon and the titular U4EA—we assume the show went with a made-up drug so as not to glamorize Ecstasy even inadvertently—came to cross paths. Brandon's just gone "locker official" in his relationship with Emily, a turn of events Em takes as license to act incredibly condescending to The Gang, and particularly Andrea, about the "incredibly hip underground club" she got a flyer for. Not sure how "hip" it is if it's courting underage try-hards with sticky bird nests on their heads, but Emily sells The Gang on the experience—even Brenda, who's already over Emily, and Andrea, who would probably rather split an infinitive in a headline than go to a rave but is successfully baited when Emily implies that Andrea's "scared."

Andrea has nothing to fear, despite Dylan's somber warning to Brenda that "some people" only come to raves "for the drugs." After everyone's scavenger-hunted the club's address by hitting up a flyer-specified market and dropped the secret password—"I'd like to exchange an egg"—they end up at a typically sanitized TV rave, hardly worth the strenuous lying everyone has had to do to their parents to get there. The dance floor's half empty, the resident drug dealer is practically marked off with road flares (he's . . . wearing a T-shirt with a "4" on it), and the wan addicts festooning various dark corners of the club are more baffling than cautionary. What's with the greige makeup? And what kind of self-respecting junkie pays a cover charge when s/he could smoke that crack anywhere? Andrea won't get a chance to investigate these questions, having spilled coffee on the map

Emily drew, so she and Steve spend most of the episode trying to exchange eggs at the wrong places and bitching about Emily. Okay, Andrea bitches about her; Steve advises Andrea that if she wants Brandon, she needs to go after him. Steve and Andrea have a charming and natural chemistry in their scenes in "U4EA" that had many fans (including these correspondents) longing to see where "Standrea" might go; pity we never find out.

But if Andrea's going to try to lock down her actual crush, she better hurry up: Emily is wheedling Brandon to try U4EA, saying "it's the best way to bring a new couple closer." Proud square Brandon passes, but does jokingly note that he'd try it if "a poltergeist" snuck into his room and dosed him, so Emily barges through that loophole, bringing him a compromised Coke he didn't ask for and eagerly waiting for it to take effect. How do we know it has? He "dances." It is very bad. Brandon's really feeling "euphoric," though, and the revelation that Emily spiked his soda does get a self-righteously square objection from him, but he's soon too high to mind. The others have had enough of the club—Kelly's announcement that "this place is never again!" is a great line, but one of the chief minuses of the place is actually a Sgt.-Pepper-jacket-wearing David, drunk on brown whiskey and barfing perilously near Dylan's shoes, and he's leaving with them. (Nice work by both Brian Austin Green and the Foley artists.) But Brandon, mysteriously shirtless under his jacket and gnawing Emily's face as they lounge on the hood of his car, isn't going anywhere. Dylan takes his keys and leaves him cab fare, and everyone departs in disgust . . . except Steve and Andrea, who turn up just in time for the place to get raided, and for Brandon to slobber on Andrea.

The next morning, Brandon's dragging serious ass, and in response to Brenda's guilt trip, he says he was drugged by Emily and baby-voices self-pityingly that "people talk about drugs like they're so cool, but it's just a big fake-out." It occurs to at least one of the authors of this book that he's doing them wrong, but anyway, Brandon's day gets worse when Dylan drives him back to what's left of his car: the front seat and one door are missing entirely, and the chassis is covered in graffiti (and signed, with a large flower, by "BARB." Junior League plays rough in the City of Angels!). Brandon sighs to Dylan that there's "no lie big enough to cover this one" (see above re: doing it wrong) and opts to come clean with "Jimbo" about what happened.

The senior Walshes are as unimpressed as you might expect with the twins' version of events, but opt to believe that Brandon got slipped a mickey. They also opt not to comment on Brandon whining that his "life is about" paying for damage "done" to his car, namely that said damage—driving drunk; buying a lemon; taking drugs and leaving his car overnight—is inevitably his own goddamn fault. Perhaps they feel Emily's arrival is punishment enough, and it's definitely uncomfortable, as Emily tries to fix things by macking on Brandon, then desperately offering to pay for the Mustang when he whisper-yells that he can't trust her anymore and he needs "space." (Remember this lack of clarity on their relationship status later.)

Brandon makes peace with Andrea by participating in a literal "this is your brain on drugs" egg demonstration, and that's surely, obviously, the end of *that* . . . Hello?

"Brandon, what do you think is wrong with her?"

Emily Loses It

SEASON 2 | EPISODE 16
MY DESPERATE VALENTINE

Brenda decides she and Dylan need to embrace activities besides Doing It—"interesting, cultural" things. The couple then attempts a string-quartet concert and an evening of Paganini. Meanwhile, an anonymous letter-writer is sending Travis Bickle–esque poems to the *Blaze*. Why are we telling you these things? No reason!

We'll also tell you that Brandon has wimpily locker-dumped Emily without telling her and, when she confronts him, just as wimpily lies that he needed to keep his stuff closer to the *Blaze* office. Emily pretends to believe him but doesn't take the hint that comes with it, buttonholing him about hanging out. Instead of simply telling her they're done, he makes vague excuses. Why? He doesn't want Emily to become "an outcast" because the great Brandon Walsh dumped her. Instead of getting over himself, Brandon heads to the Peach Pit—partly to avoid the hang-up calls he's started getting, *hmm*—and gets caught by Emily hanging out with Steve (and free fries) when he'd said he'd be busy studying. Emily makes another apologetic pitch for reuniting, saying she loves Brandon, who finally tells her straight out that it's over.

Or so he thinks. Brandon walks Emily to her bike and they find the tires slashed (*hmmm*), but when Emily cry-voices that the culprit should have slashed her throat instead, Brandon thinks it's a great idea to . . . invite her to stay at his house? Emily's parents are out of town (according to her), but there's no reason Bran couldn't drive her to *her* house instead of opening the door for her to get, and cling to, the wrong idea with a sleepover. There's also no reason for Brandon to act this flirty and welcoming under the circumstances, but we shouldn't victim-blame; once again, Emily is acting without Brandon's consent when she slips into his bed and starts kissing on him. He puts her off with some garbage about need-ing to be in love to make love (which he's done one time; shut up, Brandon), but somehow, after crossing another Brandon boundary *and* raising Cindy's suspi-cions about the slashed-tires story, Emily's still welcome to join The Gang for the homecoming-float MacGuffin-stivities.

Em elects to borrow Brandon's treasured Twins jersey for a day of hard labor and painting, and to imply to Andrea that she and Brandon Did It. After she's departed Casa Walsh, she continues to leave inappropriate answering-machine messages for the senior Walshes to hear—which is when Emily loses Jim, because if there's anything dads hate, it's people fooling around with the phone. Emily lost Brenda weeks ago, and while the terms Brenda throws around are not how we talk about people with mental illnesses, she's right to note that Brandon really barely knows anything about Emily or her family (because he's so self-absorbed, she does not add).

As Brenda warns Brandon away from a cake Emily left on their doorstep (*hmmmm*) and the soundtrack makes histrionic reference to a Ted Bundy mini-series from the '80s, Emily divests herself of possessions, including a vintage typewriter she's donating to the *Blaze*. Andrea should remember from the rap line that this could indicate suicidal planning, but instead invites Emily to the float's "inauguration."

Speaking of eyesores, the horrors the rest of the group is wearing for the float photo (Dylan's Baja top; a herd of camel toes on the girls) *should* distract from Emily squeezing in next to Brandon and nibbling on him right before the timer goes off. No such luck: he loses it on her, while The Gang just stands there eight inches away from them. When Emily delivers her own monologue on choosing Brandon and saving her first time for him, they keep standing *right there* instead of going *behind* the float to eavesdrop like normal people. Emily slinks away at last; not long after that, the hang-ups resume, the camera *finally* wheeling around a pay phone to confirm that it's Emily making the calls, like we thought it might be Cousin Bobby or something?

Jim's already fed up with Emily's phone malarkey when Andrea, Documents Examiner, shows up to report that the threatening letters sent to the *Blaze* came from Emily's typewriter. That seals it for the Walshes minus Brenda, who try to track down Emily's parents while the editing cuts tensely between Brenda and Dylan enjoying some Paganini and Emily in the Walshes' driveway, defacing the float with gasoline and white paint. (The float is . . . also white. We don't know.) Bren and Dylan pull in after the concert to find Emily brooding and flicking the lighter, and Brenda is bitchy at first, then flips into rap-line mode to assure Emily that nobody hates her and that she's a part of The Gang. Dylan keeps his eyes locked on the lighter until Emily's lured inside the Walsh kitchen to give a full confession: she made the calls, sent the letters, slashed her own tires, and hates herself.

And then we . . . guess . . . her parents retrieve her, and get her some help? Whatever becomes of Emily, it happens offscreen, as The Gang is left to armchair-diagnose her and stigmatize mental illness and therapy some more. At least Brandon takes a nice long break before his next melodramatic relationship! . . . jk, he doesn't.

"There's no secrets on this team, Walsh. And there's no shortcuts either."

Brandon 1, Steroids 0; Driving 1, Brenda 0 (Again)

SEASON 2 | EPISODE 20
A COMPETITIVE EDGE

Steve and Brandon have joined the track team, suddenly. Brandon is so committed to this sport we've never heard about him doing that he's willing to quit the *Blaze* to make time for it in his schedule.

Or maybe it's because his many sports editorials ripping on the crappy track team get him wedgied by the team's veterans. (We use the word "veterans" for a reason; several of Brandon's teammates look to be in their mid-30s.) It's soon clear there's a big story in that locker room, though, when Brandon makes a dad joke about anabolic steroids and hears only crickets in response.

Track-team captain and seeming 35-year-old Burke (Jim Pirri) thinks Brandon's a narc, but reaches out to Steve about the "power pack," the steroid cycle Burke and some of his bulkier teammates use. Steve is skeptical—we would be too; the "steroids" look like Tic Tacs—but since he's once again stuck in a dumb Issues Plot that obliges him to compete haplessly with Brandon at a sport, he feels he's got no choice. Brandon feels *he's* got no choice but to do a story on the steroid use he suspects is happening on the team, though he does have a choice in whether to summon Andrea melodramatically to the Peach Pit after hours to discuss the piece, instead of just calling her. Andrea doesn't mind; it lets her mention her award-winning cafeteria exposé yet again, and also, it's Brandon.

Brandon's initial attempt to draw out the 'roid schemers is so clumsily obvious that when Kyle Conners steps forward as a source, it's probably as much to save Brandon from further embarrassing himself as it is to put a stop to a situation Kyle thinks is out of control. The last time we saw Kyle, in "Summer Storm," he was struggling with his sexuality, so it's inappropriate to call him Brandon's Deep Throat on the story, but . . . there's no other comparable reference. Certainly Andrea thinks Brandon's piece is Woodward-esque, but, as Brandon is getting cold feet (as it were) about publishing it, the 'roiders are getting increasingly paranoid about who's talking to the *Blaze*, and Steve's stuck between the rock of Brandon's judgment and the hard place of the 'roiders thinking *he's* the mole.

After a weird athletic-department meeting in which the coach yells at the track team while Andrea stands next to him for no reason we can discern except to allow the athletes to stare daggers at her, the Brandon-Steve angst continues with a dustup in the Peach Pit's back room. Steve says he's just started a cycle, "no biggie," but also says he changed his mind about PEDs after reading the "So You're Thinking of Taking Anabolic Steroids" pamphlet the coach handed out. It's got to be the first time in history one of these publications has worked, but Steve's still in physical peril: Burke and Tony Miller (Michael Cudlitz) will beat him flat if they think he's the source on Brandon's imminent exposé. Steve implores Brandon to write something clearing Steve's name, adding that Andrea's in love with Brandon and will print anything Brandon wants. Brandon has a spasm of journalistic ethics and refuses, and Steve flings Brandon bodily into the side of the fridge and storms out, to the dismay of several guitar chords . . . and Kelly, who witnesses the fracas while doing a little pie business. We're fine with it, however.

Steve continues pressuring *Blaze* editors to say he's not the source, to no avail; Burke and Tony are sure Steve talked, and 'roid-ragefully hurl free weights around the gym—way to play it cool, guys—before inviting Steve to take a walk. They want him to take the fall for the whole team. Brandon appears to bray at the cheaters, but they ignore his tiny ass until Kyle shows up and admits that *he* is the source. And that's kind of it. Bran and Steve make up, nobody gets expelled, the track team goes back to sucking, and Kyle is reshelved until Season 3.

Also shelved after this, thank God: Brenda/car "comedy." Cindy is visibly nauseated while riding with her, but Brenda insists she's a good driver now and finagles the rights to Brandon's car when he's not using it. Only because Jim has the flu and Brandon is distracted by the steroids A-plot does she get away with it—and not for long, as she promptly rear-ends some lady at a stop sign. Her "victim" is super-nice about it, but sizes Brenda up as an inept newbie and sets about conning the Walshes for whiplash pain and suffering. And she totally would have gotten away with it if that meddling kid (Brenda) hadn't caught her vigorously sweatin' the oldies.

ANDREA'S UNDERCOVER CAFETERIA EXPOSÉ . . .

An Exposé

Blaze editrix Andrea Zuckerman is eternally eager to establish the West Beverly student paper's bona fides as an award-winner that "a lot of parents read"—and that includes repeated references to an apparently legendary article she wrote, offscreen, in which she went undercover "on the cafeteria thing."

Properly titled "The Underbelly of Cafeteria Cuisine," the caf exposé rears its notorious head repeatedly in Andrea story arcs—usually, now that we think about it, adjacent to some ill-advised action on Brandon's part, as when he submits said story for award consideration, not thinking that the attention could reveal that Andrea's living out of district and not strictly eligible to attend WBH. (In Brandon's slight defense, a high-profile extracurricular like the editorship of the school paper is probably going to get her busted eventually anyway, but whatever.) The cafeteria story comes up again later in the second season; with Brandon struggling to reconcile investigating steroid use on the track team with screwing over his friends by reporting it, Andrea reminds him that she's been in the same position, when she "had to go undercover to break the story on the cafeteria."

Given that said story and the researching of same is apparently accorded a level of journalistic respect on par with the *Washington Post*'s Watergate coverage, we have to ask: what in *the* hell could even be in that story?

We should probably first ask *how* Andrea even got that story—or whether we're all using the same definition of "undercover" here. We doubt she tried to assume another identity entirely, but how covert could this op have been when, as of the pilot episode, Andrea's already ensconced as the editor-in-chief of the *Blaze*, and would likely have been known to her fellow student workers as a reporter, if not to the caf staff? The logistical—and ethical—difficulties of this assignment are perhaps a wee bit overstated.

What horrors Andrea could possibly have revealed are probably also overstated—and therefore wisely left unspecified. Let's face it: the revolting nature of cafeteria food generally is not a scandalous secret. As well, the food-service budget for what is, ritzy Zip notwithstanding, a public school would be a matter of public record, so the menu is not confidential, and it doesn't sound like Andrea wrote a finance story in any case.

ANDREA'S UNDERCOVER CAFETERIA EXPOSÉ ...

An Exposé

So, what did this award-nominated piece uncover exactly? We have a few theories on possible topics, including:

- Serial thefts from the walk-in fridge included the entire menu for the slumber-party episode; the eggs for David and Scott's Halloween egg fight; and an industrial vat of mayonnaise liberated by Emily Valentine to deface the homecoming float (we only *thought* it was white paint).

- The "surprise" in the Tuna Surprise is choice cuts from characters we never saw again, including the principal from the pilot episode.

- The food cart serving the revolting-looking burrito that Tricia the figure skater (Gabrielle Anwar) pretended to enjoy was actually a plant designed to drive student lunch business back to the cafeteria.

- Felice Martin demanded that funding for oysters, chocolate, pomegranates, and all those strawberries Kelly's always "erotically" eating be removed from the budget lest impressionable children become inadvertently aroused; the school board caved, in closed session.

- *There is no cafeteria.*

To our minds, this last option is the most likely big reveal of "The Underbelly of Cafeteria Cuisine"—not what the meals contain or how they're paid for or who benefits from cutting worker salaries, but the fact that they're prepared and consumed in an alternate dimension viewers never see. Think about it: we see West Bev students eating sushi (Marianne Moore) or sack lunches (the Walshes); we know there's a soda machine in the hallway; background actors do sometimes carry cafeteria *trays* into the quad at midday. But we don't see the cafeteria, and aside from nods to Andrea's story, the characters seldom refer to going *to* the cafeteria, so we can only conclude that, when Andrea went undercover, she had nowhere to go undercover *to*, and wrote a fierce screed disclosing that "the cafeteria" is actually "the hood of a booty Plymouth station wagon some teacher's cousin Donny is using as a cooktop."

Hell, we'd read it.

"Andrea, if you had a little more experience, you'd know that love is not a public health issue!"

Andrea Can't Be a Safe Sex Advocate Without Having Brandon Remind Her About Her Virginity

SEASON 2 | EPISODE 21
EVERYBODY'S TALKIN' 'BOUT IT

When noisy local prudes get a public health survey shut down at WBH, Andrea and the *Blaze*'s managing editor, John Griffin (Andy Hirsch), decide to do an end run, bringing the school board a proposal to make condoms available to students at the school.

The issue lights up the next meeting of the parents' association, where the second and final depiction of Donna's mother, Felice Martin (the great Katherine Cannon), puts on her most reasonable, serene voice to deliver a polemic against condoms and in favor of abstinence. An agitated Donna pushes back: "It's like if you have a swimming pool in your backyard. You can tell your children not to go in it—you can even build a fence around it—but if you know that they're going to find a way into that water, don't you think you ought to teach those kids how to swim?" Who knew Donna had it in her either to defy a parent or to craft a cogent analogy?

The sex discussion winds through a lot of areas: how even quite liberal parents like the Walshes message sex differently to their son than to their daughter; Magic Johnson's recent announcement of his HIV-positive status; whether it's shameful for a high school junior to be a virgin. The positive attention Andrea's getting for her crusade, combined with the righteousness of her cause, leads her to try to expand the mission, soliciting students' personal sex journals for the *Blaze* and planning to distribute safer-sex information packets on the street. Jealous of the way John keeps spurring Andrea on, Brandon pulls her aside to have a meandering fight about her leaving him out of *Blaze* decisions, using aggressive activist tactics, and, finally, trying to make people think and talk about sex when she hasn't actually had sex herself. AND WHOSE FAULT IS THAT, BRANDON?! . . . Just kidding, we don't *really* think they should have boned down at the Peach Pit in the Season 1 finale, if only for food-hygiene reasons, but even Brandon should know this is a conversational third rail he absolutely must avoid.

Thanks to Brandon's braying (and no thanks to his many inept, defensive apologies for same), Andrea loses her passion to continue fighting for her proposal, which gets voted down at the next school board meeting. The tension spreads to Brenda and Dylan when he finds *her* sex journal, describing her pregnancy scare. She just wants to share her experience with anyone else who might go through it, but since she doesn't intend to publish it anonymously (?), Dylan notes that readers are going to be able to identify the father of her maybe-baby. He wins the fight by overreacting—don't rip pages out of her notebook, bro, that's a Brandon move—and Brenda tells Andrea the next day that she's withdrawing her contribution. Andrea's withdrawing generally, skipping the info-packet distribution action to stay in the *Blaze* office and mope alone about Brandon. When Kelly finds her there, they compare notes on their sexual history; Kelly reveals that there is one guy she propositioned who turned her down: Brandon Walsh. The two commiserate about wanting someone they can't have, instead of counseling each other to stop wanting someone who doesn't deserve it. Bucked up, Andrea finds that John has also stayed back, feeling like an outsider around the gang and referencing *his* sex journal, about his virginity. Andrea finally notices the obvious crush he has on her and asks him out and . . . we never see him again.

Speaking of virginity: David thinks Donna's asking him over to her house when her parents are out of town is a green light for him to try to bone her, but surprise! She intends to remain celibate until marriage. Probably won't be an issue for them, though!

And then Jackie flaps into Kelly's room, gasping as she extracts a promise from Kelly never to have unprotected sex, not even once. Turns out that Jackie's mentions of the little bug she's caught and the weird smell wafting off her sushi had the same cause: she's pregnant! Pour out some sake for Kelly's dreams of ever extricating herself from David Silver.

DonnaWatch:
HOW LITTLE DONNA GETS TO DO UNTIL HER BIG "I'M A VIRGIN" MOMENT

In *BH90210*, the 2019 *Beverly Hills, 90210* meta-reboot about the cast mounting a sequel to the show that made them all famous, Jennie's (fictional) daughter, Kyler (Karis Cameron), auditions to play Kelly's (even more fictional) daughter on the show-within-a-show. Kyler half-asses it and does okay, only to be wildly outshone by Tilda (Michelle Connor), who follows her. Jennie panics, saying she already gave Kyler the role, but Tori corrects her, saying Jennie gave Kyler *a* role: "Maybe Kyler's a Donna!" Even the (fictional) Tori acknowledges that she couldn't have played Kelly, the role she had originally auditioned for; clearly, in both *BH90210* and in reality, a Donna is a nothing character for a C-minus actor to play, normally in the background, while said C-minus actor gradually figures out how to do her job.

With that in mind, let's take a moment to recall the little Donna got to do on the show—other than tag along on Kelly and/or Brenda's plotlines—until producers locked in on what would become her defining character attribute: her intention to remain a virgin until marriage.

S01.E01: Nothing.

S01.E02: Nothing.

S01.E03: Nothing.

S01.E04: Nothing.

S01.E05: Nothing.

S01.E06: Mocks her history teacher's fashion sense in a casually cruel way (much more Kelly than the Donna we come to know).

S01.E07: Wears a bikini in the mother-daughter fashion show with her noncanonical mother, "Nancy."

S01.E08: Nothing.

S01.E09: Nothing.

S01.E10: Nothing.

S01.E11: Throws a party when her parents are out of town, at which alcohol is served; slow-dances with some preppy guy we never see again.

S01.E12: Nothing.

S01.E13: Eats ice cream with popcorn at Brenda's slumber party.

S01.E14: Nothing.

S01.E15: Nothing.

S01.E16: Nothing.

S01.E17: Nothing.

S01.E18: Nothing.

S01.E19: Bombs her SATs; starts acting out in typical "bad girl" style (smokes in the school parking lot with the burnouts); finds out she has a learning disability.

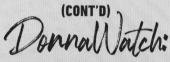

HOW LITTLE DONNA GETS TO DO UNTIL HER BIG "I'M A VIRGIN" MOMENT

S01.E20: Nothing.

S01.E21: Agrees to be Steve's platonic date to the Spring Dance; wears an incredibly ill-advised (and ugly) red satin dress with a hoop skirt that she can't sit down in.

S01.E22: Nothing.

S02.E01: Enrolls in a drama class at summer school with Andrea and Brenda; reminds Brenda and Kelly that the only absolutely fool-proof method of birth control is abstinence.

S02.E02: Nothing.

S02.E03: Gender-flips a scene from *Romeo & Juliet* with David; gets lightly critiqued for playing the scene for comedy, instead of as written.

S02.E04: Nothing.

S02.E05: Nothing.

S02.E06: Nothing.

S02.E07: Has to go buy tampons when she gets her period on a camping trip.

S02.E08: Nothing.

S02.E09: Nothing.

S02.E10: Discovers a surprising talent for the stock market; orders her friends to quit calling her dumb.

S02.E11: Starts to display receptiveness to the idea of dating David.

S02.E12: Nothing.

S02.E13: For a Halloween party, chooses a mermaid costume she can't walk in.

S02.E14: Helps David by convincing the rest of The Gang to attend Scott's surprise birthday party, at which Scott accidentally fatally shoots himself.

S02.E15: Nothing.

S02.E16: Nothing.

S02.E17: Goes to the Winter Dance with David—officially as friends, at least at first, until he impresses her with his dancing; then she makes out with him in full view of everyone and defiantly announces that she likes him.

S02.E18: Reveals that her birthday is December 25.

S02.E19: Nothing.

S02.E20: Nothing.

S02.E21: At a PTA meeting about a plan to distribute condoms at school, argues against Felice as she defends the importance of comprehensive sex education and accessible STI prevention. When David later tries to get her to sleep with him—on the theory that telling off Felice about condoms means Donna's DTF—she tells him she does not plan to have sex until marriage, retroactively justifying producers' decision (or, perhaps, an edict from above, specifically her father, series executive producer Aaron Spelling) never to let Donna do anything scandalous or interesting: **A VIRGIN IS BORN.**

"I don't know what's going on here, Walsh, but control your son!"

Brandon Saves the Peach Pit (for the First Time)

SEASON 2 | EPISODE 24
THE PIT AND THE PENDULUM

Think Jim Walsh learned his lesson about letting his sanctimonious son and his clients anywhere near one another after Brandon's hateful performance in Season 1's "East Side Story"? Think again!

This time, the client's a big-shot real estate developer, Dixon St. Claire (John H. Ingle), whose daughter Marcie (Liz Vassey!) is coordinating the teen focus group for her dad's next mall project. Brandon is late to the teen committee's first meeting because he was finishing his shift at the Peach Pit and listening to Nat grouse about how slow business is. Things might pick up if Nat didn't give free dinner to every Bev Niner with a sad puss, but anyway, Marcie forgives Brandon's tardiness because he's cute.

Not cute: Brandon demanding to speak to Jim during a formal presentation when he realizes the mall is planned for the corner the Peach Pit sits on. That's 666 La Bray-a! How dare Jim not consult with Brandon before working on this?! Jim tries to justify himself to Brandon by explaining that he can't influence the deal, or get a good offer for Nat, if Brandon interferes. This bizarre power dynamic might explain why Brandon has so little compunction generally about taking up causes that aren't his business and speaking to adults like *he's* the boss or parent.

The only things that explain the three-bedroom red blazer Brandon wears to a blue-themed frat party (whose host is played by Walton Goggins) is (1) the early '90s and (2) Brandon's condescending contrarianism. While conscientious frat objector Dylan explains to Brenda why he's not about Greek life, or college generally, Marcie takes Brandon to a giant gallery space to show him architectural models from her father's projects and to vaguely promise him a job. They french endlessly before she proposes going out to celebrate. Instead of asking what exactly they're celebrating—his new job? that Marcie lives in a museum?—Brandon sets a trap with a trip to the Peach Pit.

His plan works, at first; Marcie loves the Mega Burger Brandon makes her, and thrills to the tales of bygone stars who used to eat at the counter. Learning that Swiss cheese is the so-called innovation that sets the Mega Burger apart makes us wonder how Nat stayed open *this* long, but Marcie's sad to learn the place is about to get wrecking-balled, and sadder still when she realizes Brandon thought this guilt trip would make the mall development just disappear.

Brandon's next move is to flout the rules of order at a public hearing on the development, then snarl at his justifiably incensed father that "it's a free country" and he's going to stand up for Nat even if—or, let's face it: especially if—Jim won't. Nobody points out that Nat is an adult who has to abide by the terms of his lease, because Brandon isn't interested in facts. He wants to be right, and he wants to be thanked for it. The rest of The Gang is happy to ratify Brandon's obnoxious self-regard; they're prepping a protest to save the Peach Pit, at least in part because they're proud of Brandon for taking a stand. Even Jim is proud of Brandon, albeit also pissed off at him, Brenda reports. Treating Brandon's uninformed defiance as an act of courage (as usual) encourages Brandon to give Marcie a hateful kiss-off lecture dismissing her as a daddy's girl.

The Peach Pit Avenger isn't *just* a patronizing ignoramus, though; he's also a hypocrite, reaming his father for disloyalty, then turning on Nat when Nat—who, just a reminder, really has no choice—takes the offer from St. Claire. Jim tries once more to reason with Brandon, explaining that adults have responsibilities, but he should have hammered Brandon head-down into Casa Walsh's front lawn like a croquet wicket, as our own parents would have if we'd taken Brandon's insufferable sarcastic tone.

Jim drops by the Peach Pit to pick up a pie (on the house, of course . . . sigh) and bond with Nat over how pathetically they both crave Brandon's approval. (They may have used different words.) Nat asks Jim to look over the one-page development agreement—not how that works—and Jim is concerned enough to rush to the Pit's pay phone . . .

. . . and whatever he reports to HQ kiboshes the entire development. Brandon is thrilled for Nat, but concerned that Jim may get fired. *Now* he's worried about that? At least he gets to tell Nat the good news—in the meanest way possible, making snarky remarks about the upcoming "fire sale" and how every-thing has its price. Nat is nearly in tears of self-flagellation *for disappointing Brandon* before Brandon finally lets him know the deal fell through. Self-righteous dillhole Brandon did nothing to "save" the Peach Pit, technically, and Nat is in the same pickle (so to speak) vis-à-vis the recession that he was at the beginning, but Brandon gets credit for rescuing the little guy, and the rest of The Gang piles in to "celebrate" Nat's continuing to go broke by having him cook for them, after hours, for free.

Donna's Color Me Badd Fandom Coincides with Felice's Infidelity

Once upon a time, there was a boy band called Color Me Badd, whose brief time as a one-and-a-half-hit wonder crossed over with *Beverly Hills, 90210*; this episode starts from the premise that they are currently Donna's favorite band.

When David fails to get Donna, Kelly, Brenda, and himself on the list for an upcoming show, and the girls fail to win tickets in a radio contest, David finds out where the band's going to be staying, and you're not going to believe this, but it's the Bel Age! The only hotel in Los Angeles! The groupies are trying to figure out how they're going to find the band when an elevator opens and Donna's face-to-face with Felice. Donna has to think so quickly to explain why she's there—she says David and Mel's place is getting fumigated, so they're staying at the hotel!—that she doesn't notice Felice taking a moment before saying her hospital charity event is taking place there. Oh well, no time to question this when there are latter-day Beatlemania-esque shenanigans to montage! Eventually the WBH squad splits up to cover more ground, which is how Donna's alone when a hotel room door opens and her mother pops out, followed by some dude Felice starts enthusiastically kissing. Looks like Felice is "swimming" in a stranger's "pool"! ("Everybody's Talkin' 'Bout It" callback.)

While Donna tries to come to grips with what she's just witnessed, Kelly chances upon the band's floor and finds herself in the hallway just in time for Color Me Badd's Bryan Abrams, in the world's lightest, dumpiest jeans, to be there fighting with a vending machine. Kelly—who, throughout the episode, has been a true queen of NGAF about this band, rolling with the high jinks because she has nothing better to do—doesn't recognize him until he introduces himself with his full government name. He offers her four passes to the show, and brings her back to the band's suite for a perfectly respectful, hands-off, fully clothed conversation about what it's like for the guys to have fans—kind of mean given that Jennie Garth and the rest of the cast were, at this point, exponentially more famous than these goons. Anyway: don't worry, the Color Me Badd guys love their fans and will continue to love them for the three or four more months remaining in their careers.

When Brenda and David find their way back to home base, Donna tells them why she's no longer in the mood to stalk the band (and rejects David's suggestion that maybe Dr. and Mrs. Martin are poly, lol). Felice finds Donna in the lobby on her way out and confronts her about the fumigation lie, not knowing Donna now has ammunition with which to confront her right back. Felice tracks her devastated daughter down at the Walshes' and, while Brenda and her parents hilariously eavesdrop, Donna doesn't let the indecency of her buttcheek-baring shorts stop her from reading Felice for her sexual hypocrisy and dismissing her, which is when Cindy tries to make Donna understand the complexities of marriage by confessing about her own Season 1 emotional affair. Donna finally calms down enough to go home and, with her rage on a low simmer, accepts Felice's assurances that she will tell Dr. Martin everything. Then David shows up to take Donna to the Peach Pit, just in time for Kelly to appear post-show with some really cool guys she met . . . and in walk Color Me Badd, to serenade Donna with "I Adore Mi Amor." Her family might be on the verge of falling apart, but at least she got to enjoy some stubbly a cappella!

Also: Steve, Dylan, and Brandon decide to take advantage of an empty Walsh house by ordering an exotic dancer, Brandy, from an ad in the back of *LA Weekly*, only to have their horny plans derailed when Andrea invites herself over and proceeds to get to know Brandy (Michelle Nicastro) as a person, killing all their boners in the process such that they no longer want anyone to sex them up. (See what we did there?!)

HOW COLOR ME BADD COULD HAVE BEEN
Color Me Even Worse

We all remember how Color Me Badd, mega-selling superstar recording artists, were seamlessly integrated into "Things to Do on a Rainy Day": Donna, David, Brenda, and (to a much lesser extent) Kelly hatched a caper in which they'd go to the Bel Age Hotel, where the members of the band—playing themselves—were staying, and try to meet them; then they did! But what if producers hadn't alighted upon this elegant way of importing Color Me Badd into the action? Here are a few ways it could have gone worse:

- How fancy are Little League games in Beverly Hills? When Nat's team faces off against Jim's, the National Anthem is performed by Color Me Badd!

- The Gang's Yosemite camping trip takes a wild turn when inclement weather forces them to rent a cabin for the night, only to discover their neighbors are Color Me Badd! Too bad they're all on vocal rest and spend their evening together silently showing off fishing lures they've made.

- Brenda's barely screwed up her courage to perform her "comedy" "act" at the Fallout Club when she sees the act she's supposed to follow is Color Me Badd. She then throws out all her notes and turns her time at the mic into a roast of the band instead. Sam cries.

- Brandon befriends Melissa, a promising student whose path to the Ivy League has grown stonier since the birth of her son. Tearfully confessing the difficulties of her life, she lets it slip that the father is Mark Calderon of Color Me Badd, who has denied his paternity. The episode ends in a flash-forward to Melissa, now a lawyer, suing Mark for back child support.

- Brenda develops a benign mass on her breast that, according to her doctor, looks exactly like Bryan Abrams of Color Me Badd. Brenda enjoys a brief flash of freak fame when her story goes viral, and she and her mass are even invited to meet the band on *The Tonight Show*. Color Me Badd does an episode-closing PSA about the importance of regular breast self-exams.

- Andrea breaks both legs in a hit-and-run. The offending vehicle? Color Me Badd's tour bus!

- Samantha and Steve are invited onto a Thanksgiving TV special that will also feature Color Me Badd. Producers are aghast when Sam uses his screen time to scream that meat is murder and drown the table in what everyone hopes is prop blood.

- Reading Scott's diary after his untimely death, David finds out Color Me Badd was the only non-C&W act Scott still liked. David throws a Hail Mary and manages to book them to sing "I Adore Mi Amor" at his funeral.

- Jim has grown "so absentee" that a restless Cindy starts looking for new ways to bring excitement into her life. A chance meeting with Kevin Thornton at a Coffee Bean & Tea Leaf leads to Cindy having an orgy with all four members of Color Me Badd, plus their tour opener, Cathy Dennis.

> *"Just remember one thing: if we treat you like an*
> *adult, we expect you to behave like an adult."*

Dylan Reconnects with His Dear Old Friend Jake Hanson, Then Sneaks Brenda into Mexico

SEASON 2 | EPISODE 27
MEXICAN STANDOFF

Brenda and Dylan are starting to chafe against both her parents' curfew and their jeans, what with all the dry-humping they're doing on his futon.

Dylan's heading to Mexico for the weekend and suggests that Brenda join him; though she's sure her parents would never allow it, Dylan thinks they might surprise her. She doesn't exactly lay the groundwork for such a big ask by breaking her curfew that very night, but, spurred by Dylan, Brenda shoots her shot the next night, and her parents *do* surprise her—and Brandon—by agreeing, perhaps because Dylan represents their accommodations as "really sort of a family guesthouse" as opposed to a regular-ass hotel where they will not be chaperoned.

Brenda and Dylan successfully evade Andrea's oblivious attempt to invite the whole gang along on this dirty weekend (Andrea: "It would be a real adventure, don't you think?" Dylan: "No"), but then blow through Brenda's curfew *again*. This time it's actually innocent—a TV airing of *The Grapes of Wrath* puts them both to sleep, and when they wake up, it's 4 A.M.—but Jim doesn't care about the circumstances and rescinds his permission for Brenda to go to Baja. Somehow this doesn't get her generally grounded; Kelly hopefully asks if that means Brenda can sleep over at her place that weekend, but Donna, of all people, proposes instead that Brenda just *say* that's what she's doing but *actually* go to Mexico. This was both easier and harder to pull off in a pre–cell phone era: sure, Cindy can't just track the location of Brenda's phone, but when she calls the Taylor landline, Kelly will have to invent a reason Brenda can't talk just then, phone Brenda in Mexico, *hope she's there*, tell her to call her mother back, and hope the Walshes don't have caller ID. . . . And it actually works!

The trip is perfect until Dylan goes to check them in at the hotel, where the indiscreet manager somehow doesn't notice that he's there with a new broad and asks how Stacy is. See, last summer—sometime between Dylan's surfing injury and his trip to Maui—Dylan was serious enough about some other chippy to bring *her* there. Brenda doesn't care that this was after she had dumped him; she goes from zero to furious in an instant, and stays there until a roving musician at the cantina starts singing "Feelings" to them in Spanish and they both crack up. The trip is saved; the surfing is great; and no one would be any the wiser about her international travel except that Dylan's car gets randomly flagged for secondary inspection and Brenda, having still not replaced her driver's license after its theft in a Peach Pit robbery, *crossed the border without any ID*. Even in a pre-9/11 context, this is extremely careless, and Brenda won't be readmitted to the US until a guardian can come produce proof of her citizenship. We'll have to wait to see how big a scene Jim throws in view of the INS until the season finale.

In the run-up to this surf getaway, Dylan runs into an old friend at the beach: it's Jake Hanson (Grant Show), who taught Dylan how to surf in the first place! Jake's looking for work, so David hires him to repaint Jackie's house before her wedding to Mel is held there—an event Kelly has apparently been crabbing about so hard that Jackie has tried to get her on board by making Brenda and Donna bridesmaids (or . . . no one at the show felt like hiring anyone to play Jackie's friends). Fortunately for Jackie, Kelly and Jake fall in lust at first sight, and Kelly's mood is so vastly improved that she even gets excited about feeling the baby kick for the first time. Let's hope Kelly's pulsing loins don't show through her bridesmaid dress.

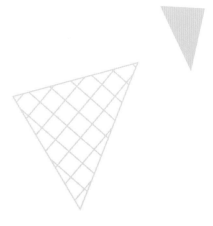

Dylan Throws Scotch at Mel and Jackie's Wedding

SEASON 2 | EPISODE 28
WEDDING BELL BLUES

On the eve of Mel and Jackie's wedding, everyone's freaking out: Andrea, because she didn't get an invitation, and now everything she believed about her status in The Gang is called into question (her mom just forgot to give the invitation to her, natch); Nat, who offered Jackie a few *dozen* pies *on the house* for the reception (oh, Nat) but was turned down; and of course Jackie, who's having second thoughts about her fourth marriage *and* has to find another venue because a pipe burst at her house.

Lucky for her that Brandon volunteers Casa Walsh without asking his parents first!

Adding to Kelly's wedding stress is the end of Jake's time at Casa Taylor, and when she invites him to the wedding, he can't say no fast enough, a depressing turn of events Kelly can't vent to Brenda about for five minutes before Brenda changes the subject back to *The McKay Khronicles*. After Kelly and Brenda fight and make up and Mel and Jackie tie the knot, Jake does show up, and a long, vague conversation on the dance floor about how Kelly's "not a kid" (actually, she is) and "a very dangerous girl" (actually, she isn't) culminates in Jake glomming onto her face like he's giving infant CPR to an ice-cream cone. At the bar, Dylan passive-aggresses at Jake about broken trust and "young girl"s who get attached, and Jake pulls a "Wait, are . . . we still talking about me?" face.

Of course, they aren't; Dylan's talking about Brenda, Jim, and the growing pile of slights and betrayals among them all. Earlier, Jim arrived at the border holding pen to pick up his most dramatic child, and happened to walk in on Dylan and Brenda fully making out (Dylan's hand is grabbing Brenda's left buttcheek). We're betting Jim seethed about that all the way back to the house, where Jim then bellows at Brenda and Dylan that their relationship's gone too far. We don't understand why Dylan is even present for this dressing-down, tbh—did Jim tell him to meet them at Casa Walsh to get yelled at some more, then drive Brenda home in silence? Why would Dylan not just go home? Is his cable out? Dylan does take his leave, making it clear with a pointed "See you in school . . . tomorrow" to Brenda that Jim may have overplayed his hand in forbidding them to see each other.

The smart move is to lie low and let Jim (and to a lesser extent Cindy, who's particularly betrayed by Brenda dragging an innocent flea market into her scheme) calm down, but what Dylan and Brenda do instead is whinge at Brandon to pick a side. Brandon ungraciously takes his parents', throwing in some condescending told-you-sos, and when Dylan forces Brandon to admit that Dylan is *persona non grata* at the Walshes' (a phrase Luke Perry renders as "potatoes au gratin"), Dylan decides he's not going to the wedding because Jim is a big meanie, nyeah! So Brenda's not going either, nyeah!

Well, that won't work, because Brenda's *in* the wedding, but Cindy puts her annoyance at Brenda's dramatics aside to write Dylan a nice (albeit oddly fonted) letter asking him to make the first move with Jim, as a favor to her— and Brenda. It's a good idea, but Cindy doesn't give Jim a heads-up that Dylan's going to approach him, and Dylan doesn't think to tell Jim that Brenda also lied to *him* about getting permission to go to Mexico, so instead of working together to . . . you know, keep Brenda from driving them all crazy, Jim and Dylan each dig in further on the other being the bad guy. By the time Jim comes up to Dylan to apologize, Dylan is fully in his daddy issues, whining at Jim to hit him because at least bruises heal or some goddamn bad-boy-pain thing. He rummages around behind the bar, then smashes the full bottle of scotch he's holding against the side of the house when Jim snarks on him. Like, that scotch isn't yours and neither is that house—go sweep up the broken glass!

But the self-pity tornado is about to deposit Dylan in his car, so he forget-you-Dads that he wants Jim's hands off his money and storms out, massive suit jacket flapping. Bren flaps after him in her Pepto-Bridesmol dress, Jim hollering at both of them that she's not to see Dylan anymore. Brenda forlornly watches Dylan peel out in the Porsche, and scandalized guitars and a plinky piano discuss the fact that that could hardly have gone worse without an actual death.

Comings

ERIN SILVER

It would be rude to say that Mel and Jackie get married *only* because Jackie finds herself unexpectedly pregnant, but it's definitely a factor. After their early animosity, David and Kelly are bonded forever not just through their parents' marriage but also the birth of their half-sister, Erin (variously played, on this series, by Arielle and April Peterson, Paige and Ryanne Kettner, Megan Lee Braley, and Mercedes Kastner). Her very birth serves the plot: Kelly decides she doesn't want to go on an intensive French course in Paris, but would rather stay home and help Jackie with the baby; Brenda goes instead, leaving Kelly and Dylan to engage in their Summer of Deception. Erin goes on to be a point of contention during Jackie and Mel's divorce proceedings; gets lost in a park by a high-as-hell David; causes fights between Jackie and Kelly when Jackie tries to launch Erin's career as a child model; and crosses paths with Steve's love interest Carly (Hilary Swank) when Erin and Carly's son, Zach (Myles Jeffrey), are on the same youth soccer team.

JAY THURMAN

It took until Season 3 for the show to give Andrea a plausible romantic prospect to challenge her tragic crush on Brandon: Jay (future *Sports Night*

and *Six Feet Under* star Peter Krause) is, like pervy drama teacher Chris Suiter, really too old to be dating a high school student, though at least he's still in college. More troubling is the fact that he's a Republican? But his purpose on the show is really just to make Brandon see Andrea as a potential sexual partner, and to establish that he pretty much does so only when she's seeing someone else.

NIKKI WITT

With Donna away in Paris, David is drawn to Nikki (Dana Barron), a West Beverly freshman newly arrived from San Francisco and living in L.A. with her aunt to get a break from drama with her parents; only much later will we learn that said drama revolves around her relationship with her abusive boyfriend, aspiring rock star Diesel (David Arquette!). Though she's initially drawn to David's musical talent and the two fool around, Nikki cedes her claim to David when Donna returns and is assigned as her Senior Buddy; whether Nikki is upgrading or downgrading by replacing David with Brandon depends on each individual viewer's personal preference. Nikki breaks Brandon's heart just before Christmas, returning to her parents' home.

s & Goings

JACK CANNER

Brandon is working at the beach club when he initially crosses paths with Jack Canner (David Sherrill), an Iraq War veteran experiencing homelessness and creeping out intolerant club members. Brandon, moved by Jack's description of losing his family and home while serving overseas, convinces Henry to interview Jack for a job; Henry, also a military veteran, is dubious of Jack's sob story, but agrees, and is proven right when Jack ghosts him. But! Brandon then runs into Jack again on the eve of Thanksgiving and invites him over to his (parents') house for the holiday (obviously without asking them first). Jim is weirdly hostile to this unfortunate stranger until we find out that Jim's father always thought Jim was soft for not having served, and Jim's taking his resentment out on Jack. (Jim's dad was a labor firebrand *and* a troop humper? . . . Okay.) Anyway, Jack goes out on the roof to help fix the cable, earning his place at the Thanksgiving table, though we never see him again.

BROOKE ALEXANDER

When she shows up a handful of episodes into Season 3, Brooke (Alexandra Wilson) seems like just the thing to save Brandon's summer: she's cute, despite a mumsy hairdo and weird wardrobe choices; and she shares several key interests with Brandon, like roller-blading, and . . . Brandon. But troubling hints that she's not girlfriend material surface early on, when Brandon's trying to help homeless vet Jack Canner and Brooke lacks compassion about Canner's situation. It's not long before Brooke's stanning Reaganomics blossoms into outright racism (dismissing Brandon's black boss, Henry, as a shiftless affirmative-action hire) and anti-Semitism (Andrea, who's Jewish, must be good with money). Brandon *isn't* really "a liberal kinda guy" except in comparison to 2D villains like Brooke, but the show can't have its hero associating with '50s-style bigotry, so Brooke and her bodysuits get the boot.

RICK (AKA RIQUE)

Brenda even *considering* cheating on Dylan is credible only with an unassailably perfect casting of Brenda's side piece . . . and the show nailed it when Dean "Superman" Cain was slotted in as Rick. Somehow, Rick mistakes Brenda for a local when he gets lost in Paris, despite the horrendous "French" accent she's using to give him directions (thus our dubbing him "Rique"). After a halcyon couple of days of sightseeing and flirting, Rique invites Brenda to come with him on the rest of his European tour; Brenda agrees, but feels guilty for smooching him (and is oblivious to what Dylan's up to with Kelly back home), and ends up standing Rique up, barely. We haven't seen the last of him, though; Rique and Brenda run into each other in L.A. shortly after Brenda and Dylan break up—and Rique's still interested, even after Brenda can no longer maintain the fiction that she's Frahnche. He's *even* still interested after it becomes clear Brenda is nowhere near over Dylan or ready for another relationship! Brenda, alas, is *not* interested in a guy with a sunny disposition and unalloyed admiration for her accountant father, and ends things. We're still a little disappointed in her, tbh.

SUE SCANLON

One of the late Scott Scanlon's million siblings, Sue (Nicholle Tom) enters West Beverly as a freshman and immediately starts running wild, cutting class with a fast crowd and changing at school from the modest outfits her mother approves to revealing looks better suited to Def Leppard videos. Later in the season, Sue accuses a teacher of inappropriate advances against her, eventually recanting and naming her actual abuser: a sexually abusive uncle whom, according to David, Scott had regarded with suspicion.

GIL MEYERS

Gil (Mark Kiely) is styled as "the cool teacher"—so cool that his students can call him "Gil," instead of "Mr. Meyers"! We've got a few things *we'd* like to call him, thanks to his rewarding Brandon's senior-year apathy toward his *Blaze*

commitments with a promotion to coeditor-in-chief, because boys need leadership motivation or whatever. Gil is also a crappy chaperone (he fails to notice anything suspicious when the entire gang is loitering around the ladies' room waiting for Donna to barf herself back sober at the prom, for just one example); he thinks a fellow named "Horthawne" wrote *The Scarlet Letter*; his boundaries with students are apparently porous enough that Sue Scanlon's accusations against him are initially believable; and his hair looks like a bishop's loaf was fired out of a T-shirt gun onto his head.

JACK MCKAY

We never found out *exactly* what Dylan's father, Jack (Josh Taylor in his canonical form), did to get sent to jail—some insider-trading thing, probably. Whatever it was isn't serious enough to prevent Jack's taking a Thanksgiving furlough, during which he proves that the entitled-jackass gene is a dominant one in Clan McKay when he brings a bottle of scotch and a lady friend to his sober estranged son's bungalow for the long weekend. (And, not for nothing, a *gigantic* pair of sweatpants . . . is he *really* on a furlough, or did he smuggle himself out of the joint in those absolute units?) But when Jack gets paroled, he seems sincere about making up for lost time with Dylan . . . and possibly about plundering Dylan's trust fund, all of which drives a wedge between Dylan and his previous father figure, Jim Walsh. It turns out that Jack was actually working with the feds to bring down some *other* shady financiers, and while we never find out exactly how *that* worked, either—only that his fiancée was actually/also his FBI handler, and that Dylan's future late wife's gangster father ordered the hit for . . . reasons— Jack's car-bomb death and the subsequent tsunami it directs at Dylan's psyche are surely definitive! . . . Until they aren't, and we all find out in the final season that Jack was in fact alive and in witness protection, with a new family, the whole time.

JORDAN BONNER

When the show felt it necessary to address the fallout from the L.A. uprisings of 1992—which, by the way, no one required it to do—Brandon travels to South-Central Los Angeles to meet his counterpart at Shaw High School's newspaper: Jordan Bonner (Michael Anthony Rawlins). Jordan challenges Brandon on his capacity for seeing past his own privileged circumstances; it doesn't really take, but he does try. Jordan also dates Andrea—mostly offscreen, and on dates that don't sound like much fun (we know they're overachieving nerds, but still, these two high school seniors are going to go see . . . *Hoffa*?). Both eventually get accepted to Yale, though only Jordan attends—on a full ride, no less— departing our lives forever.

CHRISTINE PETTIT

One of the few characters whose style holds up on rewatch, Christine (Valerie Wildman) seems like a good lady,

albeit kiiiind of a bad federal agent: she got romantically involved with her "contact," Jack McKay; she let him get blown up (as far as we and anyone else knows for six-odd seasons); and her subsequent guilt sees her not just tolerating Dylan's erratic behavior but also giving him information he probably shouldn't have. She does seem to sincerely love Jack, though, and planned to leave the Bureau to marry him, and she's warm and kind to Dylan and Kelly even when Dylan's being a prick.

DUKE WEATHERILL

When Nat starts feeling like Brandon has a gambling problem, he refuses to place any more bets on Brandon's behalf, so Brandon goes straight to Nat's bookie, Duke (Billy Vera). When you call Central Casting for a menacing rackets guy, you might not expect Billy Vera to show up in a jaunty fedora (which may be why, when Duke returns for two episodes in Season 8, he's played by John Prosky), but the same guy who's responsible for the gravelly *Family Ties* ballad "At This Moment" is the one underlining how serious Brandon's addiction has gotten. Duke, or rather the idea that Duke might make good on his promise to fuck Brandon up if he can't cover his losses, is the lone bright spot in an unsympathetic and interminable plot arc for Brandon. Alas, Nat ends up covering Brandon's nut, saving Brandon's kneecaps and disappointing your correspondents.

CURTIS BRAY & SERGE MENKIN

Finally, someone's interested in David's demo tape! Too bad it's these two sleazes: exec Curtis Bray (Raymond O'Connor) and producer Serge Menkin (Stephen Rowe). They at least have the good judgment not to sign David until he boots Steve as his manager. But Menkin refuses to go in the hip-hop direction David wants (lol), reimagining "Precious" as an even goopier slow jam. David's afraid to lose the opportunity, so he goes along . . . but then Bray hates the results and rips up David's contract. Or maybe he rolls it up to snort more cocaine with.

CELESTE LUNDY

Steve convinces Brandon to join him on a *Studs*-esque dating show, where the two end up on the same episode, both gunning hard for the same female contestant: Celeste (Jennifer Grant). After choosing Steve over Brandon on the show, Celeste continues dating him into Season 4, during which time we learn she's a little older than he is; she dropped out of community college; she's a salesperson at a hip clothing store; and she's way too good for Steve, who doesn't come close to appreciating her.

"Shh: you will spoil eet."

The Summer of Deception Finally Finds a Higher Gear

SEASON 3 | EPISODE 5
SHOOTING STAR/
AMERICAN IN PARIS

Brandon tries to fix the homeless problem one man at a time when he reaches out to Jack Canner (David Sherrill), a down-on-his-luck veteran who still has access to low-cost hair-frosting. Brandon is typically nosy about Canner's backstory, and typically dense when he's told Canner served in Desert Storm: "You were stationed in the Middle East?" No, Brandon, the Desert Storm water park outside Cincinnati. Idiot.

Anyway, Canner got back from not-suburban-Ohio to find himself no longer welcome at his job or marriage, but Brandon thinks he can fix Canner's life by setting up a job interview with beach-club jefe Henry—after rudely asking Canner in so many words whether he's willing to work. We'd like to think it's this presumptuous privilege that dissuades Canner from showing up for the interview, but the show naturally casts it as Canner being too far gone to try to save himself, and Brandon's shining idealism leading to inevitable disappointment.

Also shaping up as a disappointment: Brandon's trick *du jour*, Brooke (Alexandra Wilson). Brooke's doubling down on her dowdy mom hair and Cirque Du So Lame knee-length rollerblading unitard with a couple of (subtle for this show) hints that she's a free-market conservative at best.

But the real action is in the "Summer of Deception" section of the show. We always forget how long it takes the deceiving to get going in Season 3 . . . but in Episode 5, it is *on*. The end of the prior episode had left little doubt that Kelly (who bailed on the big Paris trip to stay home with her new half-sister, Erin) and Dylan (who supported sending Brenda on the big Paris trip so they could get some space) had frenched after the credits rolled. Sure enough, when we rejoin them, Dylan is giving Kelly a bunch of attitude for avoiding him post-smooch. Given that *Dylan's* the one in a relationship (which he hasn't even hinted at ending to be with Kelly), it seems like Kelly's doing Dylan a favor by absenting herself—and like he should dial the bratty entitlement way down—but get used to his acting like she's a bourgeois loser for caring about Brenda's feelings, because it's not going to stop.

In his defense, *sort* of, Kelly is sending Dylan mixed signals, like showing up at his house, at night, in the same kind of Marilyn-esque white getup she was wearing when they first made out, to baby-voice at him in person that they can't do "this" and "there is no 'us,'" and then make out with him again.

. . . Aaaand again, over the next few days, in her cabana, on a sublimated-sex jet-ski outing, et cetera. The other thing we always forget about the Summer of Deception is how thoroughly *un*-deceptive these boneheads are about their illicit affair; when Dylan and Kelly *do* smarten up and canoodle behind closed doors, they don't *lock* them, letting David walk in on them and obliging Kelly to trade her silence about David's indiscretion with Nikki (Dana Barron; we'll get back to it) for David's about the love-triangulation he just witnessed. On the eve of Brenda's return from Paree, "Kellan" end the episode in the same ambiguous emotional place they started: unable to resist each other and performatively brooding about it. (And yes, you *do* remember Sophie B. Hawkins's "Damn, I Wish I Was Your Lover" scoring that campout scene when it first aired; it's no longer there thanks to rights issues. Would that Dylan's repulsive Baja hoodie had met the same fate.)

Equally repulsive and unconvincingly deceptive: Brenda's subplot. She's reading in a park when a lunky American, Rick (Dean Cain, never hotter), mistakes her for a native and asks directions. Born actress Brenda decides to see how long she can pass herself off as a Frenchwoman, and the credible answer is "zero seconds," because her Frahnche accent is an utter disaster, and it isn't even the *same* disaster from sentence to sentence. Americanized contractions, the fact that nobody in the history of France has ever been named "Brendá," the desperate mugging and thinky faces whenever she's asked a question . . . anyone else would spot her as a (Texan) liar immediately. "Rique," however, apparently lives in the University of Wisconsin's concussion dorm, because not only does he believe Brendá's strangled-by-a-sentient-Gaulois accent; he looooves it. Brenda is also charmed, partly because she's, "how you say," getting eh-weh weez eet—but also, come on, it's Superman, and despite Wardrobe's best efforts to dork him up, Dean Cain is still a stone fox. Brenda takes him on a tour of the city while continuing to accumulate easily disprovable lies, they kiss, and she feels *so* guilty about it that she gives herself a UTI *and* pink-eye by going straight to bed in a bodysuit and full makeup. Invited away with Rique to the Riviera, Brendá pretends to consider it while fully intending to stand him up, but at the last moment she races to their meeting spot, only to see him getting in a cab . . . and that's that. *Or is it?!* (It is not.)

"See, I'm a liberal kinda guy."

Brenda's Back, and You're Gonna Be in Trouble (Especially If You're Racist Brooke)

SEASON 3 | EPISODE 6
CASTLES IN THE SAND

While Brenda's having a transatlantic-flight horny dream about Rique (in which, mercifully, she has admitted to American citizenship), Kelly and Dylan are waking up together on the beach.

The arguing starts almost immediately, with Kelly expressing relief that they "didn't cross that line" by Doing It and Dylan snotting that that doesn't mean they didn't connect. She keeps trying to remind him that, you know, he's in love with Brenda and Brenda is coming home soon; *he* keeps acting like *he's* the third party whose lover won't leave her spouse, like, break up with Brenda or don't, but since the answer's pretty clearly "don't," stop acting like a victim in the situation, you brat!

. . . He doesn't. Even an accidental intrusion by Andrea and her Beach Club campers while collecting seashells only presses pause on Dylan's entitlement. And while the plan, as reasonably stated by Kelly, is to chalk their fling up to summer and forget it, neither of them can play it cool worth a damn: Dylan is looking at Kelly *while* reuniting with Brenda at the welcome-home party, and Kelly is so subdued and socializing-averse that David warns her about drawing suspicion. It pains us to admit it when he's wearing an unbuttoned color-block blouse the size of a California-king top sheet, but the kid's got a point.

At least Brenda's handling herself with aplomb. Arriving back at Casa Walsh to see that only Dylan isn't at the welcome-home fête, she calmly asks her parents what's up with that, saying she's not trying to fight—she just wants to know where things stand. Jim and Cindy, impressed at her sangfroid, invite Dylan last-minute. It's awkward, unsurprisingly, although Kelly is rewarded for enduring "Brylan"'s handsy reunion with a confession from Brenda that she smooched Rique.

Even after Brenda's home, Dylan keeps checking in on Kelly, then pouting when she insists she's fine as if it isn't now his move to make . . . and Brenda seems to sense something's off, telling Kelly she thinks Dylan was seeing someone while she was in France. Kelly parries by saying it's just that she was gone for a long time (and six weeks *is* an eternity in a teenage relationship). Brenda wants closure on it before school starts, though, so she delivers a moist speech kind-of-but-not-really confirming that Dylan cheated on her before admitting that *she* had a little thing with Rique. Although Dylan's sins are more serious, he's pissed, and non-answers her extremely pointed "Are you ready to start our senior year together?" with a disgusted "Welcome home, Brenda." Should have gone to Cannes with Superman, girlfriend.

Speaking of girlfriends, it doesn't take long for Racist Brooke, in an outfit from the Lanz of Salzburg workwear catalog, to talk herself out of the girlfriend job at Brandon Inc. The semi-heartless "conservative" remarks she passed about Jack Canner in the previous episode have become outright bigotry directed at Brandon's African American boss (per Brooke, a lazy beneficiary of affirmative action who can't get fired) and Andrea (Jewish, ergo good with money). Brooke's racism is of an antique strain that doesn't really track with a '90s teenager, but racism it is, and despite her protests that she meant some of these comments as compliments (huh?) and she can change (for a guy she's dated for a week and a half?), Brandon snits that he doesn't want to see her anymore. We never see her again . . . but we're still a little resentful that she made us side with Brandon.

Brooke's lucky to get dumped when she does: She's spared the sorry spectacle that is David's debut at the end-of-summer barbecue. The Beach Club already *had* an act, but Steve and his leonine mullet pay that act to kick rocks, forcing Henry to use David at the last minute. Words really can't describe the discomfort of this musical experience, as Brian Austin Green is trying to pretend his voice hasn't dropped while pulling faces that suggest he's trying to pass a handful of jacks . . . but as Sgt. Pepper's Mustard Pants Club Band capers around cooing "be be be my love / ooh-uhhh" behind two massive keyboards, Cindy Walsh's hostage faces speak for us all.

"Well . . . do I get to be on camera?"

Brenda's Desperation to Be Special Gets Her in Big, Televised Trouble

SEASON 3 | EPISODE 8
THE BACK STORY

It's time for everyone to take the SAT again; as they're leaving a test prep class, a TV reporter named Beth (Kamala Lopez) tries to interview them, but as Brenda—of course—steps up for her 15 minutes of local news fame, Steve clocks the crew as hacks from *Back Story*, a tawdry *Hard Copy*–type operation that once did a smear job on his mother, Samantha.

After he storms over to threaten Beth, Brenda explains that he's Samantha's son, thus making her second mistake: showing Beth she will totally spill her friend's secrets. Beth shrewdly waits outside the school the next day to pretend to smooth things over after the Steve flap. Brenda must know, on some level, that she shouldn't be talking to Beth judging by the fact that they go for coffee somewhere other than the Peach Pit, though that might also be so that Brenda can smoke—a Paris habit she can't shake—without getting guff about it, which Kelly has been giving her. Beth claims to have had loftier ambitions than *Back Story*, but also that she thinks she can still do good work under its aegis—like a story about Brenda! And . . . uh, others! Brenda doesn't seem convinced, until she finds out she'll get solo face time. Later, shaking off Brandon's advice that she clear it with Mrs. Teasley before pursuing it, she wistfully says she hasn't been on "the same wavelength" as her friends since she returned from France: "If it weren't for Dylan, I wouldn't have anyone." Since *we* know why Kelly has been saltier than usual with Brenda: yikes! Then she drops her cigarettes in front of her parents and that's a whole thing—but seriously, you're a high school senior and you think they're going to buy "They're not even mine"? USE YOUR HEAD.

The next day, Dylan interrupts a spat about Kelly's disloyal relief that Brenda's parents discovered her smoking to announce that he's not going to take the SAT with The Gang: he's going to visit his father, Jack (Josh Taylor), in prison instead. This cues a Brenda snit about Dylan missing the college application deadline; Kelly takes Dylan's side on gap years, and up goes another barrier between Brenda and the new couple-to-be—so it's fortunate for her that she has Beth to distract her. Brenda goes to the *Back Story* mobile unit to drop off the video yearbook from her *first* junior year, which is somehow filled with Season 2 B-roll we know David didn't shoot, BUT ANYWAY, it's all so that Beth can manipulate Brenda into spilling more tea. Many of her friends' parents are divorced! Donna has a learning disability! Kelly had a nose job *and* a trampy reputation! When Beth tells her, "You know, you're really good at this," one almost expects flattery sponge Brenda to join *Back Story* full-time.

Meanwhile, Nikki has bounced back from her ill-fated crush on David . . . sort of, because now she's into Brandon. Brandon finds out the next day from Mrs. Teasley that *Back Story* is doing an unauthorized report on the school and has to tear ass all over it looking for Brenda so that he can . . . tell her he was right about Mrs. T? He hasn't yet found Brenda when he runs into Nikki, who asks how he is and gets her head bitten off in the process, ending with him telling her they can't date. Nikki handles this hysterical overreaction with poise and grace that let us know she's not going to last on this show. When Brandon does track Brenda down, she confidently declares that Beth is "going through channels" to get Mrs. Teasley's sign-off, because if she doesn't know the phrase "off the record," she certainly doesn't understand how tabloid journalism works.

Brenda gets home just in time for "Rich and Spoiled in Beverly Hills: The Back Story on the Teenage Inhabitants of the Most Glamorous City on Earth." Shannen Doherty acts the hell out of Brenda's dawning horror as she watches the savage edit Beth—on her producer's mercenary orders—has made of the material Brenda supplied, narrated with maximum smarm by a (pretty good) Robin Leach impersonator. "I'm ruined," Brenda gasps.

The report, we learn, has aired on the eve of the SAT; outside the test the next day, The Gang closes ranks against Brenda. (Dylan—having been cowed by Jack into conforming to society's meaningless rules, as we assume Dylan would put it—hits up the high school nearest Jack's prison to take the SAT there.) When everyone in L.A. has finished, Brandon is waiting with Beth, who went looking for Brenda at the Walsh house, to apologize in person. Not only did Beth resign from the show as soon as the piece aired, but she also backs up Brenda's version of events for her friends with a tape of Brenda's unedited interview. Let's hope Brenda's not planning to minor in communications, because she still doesn't get that Beth's original concept—Local Teens Keen—isn't really a story.

Comparing notes at the Peach Pit afterward, Steve seems to realize he might not have killed the SAT, and a master key to the school offered by good old B.J. Harrison (Chadd Nyerges), recent grad/cheater, could be handy for Steve after all. And Nikki appears so that Brandon can inform her that he got over himself and then kiss on her in the back room. He's a worse boyfriend than she deserves, but better than she's had, as we will soon discover. *Yes*, really!

HARTLEY HOUSE
LORE

If *Beverly Hills, 90210* had premiered in the 2010s, Fox definitely would have created bonus internet content related to show-within-a-show *Hartley House*: if not shareable episode clips, then a period-appropriate opening-credits sequence or possibly a mocked-up fan site. As it is, when it comes to the show that starred Steve's mother, Samantha Sanders, we must try to reconstruct a full picture from stray bits of *Hartley House* trivia as they blow by, very occasionally. The Hartleys deserve better!!!

Or . . . maybe they don't. By the time we hear about the gig that remains Samantha's biggest credit—a saccharine family sitcom in the *Webster* mold, with Samantha playing its matriarch—it's already been off the air for a while. However, because it doesn't just live on in syndication but is apparently ubiquitous, Steve sometimes gets teased for his association with something so corny, and specifically for its status as the peak of Samantha's success: the Season 1 finale kicks off with Brandon breaking up a fistfight between Steve and some no-name under-five who dares to describe Samantha as "washed up."

Steve is a good egg and his fierce loyalty to Samantha is laudable, but all the evidence *Beverly Hills, 90210* offers backs up this one-off bully's assessment. Let's look at "Chuckie's Back," the Season 2 episode in which we actually meet Samantha for the first time. There's talk of a *Hartley House* reunion—a relatively rare event at the time, well before the reboot mania of our era. Samantha knows it won't happen without the enthusiastic participation of Chuck Wilson (Matt Nolan), who played cloying moppet Chuckie on *Hartley House*. After getting expelled from every private school in the greater Los Angeles area, Chuck has ended up at West Beverly, and Samantha makes Steve a deputy to her management team by ordering him to kiss Chuck's ass so that he'll do the reunion. Much as it did Lydia in "Fame Is Where You Find It," the show portrays this episode's former child actor as a spoiled, ungovernable sociopath. (It's so funny how the people writing for this cast of "teen" superstars keep coming up with storylines about spoiled Hollywood brats!) Chuck needles Steve by asking Kelly to the winter dance; then he baits Steve into a physical fight and orders Steve to take the blame, threatening the reunion if Steve doesn't capitulate. When it comes out that Chuck knew Steve was adopted before Steve himself did (a loose-lipped functionary told Chuck so that he wouldn't be so jealous of Steve and Samantha's relationship), Samantha turns on her former collaborators, dooming the reunion and sending Chuck to one-shot guest-star oblivion.

But propping up Samantha's career is only one reason it can suck to be her son: while Andrea's busy trying to conceal her residence scam in "Down and Out (of District) in Beverly Hills," the B-plot finds Steve keeping company with Christine (Jennifer Runyon). The two have a chance meeting at the Peach Pit; Steve rescues her from not being able to pay her bill, and she's grateful that she won't be working off her debt washing dishes because she has to get home and watch her favorite show, *Hartley House*!!! Steve reveals his connection—he's not so cagey about it when it might get him laid—and they become "one-week anniversary" official. Steve resists Brenda's and Kelly's attempts to warn him that Christine seems kind of materialistic, but she outs herself soon enough—not just for being more interested in his gifts than she is in him, but that she knew who Steve was all along and specifically targeted him for his wealth. How she knew where the son of a particular former sitcom star hangs out is a mystery; it's 1991, so it's not like she would have clocked it on his Instagram. But this is just the sort of ingenuity that will stand Christine in good stead in pulling off even bigger grifts in the future.

One of the biggest moments for *Hartley House* is also one of the biggest for *Beverly Hills, 90210*. After throwing an illegal rave in a house where the compromised electrical system caused a fire that burned a guest nearly to death, Steve is ordered to do community service (???) in a nursing home. There he meets Saul Howard (Milton Berle!)—or, rather, is reunited with him, since they've met before: Saul guest-starred on *Hartley House* before succumbing to Alzheimer's disease, which is, at least partly, why he keeps calling Steve "Chuckie" (we're not ruling out the possibility that he's also just breaking balls). Steve treats this elderly man more or less like a mascot during his periods of lucidity, but soon learns all about sundowning. Attempting to startle Saul out of catatonia by *jingling car keys in his face* is a low point for Steve in this episode, but evidently the Television Academy was able to see past it and to Berle's performance: his nomination for Outstanding Guest Actor in a Drama Series was the only time *Beverly Hills, 90210* was ever represented at the Emmys. (Berle lost.)

We like to think that, in the universe of *Beverly Hills, 90210*, *Hartley House* is still extant—that it airs in a punitively early time slot on TV Land, or trades days with *M*A*S*H* on Sundance. Then again, maybe Samantha's coming out as a lesbian later in life revived interest in her life and work from fellow members of the LGBTQ+ community and earned it a slot on LogoTV; it's nice to imagine queer women filling their timelines with ironic *Hartley House* gifs, to which Steve can point the next wag who dares to say his mother's washed up.

"I'm sorry, Walsh, I didn't mean to insult your intelligence here,
but either you are totally ignorant or naive in the extreme."

Brandon Solves Racism for the First Time Since the L.A. Uprising

WBH's football team is having its best season since 1969—which you'd think would be a nice turn of events everyone can get excited about until you learn its next opponent will be Shaw High School, in South-Central L.A.; even Will (Mushond Lee), one of WBH's few non-white football players, "jokes" that he's not sure he'll survive the drive down there.

Turns out he needn't have worried about it, because two spectators get fatally shot in the stands at a Shaw game (Jim: "I thought they were supposed to 'increase the peace'"), and the paranoid school board cancels the WBH/Shaw game, completely unconcerned that this is going to negate the whole premise of the next night's Pigskin Prom. And Brenda and Donna are the ones planning it!!!

In the course of reporting on the school board's overreaction—something that's no longer within his purview since new *Blaze* advisor Gil Meyers (Mark Kiely), in a bullshit sexist move earlier in the season, strong-armed him into being coeditor-in-chief, with Andrea—Brandon meets Jordan Bonner (Michael Anthony Rawlins, far and away the best part of the episode), editor of Shaw's newspaper. Their initial interaction is hostile for the usual reason, namely Brandon confidently opining about shit he knows nothing about (in this case, "street violence") and defensively exploding when his interlocutor (in this case, a black student attending what appears to be a majority-black school) calls him on it. But Brandon bravely drives his *precious car* through burned-out post-L.A.-uprising storefronts to Shaw to tell Jordan his brilliant idea: the teams should just play the game at a neutral location. Jordan, who has already told Brandon the shooter who killed the spectators wasn't from Shaw, must then further explain what's at stake: "If we play this game anywhere *but* here, we might as well hand the community over to the gangs." So they pivot to a different show of unity: they'll each write an editorial—Jordan eulogizing his friends; Brandon eulogizing the game (*eye roll*)—and publish both pieces in both papers. Jordan's even written his already, so what could be easier? Well, both Gil and Andrea are aghast at Jordan's profane rhetoric, Gil incorrectly calling it "racist"; Brandon refuses to edit Jordan, so the idea of mirror editorials is dropped. Brandon then faffs around writing *his* editorial for so long that Gil and Andrea leave him to close the paper alone, and late . . .

. . . which is when we learn he was only *pretending* to be slow and inconsiderate (two things, it must be noted, Andrea and Gil had no problem believing him to be): Jordan appears with his *real* editorial, which is shorter and less swear-filled than his emotional first draft, and then is shocked by a closer from Brandon that "personally" invites the Shaw student body to the Pigskin Prom. Everyone is furious at Brandon: Brenda, for making his symbolic stand at an event she worked hard to plan and which may now get just as canceled as the game; Steve, because his client David is booked to perform and Steve lined up A&R guys to come see him; Gil and Andrea, for the way Brandon deceived them; and Mrs. Teasley, for his opening the door to possibly hundreds of kids who may literally not fit in the WBH gym, though she lets *us* down by looking chastened when Brandon the honky idiot stops just short of calling her a race traitor.

Gil, apparently the only faculty member scheduled to be on-site at the dance, prevents its cancellation ("I'm a sucker for girls in party shoes," he says of the STUDENTS who will be attending, GRRRRRROSS), but that night, everyone is tense. Jordan reports that a caravan of Shaw kids are en route to WBH and have been drinking. David finally stops Scott Scanlon's younger sister Sue (Nicholle Tom) from aggressively hitting on him by telling her their doing anything would be "incestuous." (Remember that word choice later.) Even Kelly, skipping the dance due to a rare dinner with her absentee father, is testy after Brenda tries to manage her expectations about it. Brenda turns out to have been, while insensitive, right, and Jennie Garth does a nice job with a weepy monologue to Dylan, who finds her at the Peach Pit after her father blows her off (which, since she wore a skintight dress with a cut-out/lace-up back she couldn't wear a bra with to dinner with a *parent*, may be just as well).

But as the Shaw students start to arrive, the hired security guards mistake roughhousing between Tony and Will as an interschool hate crime and lose a lot of their enforcement authority in the process. Donna, Nikki, and Brenda interrupt the dumb fronting between rival factions by asking Shaw guests to dance. David is joined onstage for "Switch It Up"—still a banger and hands down his best song—by a Shaw kid who makes an able hype man. Proudly regarding the potentially incendiary situation that he created and others had to defuse for him while he did nothing but bray about it, Brandon predicts that an unofficial game will be played the next day. Jordan says his late friends would have liked Brandon, and somehow their unquiet spirits do not rise from the dead to contradict him.

Who's Bad-Touching Sue?

No one remembers this as the episode Dylan turns 18; gets a bronchial infection from surfing in bacteria-infested water; learns that there's an environmental ballot initiative in the upcoming election; learns that he should have registered to vote over a month ago; and learns that Donna, who's also 18 and registered months ago, is more civic-minded than he is.

(Donna's birthday is December 25 and this episode aired in October, so are we to think she turns *19* in the middle of her senior year of high school?!) Nor does anyone remember this as the episode where Brandon gets weirdly threatened when he goes out dancing with Nikki and then glares at her resentfully from behind his club soda as she dances with guys who actually ask her. He then finds out dancing makes her horny and decides to get over himself and dance with her—offscreen, thank god, because Jason Priestley has moves less graceful than most zombies. What everyone *does* remember about this episode is that it's the one where a student accuses Gil of getting handsy with her, and it sure is credible!

Scott's sister Sue has stopped hitting on David and started hitting on Gil—for instance, asking him in the middle of the Peach Pit what she has to do to get a good grade in his class: "Take my clothes off?" The next day, she finds Gil in his classroom after hours to rant about Mrs. Teasley reporting her truancy to her mother, and about her persistent thoughts that she should have been the one who died, not Scott. Having already watched suspiciously while Gil hustled Sue out of the Peach Pit the night before, Andrea's attention is piqued when she sees Sue tearfully racing out of Gil's classroom. Later, Gil is lecturing his AP English students about "HOR-thawne [*sic*]" (we *think* he means "Hawthorne," but that no one on set knew he'd mangled it) when he gets an urgent note from the office and has to duck out. Before long, "office service" operative Brenda is spreading the scandalous news: Gil's been suspended for sexual misconduct with a female student, and word soon gets out that it's Sue.

Gil's coeditors end up on opposite sides, with Brandon predictably discrediting the anonymous accuser and trying to talk Gil out of resigning so that Sue's mother will drop the complaint. "But why would you want to do that?" Brandon brays. Gil, huskily: "Why do you think?" BECAUSE YOU DID IT is what *we* may think at this stage in the story, KNOWN SKEEVE. Meanwhile, Andrea follows her hunch and lets Sue know she's there if Sue wants to talk, even mentioning her own ill-fated crush on Season 2 Chris, the drama teacher she was totally prepared to bone until he suddenly had a girlfriend. Andrea's confrontational when she runs into Gil in the *Blaze* office, packing up his stuff, but he won't contest the charges, for the sake of Sue's mental health; he tells Andrea about another student he says "fell in love" with him and, when he firmly rejected her advances, died by suicide and blamed him in her note. Is this an appropriate story for an adult teacher to tell a minor student? No! Is this the kind of boundary-blurring that might continue to get Gil in trouble if he doesn't drastically change his behavior? MAYBE!

Sue then surprises Andrea with an invitation to the Scanlon house that night, where Mrs. Scanlon greets Andrea effusively, yanks her inside, and introduces Andrea to Sue's Uncle Henry (Cliff Bemis), visiting from Oklahoma. The evening is pleasant (for everyone but Sue) until Mrs. Scanlon suggests watching some old videos of Scott cowboying and Sue flips out: she doesn't want to talk about Scott, and she doesn't want to talk about Gil. But Uncle Henry wants to know what Sue did to make Gil think he could "make such advances." Andrea immediately defends her, but Sue interrupts to say that, actually, *she* tried to kiss Gil, and he wouldn't let her. This is all it takes to get Gil reinstated, but Andrea can't stop thinking about Sue, imprisoned at home; when Andrea goes by to check on her, Mrs. Scanlon says Sue's only seeing family.

Nothing for it but to send *family* over, and that means Andrea and Brenda (Sue's senior buddy) enlisting Donna to call on the Scanlons with Mrs. S's beloved David. There, Donna and David learn that Mrs. Scanlon's pulling Sue out of WBH: the family's moving to Oklahoma to be closer to Uncle Henry. David quietly tells Donna that Henry *was* Scott's favorite uncle until that last trip to Oklahoma; then something happened that caused Scott to say he was a jerk and never mention him again. After Donna witnesses Uncle Henry favoring Sue's younger sister Amy and scolding Sue for trying to keep them apart, Donna tries again, noting that Andrea told them kids don't make up stories of abuse: "It has to come from some-where." This affects Sue, who recounts, "He was kissing me and touching me. I don't know who started it. It could've been me. He said it was me. But then I didn't want to anymore, and I pulled away, but he wouldn't let me. He wouldn't let me go. He hurt me." But it wasn't Gil: "It was my uncle. It's always been my uncle."

Donna supports Sue as she comes out to the patio to disclose the abuse to Mrs. Scanlon, in the middle of a cookout, and with Uncle Henry just inches away with the guiltiest mug you ever did see. The good news is that Sue is done keeping her secret and trying to be a human shield between Amy and the uncle trying to groom her as his next victim. The bad news is that her extremely high-strung mother is in no way equipped to help her with her recovery. And we neeeeever see them again.

Brenda Finds Out About "Kellan" and Loses It

Fresh off Dylan and Brenda's breakup, the show is determined to act like we have even the slightest interest in other subplots at the moment, so before we get into the climactic restaurant showdown, we have to sit through some Jim Walsh midlife-crisis STUFF involving his foxy secretary, not to mention the ongoing "drama" with Steve using the skeleton key he got from B.J. (. . . hee) and his freshman buddy's mad computer skillz to break into the school's computer.

This is yet another already-exhausting variation on the "Steve takes a shortcut and it blows up in his face" plot, but it's worth noting (barely), for two reasons. One: Steve, getting blackmailed by Janitor Hudge (Jeff Doucette), handles that aspect of the situation as badly as the rest, wearing not just a snotty attitude but what appears to be a ladies' aerobics outfit to a late-night meeting with his tormentor. Two: Andrea is in a wheelchair after a hit-and-run accident (and you'll never guess who gives her free food as an analgesic) (oh, Nat), but she still has to take point on the story for the *Blaze* because Brandon is the laziest coeditor-in-chief in school-paper history . . . although, per Andrea's sources, the Beverly Hills precinct is quite conscientious, claiming it won't drop the matter until an arrest is made. If memory serves, LAPD was too busy sitting around O.J. Simpson's pool at this point in history to bother with some trifling school hack, but: sure.

Of course, in theory, a trifling school issue is what led to Brenda and Dylan's split, as Brenda's failure to be supportive when Dylan was accused of cheating on the SAT was the catalyst. In practice, it was cheating of another sort, but Brenda doesn't know that yet, and is more than happy to accept a date with Rique now that she's free to do so. She's also free of Dylan's constant sulking. Kelly, on the other hand, is now cleared to marinate in said sulking to her heart's delight, as Brenda has shrugged that Dylan can date whomever he chooses. Nobody believes her, least of all Kelly, and Dylan is still acting like *he* was the mistress—and like, because Brenda technically dumped *him*, she doesn't get to care what he does. Kelly doesn't point out that just because Dylan is inconvenienced by the feelings of others doesn't mean they don't exist, or that Brenda is also Dylan's best friend's *twin sister* (not that Brandon ever takes her side either, but whatever) and everyone's emotionally braided together, though it wouldn't do any good anyway when Dylan's in full "misunderstood poet, beset on all sides" mode.

And *boy* is he in that mode. Dylan turns up to Bio to find his lab partner—still Brenda—prepared for their experiment; *he* has forgotten the materials he was supposed to provide, and is a bitch about it when he's the one fucking up their grade. (Kids, never pair with an SO on school projects.) Dylan's other modes on his and Kelly's deeply basic planetarium date are no better, mind you: either the writers are trying to make him funny by way of an excruciating Scotty–from–*Star Trek* bit, or he's waxing philosophical about the stars making their problems feel insignificant. Stick it in a blog, McKay.

Meanwhile, Brenda is getting a bad feeling about the tax shelter–related bonding going on between Rique and Jim, and an even worse feeling when they head to the Peach Pit for a bite and run into almost everyone she knows. They head to the only *other* restaurant in town for a little late-night delicious cumin, but as they're walking in, Dylan and Kelly—having just wrapped up a truly bizarre dessert-"sharing" scenario primarily intended to underscore Kelly's increasingly disordered eating—are walking out. We're finally at the fireworks factory, folks, and the ensuing explosion does not disappoint. Dylan is outright aggressive toward Brenda about having broken up with him first! Brenda is button-mashing Kelly's sensitivity about her "slut" rep! Rique is trying to give everyone group therapy, because anyone dumb enough to fall for Brenda's atrocious Frahnche accent is also too dumb to save himself from this cluster!

Later, Rique drops some pretty decent wiz about relationships having a reason and a season, but after he spends a little too much time with Jim and *The Jerry Lee Lewis Casio Songbook*, Brenda cuts Rique loose. She swears it's not because of Dylan, and obviously it totally is, but that doesn't mean she couldn't have gotten it in with Rique anyway, does it? He's Superman! There are worse things than your dad liking your man!

For his part, Dylan is still trying to lawyer Brenda's reactions with the she-dumped-*me* line, like he and Kelly don't know Brenda and couldn't have predicted exactly this response. Kelly isn't impressed, and the next day, Dylan finds out the College Board wasn't impressed with his lawyering of the SAT situation either: he can take the test again, but they've denied his appeal. He screeches at poor Mrs. Teasley about being tagged a cheater (if the tiny-waisted jeans fit . . .) and flounces out of her office, past a catfight between Kelly and Brenda about who's sloppy seconds, out of school entirely, and then all the way out of *town*, ignoring messages from Kelly *and* Brenda on his machine and telling only Brandon that he's peacing out. We would tell you that prickly self-pity about situations you put *yourself* in is not sexy, but we regret to say that the next episode does not bear that statement out . . .

> *"Horses get bored if they're always ridden by the same person."*

Nikki's Abusive Ex, Diesel, Comes to Town While Dylan "Works Shadowcaster"

SEASON 3 | EPISODE 14
WILD HORSES

You know it's a packed episode when the brokering of a Brenda/Kelly ceasefire *and* Steve's expulsion after finally confessing to Skeleton Keygate barely crack the summary, but since neither of these developments lasts, let's move on . . .

. . . to the music showcase The Gang (*sans* a resentful Brenda) is attending. David's set is marred by equipment problems (because Steve is still his manager) and by . . . you know, David's material, but things get truly ugly when the next group takes the stage. It's Diesel and his band, Waste Management, and the eponymous Diesel (David Arquette, going for an acting volume discount) is wearing a leather vest with no shirt underneath, an intense sneer directed at Nikki, and a red keytar, which undercuts the first two things rather handily.

Nikki is drawn to her ex as if by a tractor beam after his set, cooing about the song he wrote for her as her current boyfriend, Brandon, seethes beside her, and when she finally introduces Brandon, Diesel's idea of small talk is to slag David as a "Vanilla Ice rip-off." We'd like to know where the lie is, but Brandon, who ordinarily could give two shits about David, is happy to wax self-righteous about David being "a close friend of ours." Wellll, he's really a close friend of *yours*, and that barely, but that's symptomatic of a larger problem Brandon and Nikki proceed to fight about, namely that they "always go to the Peach Pit," and that Brandon kind of expects Nikki to wedge herself into The Gang instead of having a life of her own. Nikki tries to mollify Brandon, but he won't have it and ditches her in a nightclub by herself . . . again.

Brandon certainly feels justified, versus concerned about her safety, the next day when he learns Nikki didn't come home the night before, and gets in her face about how she's a groupie who probably "made it with" Diesel. Who wrote Brandon's dialogue in this ep, Peter Frampton? Shut up, Brandon. Nikki barely has time to register what a choad her alleged boyfriend is before Diesel appears to announce that he's gotten a record deal (lol) and that Nikki's coming with him to celebrate. Brandon rolls up and asks if she's okay, and when she says she's fine—despite Diesel not only roughly yanking her toward his car in front of everyone, but also admitting he's been drinking all morning—Brandon backs down.

But not for long! He finds Diesel's squat somehow, and barges in shortly after Diesel has responded to Nikki's objections to his bringing an *actual* groupie home by backhanding Nikki across the face. This is not as cautionarily shocking as it should be thanks to overly spacious blocking that makes it look like Diesel is instructing Nikki on approach shots in tennis, but Brandon is in white-knight mode and doesn't even have to mount a stepladder to drop Diesel with a single punch (snort).

At the Walsh house later, Nikki explains that her abusive relationship with Diesel, and fighting with her parents about him, was why she left San Francisco, but she's hoping a trip home for Thanksgiving will reestablish communication. (And rid her of Brandon's paternalistic judgments, she does not add.)

Elsewhere in unearned judginess: Dylan's car breaks down outside the ranch of an obnoxious thirtysomething heiress, Anne (Alice "The Borg Queen" Krige), who offers him a bed in her guesthouse while he waits for the local mechanic to hunt up the vintage-Porsche parts Dylan needs. We'd make a joke here assuring you that "a bed in her guesthouse" is not a euphemism, but . . . it is. In fact, just about everything either of them says—about the freedom money can buy; about needing a ride, or the mechanic coming; about the horses they awkwardly ride to a secluded creek—is a euphemism. Well, unless one of them is disgorging his or her poor-little-rich-kid bio and pontificating about trust. Which is constantly.

The biggest howler is Anne's indecent proposal to Dylan: that he stay at the ranch for a while and "work Shadowcaster." Shadowcaster is a champion show-jumper, so the idea that Anne would let some rando anywhere near him, much less train the animal, so she could get a leg over is ridiculous. But using "work Shadowcaster" as a polite term for Doing It has brought us so much joy over the years that we'll just have to let it go. There's a lot we have to do that with in this plotline: the weird make-out spot next to the creek that would have them tumbling into the water after one thrust; the dinner party with Anne's terrible Reaganite neighbors that somehow leads to a cynical bidding war over Shadowcaster; and of course the fact that Dylan, who has spent *months* blaring at Kelly about their soul connection, is fine with macking on (. . . probably having sex with; the episode's unclear, but adult Anne is unlikely to content herself with grinding on the sofa) a crazy-eyed horsey lady he just met and never mentions again. Several pretentious debates about trust funds making your heart die later, Dylan realizes he *wants* strings attached in his life, and heads back to the Zip to continue messing with Brenda's and Kelly's heads.

"The man upstairs doesn't have time for a bunch
of self-absorbed kids and neither do I."

How the Zip Stole Christmas (from Frank Capra)

SEASON 3 | EPISODE 16

IT'S A TOTALLY HAPPENING LIFE

The only (public domain) holiday classic lazy TV writers love ripping off as much as *A Christmas Carol* is *It's a Wonderful Life*, and we're going to be dealing with the latter for Christmas '92.

"But how lazy could Karen and Charles Rosin possibly be?" you might wonder. Well, one of the angel narrators here—only audible to the viewer, voiced by Robert Costanzo and represented by blinking stars—is NAMED CLARENCE, EXACTLY LIKE IN THE MOVIE. He has no patience for Miriam (voice of Bonnie Urseth), an apprentice angel who's been keeping tabs on The Gang and has *a very urgent matter* to bring to his attention.

Once it's established that it's the holidays, and our "heroes" are putting together a toy drive for the Alvarado Street School, the episode complicates its framing device by jumping forward a few days to everyone on a bus to East L.A., looking pissed; and then back to how they got there. There are also flashbacks within the flashbacks, but we'll take you through it without *Rashomon*-ian pretensions.

DONNA: "An angel on earth if ever there was one," per Miriam.

STEVE: Still barred from all senior-class activities due to his legacy-key idiocy.

BRENDA, DYLAN, AND KELLY: Kidding themselves that they can all be platonic friends until both girls end up making out with him—though only one of them (Kelly) is sloppy enough to get busted.

DAVID: Pouting because it's only just occurred to him that all his friends are about to go to college and he'll be left alone, and—establishing a pattern—taking his stress out on Donna.

ANDREA: Gets into Yale; gets dumped (in a letter) by Peter "Jay" Krause.

BRANDON: Gets dumped by Nikki on her way out of town to live with her parents again. (Aw, bye girl, we'll actually miss you!) He then tries to soothe his ego by making out with Andrea, who wildly overreacts instead of just letting herself enjoy the one thing she's wanted since the day she and Brandon met. "He'll have plenty of girlfriends," Clarence (audibly) shrugs, of Brandon. Miriam: "Not if he gets on that bus." Okay, but . . . we already saw him on the bus?

Come the day, every member of the gang who is scheduled to go to Alvarado Street has beef with at least one other person attending—except Donna, to whom they each go whining and trying to weasel out of this *philanthropy*. After we're forced to watch her have this interaction with each one of them, she narcs to Mrs. Teasley, who forbids them all from flaking on—again—*the trip we have known they were going to take since the start of the episode.* Clarence thinks Miriam is concerned that they all got sidetracked from holiday merriment by their petty issues, but no: it's that the bus is on a collision course with a truck! Leaving aside how preposterous it is that any viewer would think the show was going to kill off virtually its entire opening-credits cast *in its Christmas episode*: if the issue is that an accident is imminent, then how was ANY of this personal bullshit at ALL germane to Miriam's appeal to Clarence to prevent the accident using his angel powers?!

Whatever: Clarence says he already looked ahead and exercised said power with a onetime fix, accessible only in case of "catastrophe," and rerouted truck driver Craig Clemens to the freeway. Too bad the guy who's about to T-bone the bus is *Greg* Clemens, behind the wheel of a garbage truck, and drinking. In order for us to think this would be sad and not a relief, Donna gets up and orders all her jerk friends to get over themselves. (The West Beverly High Madrigal Singers, also on the bus, probably talk among themselves about these entitled boobs ruining yet another school event by acting like they're the only people there.) Steve, who snuck out to Alvarado Street, sees Greg driving the wrong way down a one-way street and tries to get his attention, to no avail. The editor cuts frantically between Greg, swigging from a fifth of something and picking up speed, and the happy bus passengers making peace with each other. Clarence and Miriam can do nothing but watch helplessly as . . . the garbage truck phases through the bus in a spectacularly terrible "special" "effect." What does Steve, established as watching this from the schoolyard, make of this total violation of the laws of physics? No idea; we don't see his reaction. Miriam thanks Clarence for his intercession, but

Clarence gasps that it must have been "a higher power" that miraculously rescued this bus full of turds!

Mrs. Teasley lets Steve stay, but makes him play Santa. David tells Donna he figured out he can "load up" on required courses and graduate early, though it might limit the time they'll have to hang out together. Brenda and Kelly order Dylan to choose which of them he wants to spend New Year's Eve with. Donna hears jingling bells and repeats the famous line about bells and angel wings and Miriam gets hers and we reject God.

"You said choose. I chose. I chose you."

Getting Dumped Is Only the Second-Worst News Brenda Has to Endure

SEASON 3 | EPISODE 19

BACK IN THE HIGH LIFE AGAIN

Brandon's degenerating gambling addiction, David's precarious living situation in the wake of Mel and Jackie's split, and Andrea's new hair color (. . . yes, this is a storyline that spans several scenes in multiple locations) try to distract you, but they cannot pull your focus from the main event: Season 3's love triangle losing a side, thereby entering TV history in the process.

Jack is out of prison and being very vague about how his lawyers pulled off such a feat when he was still years away from parole eligibility. To celebrate, he throws a party in his suite at the Bel Age (where else) and tells Dylan to invite all his friends; Brenda tries to go, but Jim forbids her from hanging out with a convicted felon still facing hundreds of civil suits for his financial crimes, and ultimately only Kelly makes it, selling out Brenda by revealing that Jim's disapproval is the reason Brenda's not there. Since this passed hors d'oeuvres party would be boring for teenagers even if it wasn't also attended by fewer guests than servers, Dylan suggests that he and Kelly go for a swim and a make-out sesh, which is when we find out he has, at last, made up his mind, and the gentleman prefers blondes. Kelly—a little flirty and a little sincere—asks if she only won the bake-off because Brenda didn't make it out that night, and Dylan says, "I've always wanted you," like we don't know he was in love with Brenda, and not long ago! We all watched the first two seasons, Jones! Kelly declares that, before they publicly become a couple, they have to tell Brenda about their Summer of Deception. OKAY, BITCH, IT'S YOUR FUNERAL.

But this isn't the only issue Dylan has to deal with right now: Jack tells him that he stashed away a little money where no one can find it, and is confident he'll make more (when he's not in court defending himself in civil suits, presumably), but since they're talking money: does Dylan think Jim is doing a good job managing his investments? The three meet in Jim's office, where Dylan announces that he'd like Jack to handle his finances from now on. Swallowing his bile, Jim says it's not possible: given Jack's conviction, he can't be licensed as a money manager, nor a competent trustee. But surprise, the latter isn't an issue: Jack wants to dissolve the trust! Jim explains that he, Iris, and Dylan would all have to sign off on such a move; he's just as confident Iris won't sign as Jack is that he can convince her (#BigDickEnergy). And apparently Jack's motivated to persuade her, judging by his side of a heated phone conversation in which he promises an unknown caller he will "get the money out of the trust—a deal's a deal!"

Back to Brenda, whose hair is as droopy as her spirit; she can tell something's changed for her and her fellow love triangleers since the party she couldn't attend. Dylan first tells Brandon that he's going to need to look out for Brenda since Dylan's not going to be around anymore, and Brandon, the world's worst brother, doesn't warn her about what's coming before Dylan and Kelly appear together at her front door. Rather than sully the Walsh foyer forever with the memory of Brenda getting dumped there, Dylan and Kelly walk her to a park to confirm that, yes, Brenda is officially out of the throuple. She's already furious and ready to leave when Kelly tells her that's not all. Instead of taking Brenda's cue and not giving her even *more* bad news when, after all, they basically got away with it, Dylan Brandonishly brays at Brenda that she has to listen because they can't stand lying to her anymore. Out comes the truth: they started fooling around when she was in Paris. "I thought you guys were my friends!" screams Brenda, heartbroken. "I loved you, I trusted you both! . . . Why are you doing this to me?" Often in TV—even in teen dramas, where no one should be expected to be mature—breakups are presented as mutual so that the audience doesn't have to bear a grudge against the dumper through what may be many more years' worth of episodes. So, even though it is still devastating to watch the two people Brenda loves most in the world absolutely wreck her, it's also extremely satisfying when she delivers her final kiss-off: "Look, I hate you both. Never talk to me again." *Iconic.*

RIP Jack McKay*

Do you ever think about how the "Brandon is addicted to sports betting" arc came about? Like, clearly the main attraction for this part of the season was going to be the love triangle, so producers had to think of something for Brandon to do while he was not interacting with Brenda, Kelly, and Dylan, and what they came up with was . . . this?

Sports betting is never interesting (ahem, Amanda on *SVU*), but what made anyone think this would be a relatable issue for teens to watch Brandon grapple with? Anyway: Brandon loses a bunch of bets and gets in over his head. When Duke (still Billy Vera, still randomly) comes by the Peach Pit to collect, Brandon sweatily asks for a little more time, and Duke gives it to him—but also makes sure Brandon knows this dispensation will not be granted again. Duke, no! Break his tiny legs or he will never learn! Alas, no one comes for Brandon's body in any way—not Brenda, taking a self-defense class with Cindy and Donna that helps her work off some of her rage (though by no means all of it—what class possibly could?), and who could have practiced sparring with/on him; and not Andrea, who, to Brandon's consternation, has started dating Jordan. Brandon denies to Steve that he doesn't get Jordan and Andrea as a couple because of "that whole *Jungle Fever* thing" (Steve, ew), but does have the self-awareness to agree that he tends to get possessive of Andrea whenever she dates anyone. Too bad Gabrielle Carteris had to get her IRL pregnancy written into the plot and thus forestall any possibility of this obvious endgame resolving itself . . . but we'll get there.

Once again, it is the McKays in the spotlight here. Jack has acquired the biggest yacht in the marina, and is just as dodgy about its provenance as he is about his early release from prison: "I took a fall for a lot of guys who could've gone down with me, so let's just say it's payback time." No further questions! (?) He brings Dylan and Christine (Valerie Wildman) to see it, where they meet Captain Terry Wilson (George McDaniel) and First Mate Mel Borman (Miguel Pérez), the former wasting no time letting *us* know that he and Mel are not what they seem, nagging Jack: "We were told we could expect the money by now; what's the holdup?" We see agents listening in an extremely conspicuous surveillance van as Terry warns that Jack needs to speed up his shenanigans regarding the trust or "kiss [his] deal goodbye." Dutiful Dylan heads straight for Jim's office to reopen talks, Iris having given in by this point, but Jim stands firm, and proves his worth as a sober and unemotional trustee by letting Dylan spit, "I will decide what is in my best interest—not you, not anybody" at him and *not* laughing in his entitled 18-year-old face. But later, weighing the facts, he realizes that all the cons on his list relate to Jack's shadiness (which: like, fair?), whereas he has only one pro: "Dylan deserves a father." Convinced that he and Cindy can resign as Dylan's surrogate parents, Jim relents, and Dylan becomes a $10 millionaire. Given how thirsty Jack is, here's hoping Dylan's ATM PIN is hard to guess. (And given that Jackie gave up her alimony when she married Mel and now has to sell the house in a buyer's market, losing Kelly the one bit of stability she had through Jackie's many divorces, you'd think Dylan could offer to pay off her mortgage?)

Jack doesn't get too grabby with the cash: over dinner, when conversation has moved on from how little Kelly eats (••) and Jack advises her not to get so thin she's unfuckable (we're paraphrasing), Jack surprise-proposes to Christine, who delightedly accepts. Having gotten everything he wants, Jack is on the verge of confessing *something* to Dylan, but the eavesdropping agents intervene, Terry warning Jack that it's not safe for Dylan to know the truth. Instead, Jack—wearing the last in a series of aggressively voluminous turtlenecks—stops into Dylan's cabin for a nostalgic chorus of "Take Me Out to the Ball Game" and a *very* emotional bear hug. It's almost as though he knows, as we do, that right after their sing-along, an unseen figure sticks what appears to be a box of flashbulbs to the underside of Jack's Dadmobile. Sure enough, the next morning, Jack goes out to move his car, and it explodes.

Dylan's Inner Child Isn't the Most Immature Person at Jack McKay's Funeral

SEASON 3 | EPISODE 22
THE CHILD IS FATHER TO THE MAN

Stunned by the violent death, in the previous episode, of the father he'd only just begun to trust again, Dylan dissociates his trauma—into a literal embodiment of his own inner child. The inner child is *also* played by Luke Perry, in an ill-fitting "BH" ballcap and evincing the same put-upon self-pity Dylan Prime has been thinking is cute all season.

Together, they'll try to work through Dylan's grief, anger, and urge to drink again. It's a testament to the show's bulletproof popularity at the time this episode aired that the concept wasn't dismissed as a laughable reach. (Not least because both "child" and "teenager" already look craggily careworn.)

The Dylinner Child is a bad call, but he's no more clueless and self-absorbed than anyone else in Dylan's orbit. The Walshes step up to offer the Casa as a hideout for Dylan when the press starts hounding him at his bungalow—convinced Brenda won't allow it, Dylan's surprised to learn it was her idea—and try to listen and give him space, albeit with a few stumbles. But acceptable funeral behavior eludes most of the main characters: Brandon's got an arm slung casually over the end of a pew like he's at a ball game. (Which he's probably betting on; that subplot does make a cameo in this episode, somehow.)

The Taylor/Silver household is the worst, though. David kvetches that Jack's memorial is a scheduling hassle for him, because Icon Records has booked his first recording session (lol) at the same time as Jack's service; Kelly doesn't want to go at all, because Dylan's too busy grieving to pay attention to her (not how she puts it, but . . . not *not* how she puts it, either), and the feeble attempts she *has* made to comfort him haven't gotten a warm reception. (We do mean "feeble," too. "Are you okay?" Kelly, they're picking Dylan's dad up with a sponge. Would *you* be okay?)

Donna rips into David *and* Kelly for making Jack's death about their own problems and manages to herd the two cats to the service, but Dylan barely notices, because he's got his hands full. Dylinner Child has already taunted Dylan into guzzling scotch like a man possessed (which we suppose he is, technically); the guy posing as the first mate on Jack's boat is lurking around having *Mad Libs: Conspiracy Edition* conversations about promises and cowboys; and David interrupts another Dylinner Child monologue to get (refreshingly, tbh) real with Dylan about the fact that, while they're not really friends, David can relate better to Dylan than anyone because of Scott's death. Dylan has only just recovered from the shock of the writers remembering Scott's existence when the mysterious phone call that Lurking First Mate told Dylan to expect comes through, and it's time to borrow Brandon's Mustang for a covert meet in a farmer's market. Well, as "covert" as Dylan can be when he's wearing a conspicuously hideous western duster that looks like *Walking Dead* zombie rags were affixed to the underside of a SunSetter awning and dipped in day-old Sanka.

Dylan learns that Lurking First Mate is a federal agent who worked with Jack in some kind of confidential-informant setup that got Jack an early release—as is Christine, also present and looking legitimately wrecked by Jack's demise; she really did love him and planned to marry him. It's unclear what the terms are or exactly what went wrong; we've had years to parse it and we're still not sure how it worked. Dylan has known about it for about seven seconds before shrieking at armed federal agents that they got his father killed, but this meltdown—and a subsequent screaming match with Dylinner Child in the car that turns Dylinner Child into an actual (terrible; sorry, kid) child actor—give Dylan some of the closure he needs. Back at Casa Walsh, an exhausted Dylan has a couple of sweet moments with his surrogate parents before giving his glycerin-soaked inner child a hug. It is dumb.

"Perfect, huh? There's no such thing as perfect."

Kelly's Long-Simmering Eating Disorder Fells Her at Her Own Birthday Party

SEASON 3 | EPISODE 24
PERFECTLY PERFECT

Since Cindy and Jackie took all the girls to the spa where, through convenient plot contrivances, Kelly heard Mel was cheating on her mother—*and* where Kelly's masseuse promised to work on all her "problem areas"—Kelly has been very aware of her figure.

Fortunately for concealment purposes, she's also been able to explain away her poor appetite by blaming stress, but her dieting tactics have been escalating: now she's taking OTC diet pills; getting up hours before school to exercise, compulsively, in front of her mirror; and planning to treat herself to a breakfast of one banana . . . which David eats before she can get to it. She bites his head off instead, and when she's flounced off, Jackie and David have an expository discussion about Kelly's surprise birthday party that night, for which David still has to find a venue, since the Taylor house is on the market and the Walsh house is, given recent events, not an option. He outsources the planning to Donna, who settles on "where else. Peach Pit," as excited about it as we are, though who but Nat would shut down his diner for a private weeknight party on 12 hours' notice?

The combination of malnutrition and nonprescription speed puts Kelly in a foul mood that only gets worse when she keeps seeing her friends conspiring and awkwardly splitting up when she appears. Steve is dealing with his own crabby bitch, Brandon, trying to convince him to join Steve on a dating game show called *Love at First Sight* (which is definitely not *Studs*), but he takes a break to talk Kelly out of her paranoid fantasies by telling her about the party. She announces that she doesn't want it and goes home early to eat two bites of supermarket potato salad before getting disgusted with herself and washing the rest down the disposal. (Wasteful! There are two other people who *are* on solids living in the house, though we do find it hard to picture Jackie the retired model eating anything made mostly of mayonnaise.) It's at this point that Jackie's agent comes through with potential buyers; Kelly's rudeness to the father and son is at about a 4 compared to the 10 she cranks it up to when she finds the mother and tween daughter admiring her clothes in the course of checking out her closet. Once Kelly has chased off any chance of a sale, Jackie—rather gently, considering—recommends that she try to keep her wild mood swings in check and act like the 18-year-old she will be the next day; though Kelly's been *publicly* taking the pills as directed, she waits for Jackie to leave before secretly popping some more nowhere near mealtime. When Dylan comes to pick her up later, she's racing and flustered and needs Jackie to find her shoe and calm her down so that she'll leave with him . . . but she takes more pills before she goes. In Dylan's car, with the top down, she complains that she's hot and her heart is beating too fast but denies his guess that the culprit could be all the dolls.

Brandon barely makes it for the surprise after his *Love at First Sight* taping, where—as he had predicted—Steve got way too competitive with Brandon over Celeste (Jennifer Grant—Cary's daughter!), the contestant they both liked and who ended up picking Steve. Since Steve is bad at paying attention, he missed the fact that the winning couple must go on their date immediately after the taping, and takes his irritation out on poor Celeste (what is he, David?), but luckily for him, she's extremely considerate and even more into him, and suggests that they just complete their date as fast as possible so that he can make it to the Peach Pit in time for the cake. Brenda is at the party under duress and offering only the most *pro forma* expressions of friendship, and rightly so (she wryly tells Cindy she bought Kelly a sweater she assumes Kelly will return, like, Kelly's lucky she's not getting a dirty bomb). But it is she who goes to retrieve Kelly from the bathroom so that she can blow out her candles, though Kelly gets extinguished instead! . . . Not really, but she is passed out on the floor and unresponsive to Brenda's therapeutic screaming in her face to wake up.

Conscious again in a hospital bed, Kelly learns from her doctor that diet pills are safe when taken as directed (episode writer Gillian Horvath's not trying to get sued by Big OTC Pharma, people), but that he'd also like her to start eating a balanced diet and join an eating-disorder support group, something she hotly denies she needs—though, tbh, nearly everyone in this episode seems like he or she could use some education on the subject. One assumes Jackie would have seen anorexic and exercise-bulimic behavior during her modeling days and thus recognized it in her daughter; Kelly tries to get the doctor off her back by promising "to pig out a couple of times"; and when Brenda ends her heartfelt declaration of love for Kelly, despite everything they've gone through recently, she suggests taking Kelly for ice cream when she's discharged. The one time we need a PSA we *don't* get! Anyway: Kelly lives; Dylan spends the night in her hospital room; Brenda yearns for what she can't have but seems to have almost made her way through the stages of grief to acceptance. If not, she's at least at the stage where she can get over herself long enough to dance with Tony Miller.

"We're not gonna get caught, Donna!"

The Prom Episode

SEASON 3 | EPISODE 27
A NIGHT TO REMEMBER

It's the run-up to Prom '93, and neither Walsh twin has a date; Brenda's going to bag the whole thing, and Brandon has plans to play poker with Tony Miller, which seems like a grand idea for someone who just wrapped up a *gambling-addiction storyline* but whatever, it's not as though anyone actually believes the Walshes will sit out this momentous event.

And they don't—Tony asks Brenda; Brandon waits too long to ask his perennial backup, Andrea, but when *her* date, the far superior Jordan, gets the flu, the *Blaze*-ers agree to go together. First, though, Brandon and Andrea have to do one more co-EIC roleplay as, respectively, the guy who only cares about doing a journalism when there's a "beb" involved, and the self-serious keener who went undercover on the cafeteria story, which is how they end up at a school board meeting.

After an unannounced presentation by Felice Martin on a proposed dress code—that she apparently can't be shagged to enforce in her own family; more on this anon—Andrea's suspicions are raised further by Superintendent Ephardt's (Arthur Rosenberg) next announcement. Evidently, it was "moved and seconded in closed session" that all seniors be notified, in school, that any senior caught at the prom with booze or drugs, or found to be intoxicated, will be suspended "with senior privileges revoked," including walking in graduation. The board needn't have bothered with the "closed session": the drinking age of 21 had been the law of the entire land for nearly a decade when this episode aired, and illegal drugs are, you know, illegal.

Everyone's scandalized anyway, somehow. Maybe not David, who's more focused on getting a room at the Bel Age (because where else would this prom/anything occur) and hoping that induces Donna to Do It with him. But when Gil—holding AP English on the lawn, because of course he is—doubles down on the "I'm not just their teacher, I'm *their friend*" unprofessionalism we've come to expect from ol' Loaf Hair by reading the drug-and-alcohol policy in the eye-rolliest tone possible, the gangsters in the class all exchange glowers for like 45 minutes. Guys, did you expect the prom to *serve* drinks and joints? This is what post-prom is for—read the manual!

Nobody does, and at the Martin manse, Donna helpfully foreshadows that she didn't eat all day so that she could fit into her (skintight, extremely revealing) dress. Felice doesn't seem to think her dress code applies to her own child, but makes sure to remind Donna of her Catholic principles by gifting her a prom-night accessory: a *massive* crucifix the Christ the Redeemer statue outside Rio would reject as extra. It's a wonder Donna can stand up straight in that thing (or lift her head; her hair is a bulky Aquanet-opus that probably weighs four pounds), but for *now*, she's upright and enjoying some empty-stomach champagne at the pre-party that idiot Mel Silver is idiotically throwing for The Gang.

With a couple of exceptions (Celeste's tendrilly hair situation; David's bitch-face), everyone looks adorable, especially Kelly, whose hair and white dress have a lovely Grace Kelly vibe that Dylan's pretentious after-prom trip to San Francisco doesn't deserve. And everyone's having a good time, even Brenda—and especially Donna, who is cresting that first wave of champers buzz as she helps Steve polish off the bottle he snagged for the limo ride. Nobody notices how drunk she's gotten and how quickly, though, and while it's possible prom performer Cathy Dennis's terrible bangs make Donna ill (or maybe she heard that Brandon and Andrea borrowed the hotel-room key Tony won't be using, and that Andrea is working heroically hard to get Brandon to suck face with her, in vain), it's probably all that bubbly. Donna lurches off the dance floor, about to hurl, but manages to navigate a ten-minute trip to the ladies' without ralphing into a plant—the first time in history this has ever happened. It takes a while for the others to figure out Donna's in trouble, but when they do, it's a miracle they don't get caught immediately, since half The Gang is standing around outside the bathroom like they're waiting for a bus. Yeah, Gil walks past and doesn't notice anything, but: it's Gil; he sucks at this.

When the coast is clear, a decision is made to put Donna in a Secret Service–style flying wedge and hustle her out through the lobby, and it makes *no* sense. At least two of you should remember where the back door is after stalking Color Me Badd in this hotel—you couldn't go that way? And doesn't David have a room upstairs you could stash Donna in? Hell, sling her under a room-service rolly table and take her out through the kitchen! Any plan is better than this one, but it does *almost* work, until Donna does a grapey swoon right in front of Mrs. Teasley, and the jig is up. WELP, LOOKS LIKE DONNA'S NOT GOING TO GRADUATE.* (*Walk in graduation.)

Donna Martin Graduates

SEASON 3 | EPISODE 28

SOMETHING IN THE AIR

Following her disastrous failure to carbo-load before booze in "A Night to Remember," Donna is suspended from school.

There's a disciplinary hearing yet to contend with—although this pales in comparison to The Ire of Felice, directed as it is not only at Donna but also at Mel Silver for giving the kids the goof juice in the first place. And we live for the logic-proof dudgeon of Felice Martin—not least because there's still lingering awk between Brandon and Andrea after they totally didn't Do It, again, at prom, and Felice strapping her bitch on is just easier to watch.

But it looks like Donna won't get to graduate with her classmates, and this is a fair and fitting outcome! Donna should have gone to summer school and picked up her diploma on some anonymous August morning, because she broke the rules, and rules apply to everyone, even dumb babies!

Donna herself seems to agree, but this is not how it shakes out, for two reasons: the actor playing Donna is the boss's daughter; and *Beverly Hills, 90210* could seldom resist positioning golden boy Brandon as a defender of the downtrodden. The rationale for his entering the bray—er, "fray"—this time is more baffling than the customary "Brandon learns two things about an issue, then takes it up with the humorless zealotry of the convert" MO of his "activism." Here, he's taking up Donna's cause in part because the rising seniors on the *Blaze* razz Brandon and the rest of the Class of 1993 for their alleged "slacker" attitude toward capital-I Issues, inspiring "Ace" to show them he really does care, especially about his friends. If that rationale sounds weird and tortured, well, it is, but the writers have to find *some* reason to turn Donna's situation into A Movement when she broke clearly stated rules.

Given Brandon's 99-percenter attitude toward his twin's trip-to-Paris reward for acting out earlier this season, it's a bit weird that *he'd* lead a literal March on the School Board on behalf of Donna, the fellow Gangster he's probably *least* close with. Also, Donna's so-called martyrdom is horseshit. First of all, as putative villain Superintendent Ephardt points out during Donna's hearing, "The no-drinking rule was passed unanimously by this board. What kind of message do you think it sends when the first student who breaks it gets off?" WELL, REALLY. Donna knew the rule; she broke the rule. But no, after Gil makes yet another unnecessary appeal to Brandon's innate leadership (barf), it turns into A Whole Movement, with future disgraced Senator Seldom Right and Wrong Again at its obnoxious and self-congratulatory helm, and it has the following repellent outcomes: (1) even though he changes his mind later thanks to peer pressure, Dylan initially points out that nobody is going to (read: "should") care about a poor little rich girl puking at prom, and he's going to focus on getting into Berkeley, and the fact that we agree with Dylan on anything is disorienting; (2) the "Donna Martin Graduates" episode is ground zero for the Donna-fluffing (she's so pretty! her fashion designs kick ass!) that came to dominate the postcollege era of the show, kicked off here with a clonky line from Brenda about how she never knew how much "everyone" at West Beverly loved Donna; (3) it inflates Brandon's already metastatic sense of self-importance—the junior editors on the paper, Mrs. Teasley, *everyone* defers to him as the point man, an impression he's happy to further by *holding up his hand to silence the 500 people in the board meeting.* (He also compares his father to Spiro Agnew, a reference that would have gotten these authors sent to their rooms had it made sense; reader, it does not.)

Ephardt threatens to call parents *and* police and to get college recs and acceptances revoked, and to this day we don't understand why he doesn't. But: he doesn't, and the board votes in Donna's favor. The juniors get the dress-code repeal they backroom-dealt for with Brandon. Donna gets to pin a mortarboard to the back of her overprocessed head like it's Jersey in the '80s. Great meritocracying, everyone!

SEASON Four

Comings

JILL FLEMING

Brandon and Steve cap off their summer borrowing a Malibu beach house belonging to some showbiz contact of Samantha's. The morning after a raging party, Brandon is surprised by the appearance of a mace-wielding woman, who turns out to be Jill (Robia La Morte), the owner's daughter, who was not informed that the house wouldn't be empty. On a break from college in New York, Jill is one of many women for whom Steve has been horny in the past, and for whom he still reflexively makes a play in front of his actual girlfriend, Celeste. Jill ends up being the latest prize that Brandon and Steve fight over, finally grossing her out badly enough to storm out of a tennis match that gets too aggro. And while macho athletic posturing is, we may all agree, reason enough on its own for Jill to peace out, it turns out that, following her rape by a stranger, she is especially sensitive to displays of toxic masculinity. Nothing to do but to let Brandon hold her in bed all night, thus nursing her back to sexual health? Sure.

DARLA HANSEN

One of Brenda's Minnesota besties, Darla (Wendy Benson-Landes) is both part of the reason Brenda justifies her decision to attend the University of Minnesota and not California University, where all her friends from high school enrolled, *and* the bulk of the reason Brenda justifies reversing that decision and heading back to L.A. Darla is Brenda's roommate, and an obnoxious one—thanks to Darla's very active sex life (with a dude named Dylan; gasp!), Brenda is obliged to spend a lot of time in their dorm's hallway. Then Brenda overhears Darla and her friends talking trash about Brenda's bad attitude when they think she's asleep. They're not entirely incorrect, but Brenda's hardly allergic to a dramatic exit, so back to the Zip she goes, and Darla is never mentioned again.

DAN RUBIN

After wasting her high school years (1) pining for Brandon and (2) squandering the opportunity to sleep with Jordan, Andrea starts up a semi-illicit romance with her RA, Dan Rubin (Matthew Porretta), which they partially legitimize by agreeing that she will transfer out of the English section he's TA-ing. Dan becomes Her First—as gentle and understanding as any young woman could hope for—but soon the cracks start to form: they differ on what responsibility women have for date rape; he's a little too eager to bring her home to meet his snooty parents. By the time Andrea's dumped Dan and taken up with a new guy who's Latinx, the show's writers evidently decide this new direction has to be justified by making Dan suddenly racist—a wild choice for this proto-woke character, about which one of your commentators is still annoyed because she continues to think he is very cute.

JOSH RICHLAND

The enemy of our enemy is our wasp-waisted friend, Josh Richland (Joshua Beckett), editor-in-chief of CU's newspaper, the *Condor*. Richland's initially determined to ruin Brandon by exposing his suspect academic relationship with D'Shawn Hardell *and* his suspect sexual relationship with his sociology professor's wife. We're meant to see Richland as a sleaze who will stop at nothing to get a story, but that's what journalists are supposed to do, Brandon's usual framing of the job aside, and the influence Möbius that is the D'Shawn/Corey Randall/Lucinda/Brandon storyline *should* get investigated. But Brandon's able to throw Richland off the scent—far enough, anyway—by contracting Kelly as his beard, and later, Richland softens on Brandon, as everyone on this damn show eventually must. Brandon joins Richland's progressive student-government

ticket as Richland's running mate, and everything works out great! For a few minutes!

HOWARD

Strike one against Howard (Zachary Throne) is that he gives Donna and David a radio show at all. Strike two is that he takes it away when he makes up with his girlfriend, the DJ who used to occupy their original plum timeslot, consigning Donna and David to the graveyard shift (until Donna wisely quits and leaves). Strike three is that he's David's meth contact when David, who's trying to fill airtime alone in the middle of the night, needs help staying awake to meet all his commitments. Howard does cut David off when David comes whining to him for downers to take the edge off; pity he doesn't do the same with his own super-'90s ponytail.

LESLIE SUMNER

Leslie Sumner (Brooke Theiss) is a fixture of the many Season 4 plotlines that set Greek life as their backdrop. The president of the improbably named Alpha Omega sorority, Leslie makes a bad first impression with a series of weird comments about Andrea's Judaism; Andrea pushes back by wearing a Star of David pendant to a candlelight ceremony, after which we learn that Leslie is also Jewish, but one who inherited the internalized anti-Semitism of ancestors who changed the family name to Sumner from Schulman. Andrea helps Leslie realize she can be more open about her faith and heritage, freeing Leslie to participate in Take Back the Night Week events, car washes, and charity Thanksgiving dinners without fear or inhibition about outing herself as a non-Gentile.

JOHN SEARS

KEG fraternity bigwig John Sears (Paul Johansson) is the kind of all-purpose villain a teen drama transitioning into a soap really needs. He comes between Kelly and Dylan when Dylan's insufficiently interested in campus life for Kelly's taste; then he's a creep about pressuring Kelly to have sex with him! He hits, hard, on an at-risk teen girl during a fraternity function (and it isn't the first time he's done such a thing, apparently); then, after Steve intercedes, Sears vows to make Steve's life hell, tries to frame him for the theft of Professor Randall's prized baseball, and almost gets Steve blackballed from their frat! He's a looming, rapey slab of beefcake so scuzzy, the writers even blame the demise of Kelly's high school reputation on Sears retroactively. He's also the only thing that makes Dylan and Kelly's protracted hate-fuckery or Steve's dumb frat arcs even a little bit interesting, which may explain why Celeste ends up dating him.

MORTON MUNTZ & KEITH CHRISTOPHER

Both basically glorified extras, Muntz (Ryan Thomas Brown) and Keith (Robert Leeshock) are Steve's brothers in the fraternity Kappa Epsilon Gamma, colloquially KEG. If Keith's name is not familiar, you may know him better as John Sears's smarmy sidekick: he's okay with most of the shady shit John Sears does but develops conscience pangs when it's convenient to the plot. Muntz has the distinction of being the first and only recurring teen character who's slightly chubby and does the kinds of things slightly chubby characters apparently must do to conform to stereotype: moons over girls; fills water guns with mixed cocktails; is jolly.

CHARLIE DIXON & MIKE RYAN

We're not here to say that KEG president is a suspiciously precarious job, but we do see four different faces doing it. When Steve and Brandon initially go by the house in the third episode of Season 4, they meet Charlie Dixon, played by future *Better Call Saul* star Patrick Fabian. By the very next episode, Charlie's played by Sean O'Bryan—a weird choice given that O'Bryan is supposed to be an undergrad and is noticeably losing his hair. Then, in Episode 12, KEG's president has a new face AND name: that's when Brandon Douglas takes over, playing Mike Ryan. He gets the most screen time presiding over the "test" that sees John bounced out of KEG for trying to get Steve expelled . . . because by the time there's an episode about Steve learning that the president of his fraternity is closeted, Jack Armstrong has stepped into the role. Brandon Douglas, if you're out there, we would LOVE to know why you gave up the role right before this episode, in the mid-'90s!!!

STUART CARSON

While Brenda is employed in her *second* job of the series—assisting Jim at his office—she crosses paths with a client: millionaire real estate developer/caramel hair dye enthusiast Lawrence Carson (Peter Mark Richman). Offscreen, Jim and Lawrence decide their children would be perfect for each other, and only under duress does Brenda agree to go on a date with Stuart, against whom she's prejudiced due to his dorky name (?). Her concerns are alleviated when Stuart (David Gail, who'd already appeared as Palm Springs bellman Tom in a Season 1 episode) appears at the door and she sees his resemblance to Rique. Stuart dazzles Brenda with the perks at his disposal as a Los Angeles nepotism case; he worries Dylan, who remembers Stuart from "the scene" but declines to specify what, exactly, Stuart was into back when he was running with a ninth-grade Dylan before the events of the series began. For a drama addict like Brenda, however, Stuart is the perfect mate: she accepts his wedding proposal after two weeks; flips out on him when she finds a prenup his family prepared; elopes with him to Vegas only to change her

mind at the altar when all her friends show up to reverse-psychologize her out of it by fake-supporting her; then somehow continues dating him for several months and through about a dozen episodes in which he doesn't appear. A road trip on which Brenda locks them out of his vehicle proves their undoing, as Stuart shows he cannot remotely roll with adversity, and the relationship ends with her throwing his engagement ring into his parents' pool. That we then learn Stuart was raised by the kind of father who would order him immediately to jump in and retrieve it tells us everything we need to know about Stuart's childhood, but alas, Brenda won't be around to help him heal from it.

COREY RANDALL

Sociology professor and fuming cuckold Corey Randall (Scott Paulin) begins his time on the show as one of the many adults inexplicably impressed with Brandon, and assigns him to tutor D'Shawn Hardell so that D'Shawn can maintain his academic eligibility. It soon becomes evident that (1) "tutor" means "take D'Shawn's exam for him"; and (2) Lucinda, the fox Brandon's been flirting with at the gym, is Randall's wife. Both of those situations blow up on Brandon a few seasons later when Randall, still angry with Brandon for exposing Randall's role in various NCAA violations—not to mention boning Randall's (now ex-) wife—accuses Brandon of conspiracy to commit plagiarism of his own paper.

That ends about as well as anything ever does for ol' Corey, i.e., not.

D'SHAWN HARDELL

Top basketball recruit D'Shawn (future Black Lightning Cress Williams) starts out as a Brandon antagonist/poster boy for injustice in college athletics: when Brandon, naïvely shocked that he's expected to "help" D'Shawn by doing D'Shawn's work for him, refuses to go along, D'Shawn tries to blackmail Brandon using his flirtation with Lucinda as leverage. That doesn't work, and neither does making D'Shawn a bad guy, because he starts doing assignments on his own, and becomes an ally of various Gangsters (going on a fake date with Donna to make David jealous; saving the Richland/Walsh campaign in Season 5), not to mention the authors' eyeballs (the only thing better than D'Shawn in a tux at a charity ball is D'Shawn in a Globetrotters costume for a calendar shoot). Cress Williams has charisma for days and legit chemistry with Tori Spelling, so we're still disappointed the show didn't put D'Shawn to more/better use—and specifically didn't have the 'nads to put D'Shawn and Donna together.

LUCINDA NICHOLSON

The university iteration of the cool teacher: Lucinda (Dina Meyer) is a grad student who teaches a class on feminist perspectives in cultural anthropology; has a documentary in the works, which she can't finish because she ran out of money; and doesn't subscribe to bourgeois notions of fidelity, which explains why she's cheating on her husband, Professor Randall. It doesn't explain why she's fixated on doing so with Brandon, whom the show would have us believe is not your average college two-pump chump, but: come on. Lucinda's lady boner for Brandon leads to various complications, and ends her marriage to Randall—and once she's technically a single woman, Brandon commences sleeping with her. But she's no more interested in monogamy with Brandon than she was with Randall, especially not when Dylan financing her unfinished film is just a blowjob away. Antediluvian square Brandon isn't having that and dumps her (again?), but for some reason, Lucinda's still throwing herself at him in the fourth-season finale. Aim higher, girl . . . literally.

LAURA KINGMAN

When the show unwisely chooses to take a run at the issues around alcohol and affirmative consent on college campuses (and, later, adolescent-onset mental illnesses), Laura (Tracy Middendorf) is the one ground up in the gears. After a one-night stand with Steve, Laura's clingy; Steve's ghosting her so as not to wreck his relationship with Celeste . . . and then Laura's version of their night together changes to one in which Steve raped her. Did one thing lead to the other, or did Laura suffer a trauma? It's actually not that clear-cut to us, but Kelly convinces Laura not to name Steve at a Take Back the Night March, and we're supposed to be convinced that Steve isn't capable of such a thing. Laura's next act—as it were—doesn't make it any easier to distinguish between Laura's perceptions and reality, either. When Brenda is cast as the lead in *Cat on a Hot Tin Roof* and Laura is stuck playing her understudy, Laura enlists Steve to help her spread rumors about how Brenda got the part (rhymes with "shmasting smouch"), and tries to get him to Gillooly Brenda so that Laura can take over. This is where Steve draws the line . . . and where Laura breaks with reality completely, nearly hanging herself in the rafters of the theater before Steve wrestles her to safety.

JESSE VASQUEZ

Writing Gabrielle Carteris's real-life pregnancy into the plot required that Andrea finally have some sex—which she initially does with Dan. But evidently producers felt it would be too cruel for Andrea to get pregnant by her very first partner, so along comes Jesse (Mark Damon Espinoza). Andrea and Jesse originally meet when he's hired to tend bar at the Walshes' 20th anniversary party, and run into each other again when he performs the same function at Dan's parents' stuffy Thanksgiving party. When she gets rid of Dan, she learns that Jesse only works in the service industry on the side: he's a law student at UCLA. Andrea finds out she's pregnant very early in their relationship, and is pretty sure she wants to terminate the pregnancy until Jesse threatens to break

up with her if she does. He never quite regains your commentators' favor after that; in fact, we continue to resent him for it to this day! But whatever: "they" decide to keep the baby and get married, ugh.

DR. JOHN MARTIN

While Felice lends herself some gravitas in her Season 3 debut by claiming that her doctor husband is at a conference about sexually transmitted diseases, by the time Dr. Martin (Michael Durrell) makes it onto the show, he's canonically a cardiac surgeon. Generally speaking, his role is to be the sober yin to Felice's raging yang, indulgent of Donna and friendly to her various boyfriends. Later in the series, he experiences a stroke, but recovers well enough to take a position, in semi-retirement, as a GP at the free clinic where Kelly works. Later still, in the show's final season, we learn that Donna is not his only child . . . .

SUZANNE STEELE

It's hard to tell whether Suzanne (Kerrie Keane) *always* intends to con Dylan out of his inheritance by trading on an alleged (?) bond with his late father, but whatever her timeline, she turns up at Christmas and "reluctantly" confesses that her tween daughter, Erica, is the product of an affair with Dylan's father, Jack. Although Jim Walsh and Kelly both smell a rat, Suzanne has credible enough answers for Dylan to every query, and Dylan is more motivated to bond with his half-sister than he is to listen to Jim. It's also hard to tell whether Suzanne's chemist boyfriend—later husband—Kevin is always part of the scam, but between Dylan's need to have a sibling and Dylan's boner for clean-water initiatives, he's the perfect mark. Suzanne marries Kevin, Kevin gets all of Dylan's money (because that's how legitimate investments work), and Suzanne and Kevin put the "Erica" in "South America" and blow town, leaving Dylan penniless . . . until the Punta Brava caper in Season 5 gets her and Kevin arrested.

ERICA MCKAY

You'd think a girl with a poor man's Sante Kimes for a mother wouldn't be such a simpleton, but Erica (Noley Thornton in her first iteration) seems to have more hair than sense. That, or the writers just don't know how to render a late-tween girl, because Erica's idolizing of Dylan and childish paper-plate artwork read like she's in second grade . . . but then she starts her period during a swimming lesson with Dylan, in an unbearably uncomfortable sequence that bears no relationship to any 12-year-old's experience of this milestone. She's mildly sketched out by Kevin initially, but apparently unaware of her mother's grifty intentions, and as Suzanne and Kevin are hustling her onto a plane to Brazil, she tries to leave a note for Dylan—in an airport bathroom, ineffectually stuck to the door with gum. When next we see Erica, she's still presenting as a little kid, kitted out in a babyish ballet outfit.

Rescued from Suzanne and Kevin and sent to live with Iris McKay in Hawaii, she gets streetwise in a hurry: Erica next appears in the eighth season as a teenage sex worker and addict played by Johna Stewart-Bowden. After a sting operation takes down her pimp, Erica is given a Democratic-debate outfit and put on a plane to London to live with Dylan and Brenda; Dylan returns in Season 9, but without Erica, and by the time Jack returns in Season 10, apparently they've both forgotten her existence.

KEVIN WEAVER

Kevin (David Hayward) comes off like a sincere science dweeb at first, complete with fourth-period-bio brush mustache—the perfect cover for a long con that will require him to convince Dylan to cut other "investors" out of the "deal." Kevin shows his true colors as soon as he's leveraged Dylan's interest in chemical water cleanup to yoink Dylan's fortune, and when we meet him and the rest of the Scamily again in Season 5, he's more villainous than ever, smuggling animals and leering at Valerie's breasts. Did his water-cleaning technique actually work? Do Kevin and Suzanne even like each other? We'll never know. We do know he's still a dweeb; in addition to throwing around terms like "cyber-finance," Kevin collects "piratical material," and is waving a lethal cutlass at Dylan when the *policia* show up to arrest him and Suzanne.

JOEY BUSSICHIO

When Nat has a massive heart attack, his cousin Joey (Joe Greco) materializes—as it were—as the voice of reason: the Peach Pit is a loser that's never gotten Joey a dime on his investment, and Nat should take a step back for the sake of his health or, better yet, unload the joint. Maybe if Joey were around more, he'd know that the Pit is in financial peril, again, because his cuz is giving The Gang beaucoup meals and special-occasion desserts on the house. He'd also know that, in the Zip-verse, it's Brandon's job to bail the diner equivalent of the Lehman Brothers out of trouble over and over. But Joey hasn't shown up any of the other half a dozen times the Pit almost went under . . . and once Dylan buys in to solve the problem, Joey never shows up again, including when Nat impregnates a grandma.

CHANCELLOR MILTON ARNOLD

Brandon's achievements as a student are something we are told about far more than we see them, particularly when it comes to his relationship with California University's Chancellor, Milton Arnold (Nicholas Pryor—who is married IRL to Christine "Samantha Sanders" Belford!). A Nobel Prize–winning economist who has lived and taught all over the world, Chancellor Arnold takes a shine to Brandon when the latter is invited to participate in a hazily defined "Task Force"; from what we see, it involves a lot of retreats where no actual work is done and culminates in a trip to Washington where

Brandon gets to meet Bill Clinton (unconvincing Bill Clinton impersonator Tom Biehn) and shake his hand for what feels like ten minutes. Anyway: Brandon and the Chancellor are so tight that Brandon's Season 5 foray into student government finds him smeared as "the Chancellor's lackey," which, to be honest, isn't entirely unfair.

CLARE ARNOLD

The Chancellor is such a fan of Brandon, in fact, that he gives his blessing to Brandon's dating his daughter Clare (Kathleen Robertson), who when we meet her is a senior in high school. Brandon and Clare connect at a Task Force event where Kelly is basically bearding Brandon to deflect suspicion about Brandon's actual girlfriend, Lucinda—a plan Lucinda herself hatches and that is never really justified; are we supposed to think none of the participants in the Task Force is single? Or that none of them has a partner who has better things to do on the weekend than go sleep on a bunkbed in a single-sex cabin and watch some deans square dance? ANYWAY, Clare is not deterred by Brandon's putative relationship and pursues him hard: she invites herself over to the Walsh house, handcuffs herself to Brandon's bed, and enlists her dad to pressure Brandon into taking her to her prom. There's some lip service paid to the idea that Clare acts out because her genius-level intellect hasn't afforded her many opportunities to hone her social skills. But when

Clare becomes a full cast member in Season 5—skipping her freshman year and joining The Gang as a college sophomore because she's just that much of a brainiac—she's perfectly well-adjusted and totally over Brandon. Clare moves into David's old room in the beach apartment—and moves in on David, dating him for a while following his breakup with Donna. But Clare's longest relationship on the show is, in a classic odd-couple scenario, with Steve.

RUSH SANDERS

Steve's father Rush (the late Jed Allan) is, in both casting and character conception, maybe the best child-parent match on the show. The two share sliding standards of morality, a belief that most problems can be solved with money, and even some physical mannerisms—a particular head-wobble move they both do, for instance. Rush is sometimes presented as a producer of some sort, but later we learn that he also owns a free weekly paper (which he just straight-up hands to Steve and Brandon to run) and a holding company that operates a sweatshop, so let's just say he's a generic rich guy. He wears an opal pinky ring and loves to golf—you know, like that. While it is revealed in the first season that Steve is adopted, and we see him journey to New Mexico to try to meet his biological mother in the second, we later learn that Rush was the one who impregnated her after a chance meeting, and that before divorcing Rush, Samantha agreed to raise the baby.

ROY RANDOLPH

We should probably hate Roy Randolph (Jason Carter, whose fake-sounding British accent is in fact legit). He's ostensibly the reason Brenda leaves the show, as he offers her a spot in a summer acting program and she never sets foot on American soil again. He's also legendary for getting it on with his leading ladies, a reputation that drags Brenda down when she re-auditions for the Maggie the Cat role at his home and everyone draws their own slut-shamey conclusions therefrom. Randolph's description of acting as "dreaming on shhedjool" is deeply off-putting, and he wears a lot of vests. But he's got a budget–Roger Rees energy that's kind of entertaining, and he has the proper appreciation for the "queen" aspect of Brenda's drama-queenery.

ARIEL HUNTER

Whenever any character praises David for having waited so long to have sex with Donna, please recall that, actually, if he hadn't stopped waiting and fucked someone else instead, maybe Donna would have been interested in sleeping with him sooner than the Season 7 finale. Ariel (Kari Wuhrer) comes into David's life as a low-level A&R rep at a record label. Initially, she puts him in contact with a semi-established band to come on as their new keyboard player, though a newly sober David balks when he finds out that they use drugs. She also arranges for (real) R&B star/producer Babyface to play at CU's spring carnival, with David backing him up. Donna is put off by how flirty Ariel is, and is not being paranoid, discovering David and Ariel having sex in the back of a limo and dumping him on the spot. David's karma only gets worse from there, as we learn in the Season 5 premiere that Ariel also gave him crabs.

Brenda tells Dylan she won't be gone forever. But guess what? SHE IS. SHE IS GONE, FOREVER. Occasionally, we hear tell of Brenda's offscreen adventures in various European capitals, but after a while, characters just stop mentioning her. We will never forget, and it's largely because of her that the show's first four seasons are still its best.

Goings

BRENDA

Poor Brenda has about as much drama as any nighttime-soap diva could bear. After her painful breakup with Dylan in Season 3, she moves halfway across the country for a fresh start, then almost immediately moves back. She falls in love with a new guy and very nearly marries him after knowing him less than a month. She gets radicalized as an animal-rights activist and even gets arrested for an action on a CU lab, though an undercover FBI agent helps her escape serious consequences. But ultimately the most important bend in her story arc comes when she gets cast as Maggie in *Cat on a Hot Tin Roof*. She so endears herself to visiting superstar director Roy Randolph that he invites her to a summer program at the Royal Academy of Dramatic Art. In the last scene of Season 4, Brenda goes to say goodbye to Dylan, who's just broken up with Kelly again. Before kissing him and sinking out of frame,

"If we're going to do this, please go slow."

Brandon's Magic Arms Heal a Rape Survivor

Kelly, Donna, and David's plan to share an apartment has hit a snag: Donna is so certain her mother won't permit her to room with David that she's going to let her parents go live in Houston for a year and hope it means they'll never pop by! (Cut to: them popping by in a couple of months.)

It's not until David follows Donna into her bedroom and starts casually getting ready for bed that she informs him that he's going to be sleeping in his *own* bed, in his own room. "You said we'd do it on prom night and you've been putting me off all summer," David whines. It doesn't work.

Donna's best friend isn't making sexual maturity look so good: Kelly takes several tries and multiple locations to tell Donna how and why she and Dylan broke up in France. Depressed after finding out he didn't get into Berkeley (that's why you play ball with the ETS, Jones), Dylan moped around their hotel, reading/ignoring Kelly, telling her when she got bored that she should go to Paris without him. Several days and decimated boutiques later, Kelly returned to find him flirting with a French chippy (*chippée*?) named Brigitte. Kelly retaliated by using a drive with the hotel's bartender to make Dylan jealous. It worked; they fought; Kelly slapped Dylan for suggesting that she boned the bartender (so . . . mission accomplished?); and Kelly ditched Dylan a week early. Now that she's back, she's not sure Dylan even did cheat on her, so she goes over to his house, where they agree they're even and make up instead of acknowledging how little interest they've had in each other since their relationship went public. When Donna sees the two of them reunited, she hisses at David that this is a disaster: she just told Brenda that Kelly and Dylan broke up! David points out that it hardly matters with Brenda half a country away.

Speaking of Brenda: she hates everything at the University of Minnesota, including herself for going there. When she's not being rude about the rain to her midwestern friends as though she blames them for it, she's disdaining their parties and clothes. "Brenda, if you hate it here so much, why'd you come back?" one of them asks. Great question! Chafing Brenda's ass the most is her roommate/former BFF Darla (Wendy Benson-Landes), who's dating a former academic decathlon opponent named (*gulp*) Dylan (Michael MacDermott)!!! Darla has apparently visited a bordello supply emporium to purchase a red tassel either she or Brenda can put on the outer doorknob to let the other know she's inside fucking, and Darla and Dylan are basically fucking all the time; evidently this guy's got a fetish for girls in XXXL men's oxfords. The one night Brenda does get to sleep in her bed, Darla and her coterie briefly stop in and drag Brenda as the most "stuck-up bitch" they've ever met—which, given what we've seen, is totally fair. They also wake her up in the process: she hears everything, and between that and her finding the tassel on duty in the middle of the following afternoon, Brenda decides to end this experiment, pack her one suitcase, and head back to Los Angeles and a real bummer of a relationship update on her ex.

Brandon and his new boot-brush haircut are enjoying his last days of summer freedom at a beach house Steve's borrowed from an old contact of his mother's, to which the owner's daughter, Jill (Robia LaMorte), has also returned, from New York City. Jill and Brandon are flirting, and Steve—who first developed a crush on the slightly older Jill when he was 13 ("She was the fastest thing on this beach," says this 18-year-old, channeling the 52-year-old men in the writers' room, presumably)—has mostly quit trying to hit on her given that Celeste is staying with them too. Instead, Steve's sublimating his horniness and jealousy into overly aggressive . . . tennis? Over gin (the game, at which Steve is also too competitive), he asks Brandon what Jill's like in bed. "I haven't slept with her yet," says Brandon, who might have considered ending that sentence one rather presumptuous word sooner. Brandon then tries to coax Jill into sex by reminding her how soon she's leaving. "Maybe I just don't want to start something I can't finish," Jill dodges. "Don't worry about that," smarms Brandon. "I've been told I'm a real good closer." By whom, *SHERYL?*

The next day, when Steve gets so het up about tennis that he starts forehanding balls into Jill's face, he and Brandon end up braying at each other over the net; Jill screams at them to stop and goes back to the house, packing to leave a day early, but because no woman can *stay* mad at the Zip's golden boy, she ends up apologizing *to Brandon*, and that night tells him and his extremely empathetic eyebrows why she's "been kind of upset lately": six months ago, she was raped by a stranger. (Fuck this episode for putting "I probably shouldn't've been there alone; that's what everyone says, anyway" into the mouth of *a rape survivor*.) Steve and Brandon's display of toxic masculinity triggered her, but overall, she's grateful that their not knowing made her feel like she was "back in the land of the living." She asks Brandon if he will sleep with her—literally just sleep—and one night with his tiny arms wrapped most of the way around her cures her PTSD. His arms aren't enough to make her stay any longer in Malibu, nor to ever follow up on her invitation for Brandon to visit New York, because we neeeeever see her again.

Nana Does Sex

Dylan's not conventional, *maaaaan*, which is why he's the only one not living a conventional college story in this episode: he finds out he's killing his 1961 Porsche by driving it too much.

Advised by his mechanic to buy a regular car for everyday driving, Dylan confirms that Jim will make funds available to cover the cost of whatever beater Dylan wants to buy. Then Dylan buys a new Porsche, drives it over to the Walshes' with the sticker *still on*, and makes a whole show of flouncing off when Jim dares to question what he spends his money on. Kelly—who's been enjoying persistent attention from former WBH BMOC John Sears (Paul Johansson), now a CU senior and Steve's frat brother-to-be—barely cares, but agrees to go for a drive with Dylan while he pouts about his surrogate father, at the end of which Dylan's resolved to trade the car in for a Ford Bronco (a make and model that, back in 1993, is not yet associated with any scandalous freeway trips), and then Kelly tells Dylan she thinks they should see other people. (He replies that Brenda suggested the same thing before *they* broke up, which, like, yes and no?) He goes squealing off into the night and, when he stops at a red light, gets carjacked at gunpoint. Something that rarely happens to people in used Camrys, Dylan! Sometimes we bring heartache upon ourselves!

In addition to trading in her high school boyfriend for his exact opposite, Kelly's other very relatable college freshman story involves an inconsiderate roommate: David, working the night shift at the radio station, is keeping vampire hours, skipping classes, and messing up the apartment when the blondes are out. He petulantly refuses to accept the reasonable house rules they want to establish, but later apologizes to them on the air. When station manager Howard (Zachary Throne) hears, he offers David something to help with his work-life balance: just caffeine pills, for now, but if David ever needs anything stronger, he only needs to ask! What David *needs* is a *strong* kick in the slats, but that probably isn't what Howard means.

Brenda, weary of living "like a nun," lets Jim fix her up with the son of one of his rich clients, though she almost backs out when she finds out the kid's been saddled with the panty-drying name Stuart. A 24-year-old slab of beef in the Rique mold, Stuart is played by David Gail; Brenda likes what she sees, and though we're in the worst styling period for Shannen Doherty—girlfriend's split ends should get the show's hairdresser tried in the Hague—Stuart feels the same about her. Not until Stuart orders champagne does Brenda start to thaw; not until dessert does she figure out she should shut up about her ex; but by the time Stuart's bringing her home way past curfew, she's *also* ready to take up with a guy who's Dylan's exact opposite. (Stuart and John never share a scene, but one feels they would bro way out.)

Over in the dorms, Andrea's deep into her crush on a *third* teacher: Dan Rubin (Matthew Porretta), her English TA and dorm RA. Since we don't have access to the CU employee handbook, we can't confirm whether Dan really is permitted to date students, as he says, but Nana's hot pants aren't trying to hear about professional ethics right now. Andrea and Dan are well on their way to afternoon delight when she announces that she's a virgin. He denies that it's "an incredible turnoff," but says her first time should be more "special" than the frantic wrestling they've been doing. Andrea lets him quit . . . uh, hitting it, but that night she's too horny to sleep, and a 12:30 A.M. in-person "u up?" is appealing enough to overrule Dan's daytime scruples. The next day, Andrea is dismayed that Brandon can't read her devirginization all over her face (as it were), and even more dismayed that she has to arrive in Dan's class, receive no more acknowledgment of their new status than a smile, and *then*, on top of everything else, stay awake for a whole lecture on *Faulkner*. Andrea breaks off her next confusingly choreographed love scene with Dan to whine, "I just can't have you as my teacher in English class and my lover in the dorm! It's too hard!" (That's what she said—literally.) Dan says Andrea will just have to change classes! And while her storyline is, like almost all her friends', deeply typical of what college freshmen go through, Andrea needs to drive the word "lover" over to a furnished apartment occupied by a 45-year-old two-time divorcé, where it belongs.

"We had their wedding picture turned into a giant jigsaw puzzle: if they take it apart, it'll take them a lifetime of marriage to put it back together."

Brenda and Brandon Mark Their Parents' 20th Anniversary with the World's Worst Gift

SEASON 4 | EPISODE 8
TWENTY YEARS AGO TODAY

Jim and Cindy are celebrating 20 years of marriage with a big party, around which everyone else's ongoing issues arrange themselves.

Kelly declines to bring John as her date when he tries to invite himself along, because Dylan will be there. David is forced to bring Erin after Mel dumps her on David to go to Mexico with his new model girlfriend; when Jackie thinks Erin's running a fever, she gets enraged and starts making threats about custody. Andrea gets a new perspective on Dan when he uses this *wedding anniversary party* at which he is drinking for free to denigrate the institution of marriage, like the *very* interesting grad student he is; Andrea's trying to choke down her doubts when the party's bartender, Jesse (Mark Damon Espinoza), starts flirting with her.

Everyone manages to keep their personal shit away from the couple of the hour except Brenda and Stuart, after he proposes and she accepts. (The show leaves no ambiguity about the timeline: "We've only known each other for two weeks!" is the last thing Brenda says before "Yes!," thrilling to the confirmation that she's finally found a partner as dramatic as she is.) Brenda's social-climbing Grandma Walsh (June Claman) announces the engagement from the stage, to everyone's shock and Cindy and Jim's clench-jawed fake smiles. While Brenda's female friends pretend to support her, Dylan finds Stuart by the cake to make dark references to "the scene" from which they used to know each other and hope, for Brenda's sake, that Stuart's reformed. Did Stuart . . . do coke? Deal coke? Traffic runaways? Host cockfights? Don't bother speculating; we never find out.

All of the above is mere window dressing for the main thrust of the episode: a cautionary tale about ill-considered purchases. No, we don't mean Dylan's—although he has been gun-crazy since his carjacking, and buys an illegal Walther out of some dude's van. He's at home cleaning it when Brandon comes by to stash the episode's focal point: Jim and Cindy's wedding portrait, which their children have blown up, turned into a puzzle, and framed. It's wrapped in brown paper, so why not just bring it home with him and trust that his parents would assume it's a gift and not open it? Or, if he thinks their natural curiosity is ungovernable, just put it in a closet they won't have cause to open before the party? So that Brandon has to remember, like an hour after dropping it off, that he urgently has to retrieve it, that's why. So over Brandon goes. He doesn't see Dylan's car, and Dylan, in the shower, doesn't answer the door. Why doesn't Brandon have a key to his best friend's house, five minutes away from his own? Why doesn't Brandon decide his adult parents won't mind receiving their gift *after* the party? So that Brandon is obliged to *break in* to Dylan's house, causing Dylan to come racing out of the bathroom, in a towel, and pull a gun on him. This proves to be Dylan's rock-bottom moment as a gun nut; he pledges to get rid of the Walther, and Brandon can laugh about his near-murder. Guy stuff, right?

Back to the gift, which is leaning on an easel in the foyer to greet guests as they arrive. The puzzle's cuts are all curves; it would not challenge a first-grader. So it's not fun. It's in a frame, presumably to be hung up, but the portrait is marred by the lines of the puzzle pieces. So it's not aesthetically pleasing. Before going to bed after the party, Brandon curiously pulls out one piece, and because there aren't any knobs and notches holding them together, the rest of the pieces fall on the floor. Therefore, presumably when the puzzle is perpendicular to the floor, the pieces aren't going to stick together, *and* the shop didn't cover the image with glass or plastic to secure them in the frame. So figuring out how to display it is a hassle.

This puzzle is the worst gift in the history of television, if not the world. Happy anniversary, Jim and Cindy: judging by your children's gifting instincts, your marriage is a failure.

Is Laura Just Steve's Clinger, or Did He Date-Rape Her?

Improbably, given his inability to pronounce the word "sociology" without an "h," Brandon has impressed his prof, Corey Randall (Scott Paulin), who's assigned him to tutor a promising new basketball recruit named D'Shawn Hardell (Cress Williams—😜).

Since Brandon's having a hard time motivating D'Shawn, Randall invites both of them to dinner at his place; this proves awkward because (1) Brandon's recently learned that Lucinda (Dina Meyer), the sexy grad student he met at the gym (and whose horniness for him is even more improbable than his aptitude for sociology), is Randall's wife, and (2) Brandon and Lucinda are so obvious in their flirting that D'Shawn has made some reasonable assumptions about what's going on between them *before* he sees her fondling Brandon's arm in the gym the next day. So D'Shawn announces his intention to dime out Brandon to Randall unless Brandon takes his exam for him. At first, Brandon plays dumb/defensive with D'Shawn, then tells Lucinda they've been discovered and that his precious integrity is under threat. She's pretty sure Randall intended Brandon to take D'Shawn's exam—why else would it be a take-home?—so Brandon should "stop being a baby": do his part to preserve D'Shawn's athletic eligibility *and* start boning her. Instead, Brandon decides to stomp back to D'Shawn, tell him the truth about himself and Lucinda, and dare him to narc; then he stomps home, throws some clothes in a bag, and orders Brenda to tell their parents he's going camping. (It's almost Thanksgiving, which means CU students are about to have their first of about 15 weeks off from school.) We don't yet know where Brandon's actually headed, but given that he "happens" to find an old photo of Emily in his underwear drawer, he's probably about to make the Bay Area the Bray Area.

Before sending students off for turkey, CU is raising its consciousness on sexual consent with the awkwardly titled Take Back the Night Week. Brandon's perspective on rape culture is the most reflexively idiotic (he advises Dylan to attend a date-rape seminar because "there are a lot of babes there"), though Andrea isn't much better when she suggests that "we" infantilize women by absolving them of responsibility when they get so drunk that men who sleep with them do so without their affirmative consent. Dan disagrees, and though he and Andrea make up by the end of the episode, add it to "doesn't believe in marriage" on the list of reasons Andrea's becoming disenchanted with him.

Kelly ends up in a discussion group with Laura Kingman (Tracy Middendorf), who shares the story of the KEG guy who pressured her into having sex with him. Kelly encourages Laura to name her assailant at the upcoming Take Back the Night rally because she believes it's John, whom Kelly herself enraged when she didn't agree with him on the minimum number of dates required for her to fuck him. What we know, but Kelly doesn't, is Laura's situation: she recently went on one date with Steve, at the end of which they boned. Since Laura defied his attempts to ghost her afterward, Steve tried to get rid of her by telling her he has a girlfriend. When Laura names Steve, not John, as the culprit, Kelly immediately stops believing Laura, arguing that Steve's "not like that" (. . . isn't he), and running to him the next day to tell him about Laura's claim, which she thinks will probably result in his expulsion. Steve realizes he needs to get out in front of this: he brings poor Celeste to the Peach Pit, tells her his version of events, and gets dumped, *finally*. (We wish we could say she goes on to end up with someone worthy of her, but . . . well, you'll see.)

At the rally, Kelly positions herself near enough to Laura to give her a warning side-eye; when Laura, successfully intimidated, hesitates before taking the stage, Kelly leaps up in her place, contrasting the unambiguous story of her own attempted date rape in Season 2 with times she willingly slept with guys and subsequently regretted it, and identifying Steve as her date-rape savior. As the night-take-backers applaud Steve, Laura runs out, and he follows to thank her for not delivering him to what he'd previously, cringingly, called a "lynch mob." Laura bitterly says that though she didn't say yes to Steve, she didn't say no either, and since we didn't actually see how the "seduction" went down except in very different black-and-white recollections from each individual's viewpoint, we are expected to side with the series regulars. After Kelly's interrupted Halloween date rape and Jill's stranger rape, this is the show's third attempt (to date) at telling a rape story, and though we hardly need tell *you* fine readers this, the actual rate of false reports is a lot less than 33.3 percent. Do better with Take Back the Night Week '94, everyone.

"It looks like we're having a lot more than turkey for Thanksgiving, aren't we now."

Brandon and Emily Reunite While, Back Home, Everyone's Thankful That Steve Prevents John Sears from Raping Rayanne Graff

SEASON 4 | EPISODE 12
RADAR LOVE

A lot of memorable plot goes down in "Radar Love," and a lot of awkward filler too: like Kelly rudely picking a fight with Dylan at Casa Walsh Thanksgiving because he accepted Brenda's invitation to dinner and not hers. Girl: you broke up with him, because you hate each other, and he's in his poet-shirt phase. Stop caring what he does!

Andrea's already starting not to care what *Dan* does; she and her unflattering *Game of Thrones* choker necklaces are super-nervous about going to Dan's parents' house for Thanksgiving, ostensibly because it signals that Dan's really serious about the relationship and she doesn't feel the same. Andrea's doubts here feel utterly contrived, but in that regard they pair nicely with the reappearance of bartender Jesse at the Rubins' catered Thanksgiving. He flirts with Andrea, and she has a *lot* to think about! (Like throwing the green velvet tunic vest she's wearing in the garbage; it's doing nothing to hide the real-life Carteris pregnancy that occasioned all this drama in Andrea's love life.)

Pity Andrea can't go undercover à la the cafeteria story to write an exposé on why the KEG House goes through presidents like Spinal Tap goes through drummers, because in "Radar Love" we meet yet another one—Mike Ryan (Brandon Douglas), no better equipped to contain the chaotic evil of John Sears than the ones before. KEG and Alpha Dumb Baby team up every year to throw a Thanksgiving party for the residents of a halfway house for at-risk teen girls, and you might miss it among all the soporific filler blathering about decorations and raffles, but it does become ickily clear that Sears views the event as a hookup smorgasbord . . . and that his KEG brothers know he does. His skeezy plans for this year's event are no different, but the twist is that Sears is targeting Denise (A.J. "Rayanne Graff"

Langer, pre–*My So-Called Life*) with his oleaginous "you're so *mature*" rap—and that Steve has some audience-goodwill ground to make up after the Laura arc implied that he could have raped her, so now it's time for Steve to *prevent* such an assault. With an assist from a couple of his KEG brothers, Steve manages to keep Sears from preying on Rayanne; this pisses Sears off and sets up the black-ball showdown between him and Steve, although in our opinion the KEG-ers who know full well Sears is a sexual predator, but content themselves with farcical distractions instead of kicking him out or reporting him to the authorities, are the ones who should get blackballed.

Brandon's blackballed *himself* from Thanksgiving and blown town, a move so out of character (storming out of the whole Zip is much more Dylan-ish) that production panicked and threw a montage at the problem. At least, that's our best explanation for the almost punitive amount of highway B-roll that accompanies Brandon's northward journey, during which Bran hallucinates Emily Valentine, bores a family at a campground with his misadventures, and shows up on the doorstep of the Valentines' old house, only to find that they've moved to Greece. (What?) Not to worry, though; after almost missing each other while sitting back-to-back on a cable car, Brandon and Emily reunite and get caught up on their lives since Emily, um, stalked Brandon and had to be institutionalized. Which was barely two years prior, not for nothing, but Emily's parents still fucked off to Europe and left her on her own in a big city to "find herself"—and what do you know, she's blundered right into her stalkee, so that's working out just great.

Brandon and Emily still have solid chemistry, probably helped along by Jason Priestley and Christine Elise's real-life relationship (and Emily's much improved auburn-long-bob situation), and that *almost* sells the retconning of a girl Brandon dated for a few months in high school as the love of his life, when she in fact had fairly serious psychological problems that nearly sent Casa Walsh up in flames—but all is not well. Emily confides to her sitcommy neighbor, Rhoda—er, "Rosie" (Melissa Christopher)—that she still loves Brandon, a red flag that doesn't stop anyone from making fire jokes when Emily burns dinner. Emily does *not* confide to Brandon that she's about to go study in France. What! Will! Happen! (She will not take off that dumb beret indoors, is what will *not* happen.)

"The winds tend to affect people in strange ways."

Everything Is the Santa Anas' Fault, Including Donna Almost Doing Sex

Ah, the blowing (heh) of the Santa Ana winds—the "Mercury's in retrograde" of the *Beverly Hills, 90210* writers' room, used to explain everything from disproportionate grouchiness to ill-advised hookups.

In Dylan and Kelly's case, the Santa Anas are to blame for both those things; "Kellan" is back on, despite their evident lingering hatred for each other. Not sure what's behind the postcoital strawberries and cream, however, since it's highly unlikely a functionally orphaned late-teen boy like Dylan would keep a bowl of whipped cream in his fridge.

Nor is it probable that Jesse and Andrea would cap off a successful round of meet-the-families first dates by going back to his apartment to Do It *after eating burritos*—talk about your hot winds causing strange behavior!—buuuut that's what happens. The production's attempts to hide Nana's IRL pregnancy behind various strategic shrubs, baseball gloves, and bizarrely shaped blazers aren't credible either; in fact, the only thing we really buy in this storyline is Dan's mien of disgusted befuddlement as he watches Andrea and Jesse canoodling from his doorway down the hall. But Dan is also, suddenly and conveniently, a racist cretin, so even that's not terribly believable. At least we never see him again!

We *do* see Steve up to his pepperoni nips in self-created problems, as usual, and he's brought himself more grief by calling on Brandon for help and thinking he'll escape without a snotty lecture. Brandon, still smarting from Emily's departure, is mean about the KEG House and brays that he's getting "tired" of always having his best friend doing stupid shit. Steve resists friend-dumping the golden boy (we may be projecting) to ask a favor: can Brandon intercede with Professor Randall and get Steve off the hook for fraternity-prank-stealing Randall's prized baseball? His KEG brothers won't help him, because hazing is illegal, so they have to shun him to save themselves. Brandon doesn't think he has any pull with Randall under the circumstances, namely his having (1) frenched Randall's wife *and* (2) refused to take D'Shawn's "soshiology" test for him, and he's right . . . although his pitch might have had a shot if he'd been less of a bitch to either party in the Randall marriage. Lucinda lets it slip that the campus cops were tipped to the ball heist, so Brandon does get Steve some leverage against John Sears, who obviously set Steve up. But Brandon hilariously thinks *he* has leverage against *Randall* because Randall waved D'Shawn through Soc 101 with a B-plus. Brandon threatens to expose this sin to the entire world if Randall doesn't play ball (as it were). Brandon can't prove it, decades of "A to play" institutional protections will ensure he never can, and even if he could, nothing would change (except maybe D'Shawn taking the fall for athletic-department corruption); but sure, let's act like Brandon's a hero for spotlighting this grave injustice. (And look, it is one, but what Low Pockets over here knows about it wouldn't fill a thimble.)

Speaking of inexperience: will the Santa Anas induce Donna to have sex with David? You know they won't. You also know it takes for-goddamn-ever for Donna to get to the same place she started from with the issue of her virginity. Nor will it be a surprise that David, who has been actively unpleasant most of the time since he decided to graduate with the rest of The Gang, is still acting resentful about Donna's perfectly valid choice. They could get around said choice on any number of technicalities, by the way, and maybe David should investigate those instead of whining that he deserves a medal for waiting. Then again, the show traditionally refuses to acknowledge any bases between first and home, and it's just as well in this episode, because Donna's blocking and line deliveries make her seem child-like to a disturbing degree throughout.

But David thinks he's got a shot: it's their two-year dating anniversary (not a thing), so the gang has to attend an event dinner marking the occasion (ditto), not to mention Brandon's overly hale introduction of the fortune cookie/ "in bed" "game" (that the rest of us had already learned about by, like, fourth grade). Undeterred by awkward STUFF, Donna coins a new euphemism for sex when she coos that she's "not gonna take [her] antihistamine tonight," but before David can convert for the first down (so to speak), the Martins drop by unexpectedly. Felice's histrionic betrayal at the realization that David is living at the beach apartment sends Donna scurrying back to the safe ground of chastity . . . and David into the arms of sweet methamphetamine.

"It's easy: stop doing the meth."

Erica Becomes a Woman; Methy David Loses Erin

> SEASON 4 | EPISODE 17
> THICKER THAN WATER

Andrea thinks she has the flu. You've seen TV before, so you know that's not what she has, because it isn't possible for a straight lady on TV to experience nausea and not have a fetus on board, but Andrea— the only heterosexually active college girl (not to mention pre-med student) in the history of the *world* not to have an unplanned pregnancy be her *first* thought—is flabbergasted by the revelation that Jesse's boys can swim.

Dylan's recently arrived (alleged) half-sister cannot swim, literally, but we'll get to that. A woman named Suzanne Steele (Kerrie Keane) turned up a couple of episodes previously, claiming that she and her tween daughter, Erica (Noley Thornton, laboring under a heap of Ren Faire hair), had lost everything in a flood— and that Erica was the product of a fling with Jack McKay back in the '80s. Dylan, always craving any connection to Jack, chooses to believe Suzanne's swindlish backstory in order to bond with the sibling he didn't know he had, which is sweet, in theory. In practice, the relationship between this *very* world-weary 19-year-old and a young girl who still makes paper-plate crafts even though she's old enough to menstruate comes off a little weird . . . especially in this episode, when Erica *does* menstruate, for the first time, during a (somewhat creepy, sorry) swimming lesson with Dylan. ("'Thicker Than Water,' GET IT?!" Ew, show, *yes*.) When we were that age, we'd been eagerly prepared for the first-period eventuality for months, stocking our purses with "products." Erica is a simpleton, however, and not only doesn't have a Kotex but also doesn't ask one of the other *women* in the *women's restroom* for help, so Dylan has to blunder through the situation and it's awkward and weird. It's also awkward when Jim Walsh's background check on Suzanne turns up her $25K stash, but Suzanne has an answer for that, and even admits she's not 100 percent sure that Erica is Jack's daughter, an admission that makes her seem more trustworthy. The risk (and her careful selection of a lonely target) pays off.

Things aren't going so smoothly for David. He and Donna have broken up thanks to his drug use (and his being a bitch in general), and he's whinging about their split during his radio show (siiigh). Told to shut up about his personal life and play less-depressing music, David yells at station manager Howard that Howard gave him the meth in the first place, and now he expects Howard to come through with some downers to take the edge off. No dice, so he heads home to reject Donna's doormatty invitation to join a Big Bear ski trip by implying that they broke up because she wouldn't put out. Finally stung enough to rip him a new one, Donna smooches a ski-shop dweeb, leaving David to deny to Kelly that he's using, then take forever to help himself to his dad's codeine stash while The Soundtrack Strings of Foreboding wonder why the pills look so much like Altoids.

So, obviously it's an awesome time to task David with babysitting, but thanks to Mel and Jackie's conflicting schedules and custody battling, Kelly and David find themselves at the park with Erin. It's evident David isn't up to the challenge when he needs Kelly's help to fend off an old lady who wants to hug Erin and give her a cookie, but Kelly has a mysterious appointment she apparently can't reschedule, so off she goes. When she returns, David and his stupid backward Kangol are sprawled out on a park bench like a rejected draft of the Sistine Chapel ceiling and Erin is nowhere to be seen. The chess players in the park agree with us that David is a careless dingleberry, based on the side-eyes they cut at David as he and Kelly frantically search for Erin; everyone else in the storyline insists, infuriatingly, on reassuring David that Erin's disappearance isn't his fault, which it completely fucking is and would be even if the reason David passed out *weren't* drug-related.

Erin is eventually located in a house near the park, unharmed, and as they trudge into the apartment, Kelly once again tells David he's not responsible. Finally, even David tires of this version of events in which he's not a trifler and, with the help of an entire onion, confesses "tearfully" that he didn't just fall asleep—he crashed out on pills. "I need you to help me, Kel, please," he whispers, agonized, and it's probably unkind to note that David has hit this rock bottom after only a week, but at least that's the end of it, right?!

Andrea Chooses Life and Dylan Buys the Peach Pit (Sort Of)

SEASON 4 | EPISODE 19
THE LABORS OF LOVE

The so-called rock bottom of losing Erin at the park failed to straighten David out; he's still mething, and being enough of a bitch about it (and everything else) at home that, when Kelly finds his stash, she decides to force the issue by moving out—and taking Donna with her, despite Donna's protests that she still loves David, and what if he really *was* just holding those drugs for someone else?!

That very obvious "they're not mine" lie is older than dirt, but at least it's recognizable addict behavior . . . unlike David's visit to Howard's dealer, during which David offers to write *a check for methamphetamine*, and then, when that offer is predictably rejected, *asks for a credit line*. Sir, this isn't Macy's. But while Dealer Guy isn't about to fall for David's shit, dumb baby Donna is the perfect mark, going behind Kelly's back to write David a check—made out to David—for their share of the rent, so David's addiction lives to waste orange juice another day.

An actual baby, meanwhile, is causing problems in Andrea and Jesse's relationship. Andrea plans to terminate the pregnancy, and it's the in-character choice for her, but given the cartoonishly morose couples in the women's clinic waiting room; TV's, and particularly Fox's, notorious aversion to women affirmatively ending pregnancies at this time; and Gabrielle Carteris's actual pregnancy being visibly advanced enough that the baby could stroll out of her womb and order a steak medium well, it's clear the episode will have to contrive a change of course. The first detour is the fact that Andrea went to the clinic without an appointment and expected to get the abortion that very day, and when that can't happen, it opens the door for Jesse to make his case, again, for keeping the child—which he does in his usual presumptuous and retrograde fashion, shouting over Andrea and saying that if she has the procedure, she shouldn't "come back here." And she shouldn't, because he's an asshole, but after a sick-making conversation with her fetus and some ugly crying, followed by a visit from Jesse in which *he* forgives *her* for exercising her right to choose (then is smugly gratified to discover she hasn't yet), they announce to The Gang that they're getting married and having a baby. Not the road you'd hope Andrea would go down, but if the character were truly capable of acting in her own self-interest, she wouldn't have cherished a crush on goddamn Brandon all these years.

Said horse's ass is burning his tiny votive candle at both ends, covering for Nat at the Peach Pit as Nat recovers from a heart attack (with the rest of The Gang also taking shifts; did Nat not have *any* other employees prior to his coronary? Did he . . . ever go home? Oh, who cares) while struggling to meet his school obligations. Jim throws some wintry shade about Brandon neglecting his classes, wondering drily how the Peach Pit could ever function without him, which earns him a snotty lecture from Brandon about making a commitment to Nat. Yeah, Jim—don't you know Brandon's going for a save-the-Pit hat trick?

Well, he's not getting it, because the diner's finances are in shambles (you mean letting The Gang eat for free isn't good business???) and Nat's cousin Joey, who hasn't seen a dime on his retconned investment, wants out. Enter Dylan's trust fund, and while Jim is just as dubious about Dylan investing in a sector he knows nothing about as he was that Brandon could keep the Pit open by sheer stubbornness, eventually Jim submits (after a legit amusing crack from Dylan about not making him fire Jim as his manager again). Told the great news in Nat's hospital room, Brandon's face crumbles, which is rather satisfying . . . as is a scene later on when Brandon sighs that he did all the work and Dylan swoops in for the "touchdown," and Brenda joins us in noting that he wanted the Peach Pit to stay open, and now it can, so Brandon should cram it. (She's nicer about it.) Dylan himself explains to Brandon that he can't just let the money sit and earn interest, or buy a bunch of Porsches with it. Like, he can't do that because . . . ?

Our nobly unappreciated hero will just have to get affirmation elsewhere— like from the seemingly brain-injured Dean Trimble (William S. Taylor), who says Brandon is critical to "the mix" on CU's Task Force (composed otherwise of houseplants, apparently), and from the newly divorced Lucinda. She has an entire campus to choose from, but it's the passive-aggressive know-it-all in the credits she wants, somehow, even knowing Brandon is going to unhinge his jaw and swallow her face whole, and that's exactly what he does.

Too Mega to Fail:
THE PEACH PIT'S FINANCES

We're told the Peach Pit is a veritable Beverly Hills institution when Dylan first brings Brandon there to see about a part-time job. Also an institution: the Pit's owner, Nat Bussichio, who inherited the joint from his father, Sal. But as good as the Peach Pit's Mega Burgers and Nat's pies are, that's . . . how bad a businessman Nat is: over the course of the series, the diner narrowly avoids closing twice that we know of. Its sister nightspot, the Peach Pit After Dark, is run by the opening-credits cast with zero relevant experience, and changes hands numerous times, each majority investor less qualified than the last in any aspect of running a nightclub. One of its owners should have renamed it "the Money Pit," and in the real world, the place would have gone bankrupt and closed down half a dozen times.

Of course, that *can't* happen in the Zip-verse; the production built the sets already, and fiscal realism is not a priority of the teen drama or nighttime soap. That said, the show continually tries to wring drama out of the property's ongoing financial woes, and the revolving door of ownership suggests that *Beverly Hills, 90210* itself knows its characters suck at this. But who sucks the hardest? Of all the angel investors and managing partners, who's the most likely to land the Peach Pit After Dark in receivership, and him-/herself in debtor's prison?

FROM LEAST TO MOST INCOMPETENT, THE PPAD OWNERSHIP GROUP:

DYLAN MCKAY. Yeah, he's been going to the Pit since he was a kid, so he has sentimental reasons for bailing Nat's business out both times it happens—and the first time, after Nat's near-fatal heart attack, has the added benefit (for us) of making Brandon do all the keep-the-place-running work while Dylan gets all the save-the-day glory. Actually, the second time has a similar plus side: Noah (Vincent Young), who's scrambling to make the mortgage payments, has already sold the whole kit and caboodle to some lady named Jeannine Stein—including the diner portion of the business—but Dylan isn't trying to let that happen to Nat, and buys the mortgage from the bank. We don't know either; we just know it humiliates Noah and forces him to work for the character he was theoretically conceived to replace in the cast. Dylan is in recovery and probably should not be running a bar, but he puts out more fires than he starts, which isn't something everyone on this list can say.

STEVE AND RUSH SANDERS. It's Steve's idea to expand the Peach Pit into the empty former rug emporium next door, primarily to throw raves for extra cash (oh, the '90s), with Dylan as his financial backer. But soon Steve is prohibited by law from organizing parties of any kind after the fire at the abandoned house, even though his father, Rush, has somehow ended up with the Peach Pit After Dark lease thanks to Dylan's post-Scamily financial straits (and addiction issues), and Clare and David somehow end up managing the club. Rush should never have embroiled himself in this volatile an investment, but to his credit he seems to realize that, and dumps it when Valerie (Tiffani Thiessen) makes him a half-decent offer.

THE BUSSICHIOS. Nat apparently does just fine with the business he inherited, complete with celebrity headshots and tall tales of Marilyn Monroe's contributions to the menu, until the economic downturn of the early '90s. French fries seem like a recession-proof sector to *us*, but Nat chose to remodel at a bad time, and as of midway through the second season, he's paying staff instead of himself and delaying mustard re-orders (gasp!). When a bigshot developer rolls up with plans for a mega-mall and a sweet check for Nat, that should solve the problem . . . but then Brandon has to start braying about principles and "the little guy" and throw a wrench in the deal for both Nat *and* Brandon's real dad, Jim. The Peach Pit is saved in that instance thanks to some kind of offscreen out-clause finagling (we suspect the fact that the prime intersection the diner supposedly sits at doesn't exist triggered a force majeure clause), but the events of "The Pit and the Pendulum" point to two major issues with Nat's management: (1) he cares much too much what Brandon, *an employee and high school student*, thinks of him; and (2) his balm for anyone's emotional lows (or celebrating their highs!) is free food. This is a teen drama, so someone's crying into their Coke float every five minutes . . . and Nat's sending over a free burger, or packing up a free pie to enjoy at home.

We find out later that Nat's cousin Joey buys in at around this time; we never see him, and he never sees a dime, possibly because Nat's best "customers" don't pay most of the time, possibly because the Pit is drowning in health-department fines thanks to Brandon's chest hairs falling in people's omelets (seriously, dude: undershirts!). Or maybe it's that Nat's insurance never dropped back down after Brenda got robbed at gunpoint. In any case, by the time Nat has his heart attack, the restaurant's running at around break-even, and after Dylan buys Joey out, we don't hear much about the original Peach Pit's profitability (or lack of same).

VALERIE MALONE. If she can't *have* Dylan, Valerie's going to act as much *like* Dylan as possible once she gets her cut of the Punta Brava money—living in a hotel, driving a black sports car, and owning (part of) the Peach Pit after she buys out Rush. It isn't great that she mostly purchases the club to control Ray Pruit (Jamie Walters), which fails; or that she hires her high school boyfriend, Tom (Kane Picoy), to manage the place; but Val's dumbest move—running an illegal-gambling ring out of the club—actually occurs when she's "only" the manager, not the owner. The way she ends up relinquishing control of the After Dark is classic Valerie: she takes advantage of a mentally unwell David's post-inheritance spending spree to sell him half her stake; comes on to him to get him to

Too Mega to Fail:
THE PEACH PIT'S FINANCES

buy the other half; then invests the proceeds with Derrick Driscoll (Corin Nemec), who turns out to be a con artist who absconds with the money.

NOAH HUNTER. Noah manages to do a lot of fucking up in a short ownership time frame, starting with boning Valerie in the PPAD office after his half-brother, Josh (Michael Trucco), had roofied her and continuing on to presiding, albeit unwittingly (which is how he does everything, tbh), over Valerie's gambling concern, then getting busted for it; letting Gina (Vanessa Marcil) talk him into a gentleman's-club side hustle, which turns into extortion; and using the bar he owns to drown his sorrows about his father's death and his own ensuing broke-assedness, then drive around Los Angeles wasted.

DAVID SILVER. Invests in the After Dark during what we are given to understand is a manic episode, then ends up running the place alone after Valerie, well, Valeries herself into another pickle. David's tenure is nasty, brutish, and short: during his brief stint between proper housing arrangements, he's living in the PPAD office, and an overloaded outlet + a space heater David drops some clothing on = a fire that doesn't cause any injuries, but trashes the office, and for which David isn't insured because he's behind on bills. That includes rent, and when the building's owner makes it clear she's sick of his bullshit, he reaches back into his meth-addict toolkit and forges a couple of Donna's checks. That's obviously not the solution he'd envisioned, so his next stop is a loan shark, and while someone on this show should probably break David's legs (if they can even find them in his giant pants), Noah steps in during the period while he's still an oil heir, and buys the building and David's debt. Not that David's done crapping up the After Dark, since his douchey radio show is for some reason parked on the *dance floor* at this *nightclub*, but that's technically on Noah.

"You're on the ledge, Silver. Don't jump."

David Is Saved by a Magical Drug Toilet (and Dylan)

Stuart is back! "Who? . . . Why?" Exactly. We assumed that that relationship ended, as it should have, after the abortive Vegas-elopement caper, but here he is, aiding and abetting some Valentine's-themed STUFF nobody asked for. (With the possible exception of Gabrielle Carteris, who may have requested other storylines get bulked up so that her 15-months-pregnant ass could rest.)

Certainly nobody asked for more of Lucinda's pronouncements about cultural Valentine's Day myths, or the documentary she's trying to get funding for, so it's almost a relief when Brandon takes a break from misusing the term "politically incorrect" (and from continuing to passive-aggress in Dylan's direction about the Peach Pit deal) to gnaw on the lower two-thirds of Lucinda's face.

And at least we have reasons, if not excuses, for runaway bride Brenda and her homewrecking twin to make Andrea's impending nuptials about themselves? Granted, they'd probably do that anyway, but Andrea's too preoccupied with her parents' feeling that she's "throwing [her] life away" by marrying Jesse to notice—so preoccupied, in fact, that she's fine with the production recasting Grandma Rose with Bess Meisler. We are not fine with it, as Meisler's attempts at Yiddish sound like she has Katharine Hepburn stuck in her throat, but New GR does give *her* blessing to the marriage after guessing that it's happening because Andrea's pregnant. Not exactly a long-shot guess—Carteris looks like she's got an exercise ball jammed under her smock in the scene—but hat tip to Carteris and Mark Damon Espinoza for acting stunned at Grandma Rose's acuity.

Would that she'd prevented Andrea from picking her own outfit: The bride has paired a tent from the Dorothy Zbornak Wedding Collection with steampunk white booties and yet another Winchester House of an updo, and when her parents show up at city hall minutes before the vows, the hope is that they've brought a change of clothes. Alas, no, but they *have* brought their sign-off, which would have more emotional weight if we had ever seen them before, or ever saw them again. Andrea's mom doesn't even get any lines! Brandon, entrusted with giving-Andrea-away duty but now no longer needed in that role, slides over to be Jesse's best man instead, and once it's official, the most inept hora in millennia of Judaism occurs . . . at the Peach Pit, where else.

David's too busy approaching his *real* rock bottom to interact with any of this, although for much of the episode, he's getting by with it. Mel takes what he thinks is a hard line with David, but still writes him a rent check, which David then parlays into cash back with the landlord. What's more unrealistic—that anyone in the transaction fails to notice David's extremely long pre-lie pauses? Or that $600 a month *total* for a beachfront 3BR is absurdly low, even for 1994? David's (cheap) house of cards starts to buckle at a Valentine's dance, of all places, because although Donna's still his staunchest defender, even she is not okay with David's inviting his new drug buddy Happy Jack (Eric Wylie, creating the template for Travis in *Clueless*) along on their date. And it's not because the law of economy of characters states Jack is a narc, although it does and he is; it's because the drugs have changed David and made him mean. We're not sure how she can tell the difference, because David's always that pissy to her, and the colloquy he has to endure with Dylan in the parking lot about emotional debts and metaphorical ledges doesn't improve David's attitude.

Neither does his next stop; David's dealer is folding the tents because he heard the dorm's getting raided. This genius then gives his entire stash to David "for safekeeping," and though David spirits it out of the building moments before the dealer gets arrested, he is freaking out! He finally calls Dylan, and when Hard-Living Sensei arrives, he drops a bunch of home truths on David about his addiction, then tells David that *David* has to flush all the drugs down the toilet, because symbolism . . . so, after the camera's POV flips to toilet-cam, David does. And that $600 rent is *really* a bargain given how sturdy the plumbing is in this joint; David and Dylan spend what seems like 20 minutes dumping all manner of controlled substances, most still in plastic bags, into the toilet, and magically, it never backs up.

As the last of the meth is gurgling its way out to the Pacific, the cops come in and arrest them both, then tear up the apartment—but neither perp says anything, and the cops don't find anything, so except for the mess the search left behind (which Kelly thinks she can sue LAPD over, lol), David is free and clear. He vows to get help, Kelly and Donna believe him, and the toilet gets a syndicated spinoff that runs for four seasons.

"When push comes to shove, you gotta go with the flow."

The '60s Flashback

It's difficult even for great shows to nail a late-'60s flashback episode, between the overwrought symbolism of the era, the requisite terrible wigs, and the pointed name-checking of key events few writers can resist. For a not-great show like *Beverly Hills, 90210*, it's nearly impossible, as "The Time Has Come Today" wastes no time in proving . . . Just kidding; *all* it does is waste time.

That's partly down to inexperienced episode director Jason Priestley, doing triple duty behind the camera, as Brandon, and as flashback Vietnam War hawk Will. It's also partly on Shannen Doherty, who's nominally carrying the episode as Brenda and her '60s alter ego, Wendy, but who with 1.5 feet out the door by this time gives maaaaybe a quarter of a fuck about both characters combined. And partly it's the music, or rather the lack of it; not that the episode worked as trenchant commentary when it aired with *all* the contemporary songs in place, but almost none of the era-appropriate soundtrack made it onto the DVDs, so entire scenes either don't make sense or have placeholder lite grunge playing . . . during a be-in.

But mostly, as usual, it's the writing. The setup is workable enough: after narrowly escaping federal charges in an animal-jailbreak misadventure, Brenda is skipping a Gang ski trip, pretending she's grounded because it's that or tell her friends she doesn't really like them anymore. Brandon chooses to put himself in the middle, then snot off to Brenda about how tired he is of her shit, so Brenda's desire to skip more of *that* makes total sense—and positions her to find a diary hidden in her window seat. The diary belongs to Wendy, the Brenda analog of one of Casa Walsh's previous owners, and as ShanDo reads Wendy's first entry (with all the oomph of a roll call), it's plain we're in for a self-serious checklist of momentous highlights of the late 1960s, intended to parallel the lives and loves of their present-day counterparts.

But it's not plain whether the writers understand their own timeline, or actually know when, say, Robert Kennedy was killed—and the parallels are inconsistent. What are we to take from the fact that 1969's not-David prevails on not-Donna to sleep with him, then never talks to her again—or that Brandon's analog, Will, is a pro-government martinet who ends up getting killed in Vietnam? (We're not saying he deserved this fate, but the character *does* kick in a television set.)

Is not-Dylan's draft-dodging and cheesy patter about "bourgeois ideas of monogamy" supposed to be funny? (His wig, which is more "Meg Ryan in *When Harry Met Sally*" than "'60s hippie," is *extremely* funny, and does exactly nothing to subdivide the acreage of his fivehead.) And who signed off on "Sal" (Joe E. Tata again) Bussichio's Chef Boyardee accent?

What's the point of any of it, is what we're really asking. Well, no episode with not-D'Shawn dressed in an Uncle Sam costume at an antiwar protest is a *total* write-off, but the true function of "The Time Has Come Today" is apparently twofold: (1) to put Gabrielle Carteris, by this point three years pregnant, in a flowy costume and give her one tiny scene swaying next to a giant ankh; and (2) to establish, via Brenda's overinvestment in not-Dylan and not-Kelly's relationship in the diary, that Brenda is still in love with actual present-day Dylan.

"Let's get one thing straight: I have never had a cappuccino."

Steve Outs KEG's Gay President

SEASON 4 | EPISODE 26
BLIND SPOT

Now that David is no longer on drugs, he cares about school— specifically about polishing his piano skills, to which end he starts taking lessons with an instructor named Holly (Sydney Brown), who is young, pretty . . . and blind!

Donna—who has apparently resumed being David's girlfriend, offscreen—is already jealous of Holly, having seen the back of her head, when David introduces Donna as his "other roommate." Donna then hatches a plan to get back at David by going on a fake date with D'Shawn, breaking our hearts in the process as we see their scorching chemistry and know nothing will come of it. In fact, both these new scene partners are here just to push Donna and David back toward each other—D'Shawn by saying David can be passionate about both music and Donna, and Holly by telling David she doesn't need to see Donna to hear the hurt in her voice. As for Holly: whatever. But D'Shawn deserves better, and nuts to the show for never enmeshing Cress Williams with the opening-credits cast because producers were too scared to portray an interracial relationship between people who, like, kissed sometimes.

Speaking of "too scared": the A-plot. Brandon's stupid Mustang breaks down on the way to a Dodgers game, so he and Steve have to go into a nearby coffee-house to call AAA. Steve quickly notices that the joint is a full-on sausage party: this must be one of those *gay* coffeehouses! Across the floor, another patron notices Steve, seemingly in the midst of a spat with his boyfriend Brandon, and tells *his* companion he's happy to know he's not the only gay guy at KEG. Not until both he and Steve are back at KEG house does the viewer understand that this other dude is KEG president Mike Ryan, because Brandon Douglas isn't playing him anymore; a new actor named Jack Armstrong is. (Bye, Brandon Douglas! Too bad you departed this character right before he got this big showcase episode about how totally gay he is!)

Mike tries to induce Steve to come out to him by offering him a cappuccino—he thought he recently saw Steve with a cappuccino!—and Steve (or Ian Ziering) is so determined to prove his straightness that he keeps pronouncing it "cup-o-chino" as he hotly denies Mike's assumption. When he tells Brandon about this crisis, Brandon reminds Steve that Mike defended him when John tried to have Steve blackballed at KEG, so Steve owes it to Mike to keep his confidence. Steve agrees, but then another KEG troglodyte, Artie (Todd Bryant), suggests that the boxer shorts Steve's been assigned to wear for Alpha Omega's charity beefcake calendar are somehow gay. (Does a duck decoy motif mean something in the LGBTQ+ community we're not aware of?) Steve deflects Artie's teasing by throwing Mike under the bus offscreen, and when his supposed "brothers" paint his bedroom door pink, Mike decides to resign his presidency and leave the frat. Sick with guilt and regret, Steve urges Mike to stay and fight. When the brothers meet to decide the matter, Artie paints a terrifying picture of KEG getting a reputation as the gay fraternity and alumni pulling their donations. Mike counters by situating himself among the pioneering brothers who, with their membership, broke barriers of race and creed. The brothers support Mike; Artie departs to find a more homophobic frat—which, let's be real, will probably be pretty easy; and the beefcake calendar is saved. (If you crave more documentation of young Brian Austin Green's sunken chest and spindly marionette arms, the February pictorial is your dream come true!) Even Mike shows up to pay homage to the Village People as a shirtless construction worker, and God bless him for letting us objectify him one last time before we neeeeever saw him again.

"Please: you're not that good an actress."

Crazy Laura Sabotages Brenda

Bad news: Andrea, now 14 years pregnant with a Volkswagen Jetta, has to go on bed rest for the duration . . . Okay, only the second half of that is true, and none of it is interesting, so let's move on to Suzanne's engagement to Kevin the Chemist (David Hayward), itself only of note because the final piece of the Scamily puzzle is now in place.

Kevin lays the groundwork for his and Suzanne's big con by complaining that the lab where he works doesn't support his bioremediation research, then performatively quitting, opening the door for Dylan to "partner" with him—and for Dylan to grow disenchanted with Kelly when she's not as psyched about the Scamily as he is.

The Task Force also seems like a scam, in our opinion, since there is absolutely zero need for Brandon to go to Berkeley on the state's dime to—no shit—"be part of the final strategy session" for a keynote address. Wh . . . at? It's a speech. There's no "strategy." Sadly, this plot is proceeding whether we like it or not, with a sidecar hitched to it that contains the Chancellor's daughter Clare (Kathleen Robertson). Clare is a precocious high-school senior with a thing for Brandon *and* a thing for handcuffs, and she semi-blackmailed Brandon into being her prom date in a previous episode, but when she breaks into Casa Walsh and announces to Brandon that they're going to Berkeley as a couple, Brandon's had it and rats Clare to the Chancellor for her wild-child ways. The plan backfires: the Chancellor doesn't take it well, and Clare thinks it's hilarious that Brandon thought tattling would work. What *will* deter Clare? Could it be a blonde beard with a cat-butt mouth?!

Not yet; Kelly's busy rolling her eyes not just at the Scamily but also at Brenda scoring the lead in *Cat on a Hot Tin Roof*. Word got out that Brenda biffed her final audition, but when Brenda readily admits that she went to director Roy Randolph's (Jason Carter) house and asked for a second chance, the rumor mill starts churning in earnest—no thanks to Steve, suddenly Laura's acting coach and emotional champion. He's furious that Laura's a mere understudy to Brenda's Maggie the Cat, and more than happy to plant a seed in the rest of The Gang's mind about Roy's predilection for boning his leading ladies. Roy has other shit to answer for—referring to acting as "dreaming on schedule," for one, not to mention agreeing to Brenda's pretentious request that the ensemble "refer to [Maggie] by her proper name, Margaret . . . at least until [Brenda gets] to know her better" instead of kicking her in the shins—but Brenda's so-called friends aren't privy to any of that. They only know how badly Brenda wanted the part and how nourished she is by drama in all its forms. Dylan is the only one who doesn't buy that Brenda hit the casting couch (Brandon, shittiest sibling ever, claims he doesn't judge Brenda after his affair with Lucinda, but also basically doesn't believe his sister and fails once again to take her side with any force).

Laura mostly seems mad that *she* didn't think of that approach to auditioning, but then, Laura is increasingly mad in the Byronic sense, leaving Brenda a message rescheduling rehearsal and suggesting while flashing crazy eyes that Steve kidnap Brenda, or worse, so Laura can take over. Brenda quickly cottons to what's going on and confronts Laura and Steve; Steve is unrepentant at first—and kind of hangs a light on how none of The Gang should really know each other anymore by snarling at Brenda that he's "your brother's friend, not yours!"—but Laura's felonious solution to her Brenda problem is too much even for Steve. Steve confides to the others that Laura wants him to "pull a Tonya Harding," and that he agreed to do it so that Laura wouldn't take matters into her own hands.

But when Brenda takes matters into *her* own hands (not like that) and gets Laura booted off the production, Laura lets slip the bonds of sanity for real. As Brenda is making up, sort of, with Kelly and Donna for doubting her chastity, Steve is checking on Laura, and Ian Ziering is overacting reading the note she's left in her room about her "final performance." He runs bodily into Brenda outside the auditorium, then dashes off to get security as Laura watches from the rafters, wearing Samantha Sanders's old Maggie costume and committing 100 percent to cross-eyed faces, and Brenda tries her best soothing noises to coax Laura down. The bizarre workout-video score is very concerned that Laura's not receptive to Brenda's rap, and Laura's affixing a noose around her neck when Steve sneaks up on her and manages to grab her before she can jump. Laura is escorted into an ambulance as a shell-shocked Brenda tells Steve she can't forgive him yet, and dissolves in tears. Steve smells a guilty fart for ten minutes, and we neeeeever see Laura again.

Brenda Goes, Forever

Where to begin with this plot-packed two-parter? Seriously: Celeste returns, reveals that she's dating John Sears (who apparently converted all his liquid assets to charity carnival tickets, because he shows up daily to mess with Steve), gets the 411 on John from Donna and Brenda, and has them join her in flashing their bras at him so that Steve can drop him in a mud pit, and that's basically the *least* eventful plotline in the episode.

Andrea's baby? Gets born, via cesarean, *way* too early (she's . . . 2 lbs. 8 oz.): another footnote! Donna catches David boning Ariel (Kari Wuhrer), a hot record-company rep, and ends their relationship of two-plus years: who has time to care?!

The main action revolves around the players in our confounding quadrangle: Brenda, Brandon, Kelly, and Dylan. Brandon goes to DC for the MacGuffin Task Force that has been boring us all season; there, he is set upon by both Clare and Lucinda. Meanwhile, Kelly and Dylan—who've been clashing since Erica and Suzanne appeared—finally break up, apparently for good this time; Kelly decides to surprise Brandon in DC, rescuing him from a fate of . . . sleeping with Clare because he's gotten too tired to fight her advances anymore. (Clare and Lucinda spot them walking out of the hotel together, and given how openly they were both hitting on Brandon in front of one another, we feel certain that if this episode had aired 20 years later, we'd have seen Lucinda and Clare shrug and just decide to have undoubtedly better sex with each other instead.)

Freed from Kelly's disapproval of the time he's spending with Suzanne and Erica and judgment of the ways he spends his money, Dylan may pursue the opportunity Suzanne's scientist fiancé, Kevin, has presented him with and found a company to develop bioremediation solutions to environme— you know what? It's not important. Jim has assembled investors who are interested in the deal; Kevin gets Dylan to admit he doesn't entirely understand the prospectus, and after a few conversations and his wedding, he has convinced Dylan to fund it all himself, because who better than the guy who can't grok the paperwork? Horrified, Jim fires Dylan as a client. Dylan and Kevin head straight to the bank to open a joint account and transfer all of Dylan's money to it; Kevin barely waits for Dylan's car to leave the parking lot before going straight back in and cleaning Dylan out. Kevin and Suzanne (who apparently hatched the whole plan herself and then . . . came to Los Angeles to find a crooked chemist so that she could pull it off? Unclear) bring Erica to the airport, lying about why they have to get on a plane to Brazil without telling Dylan where they're going, but Erica remains suspicious enough to write a note with his contact info and stick it to the inside of a bathroom stall with a wad of chewed-up gum; alas, it flutters to the ground as soon as she leaves. Too bad she never learned Dylan's phone number.

Brenda finishes her run as Maggie the Cat and gets an offer from her director, Roy Randolph, to enroll in a summer program at the Royal Academy of Dramatic Art. (Please, Lord, let it be an intensive course in accents.) Brenda has said nearly all her goodbyes—promising the heartbroken Donna that she will be back—when she joins her parents to watch Brandon, on TV, shaking hands with "President Clinton" (actually a seven-foot-tall white guy in a dust-bunny-colored wig, but sure, close enough). Jim and Cindy are, as ever, enraptured by Brandon, and when Brenda goes to say her very last goodbye to Dylan, she tells him she's never seen them look at her that way; the only time she's felt the kind of approval Brandon takes for granted is when she's onstage, and she wants it, BAD. But that's not all: "Dylan, I love you," she says. "I've never stopped loving you. And I know now I never will." "I'll applaud you from afar," Dylan replies. Brenda asks him to give her something to come back to, and while we see them kiss and sink out of frame, apparently what Dylan gives her on this particular day isn't worth coming back to, because she never does: not for graduation; not for anyone's wedding, including her brother's; not for the funeral when one of her oldest friends loses her dad; WE NEEEEEVER SEE HER AGAIN. And at least one of us never got over it.

SEASON
Five

Comings

VALERIE MALONE

With the departure of Brenda at the end of Season 4, the show had a brunette vacancy, and filled it with Val (*Saved by the Bell* alumna Tiffani Thiessen). If you'd wondered why Jim shoehorned in a reference to the Walshes' best friends in Buffalo at the *Cat on a Hot Tin Roof* wrap party, this is why: Val is that family's eldest daughter, and needs to escape the darkness following her father's death by what we are told was a self-inflicted gunshot wound. Though the early going of her debut episode finds her cheerfully playing country mouse, the closing moments let us know she has hidden depths of wildness: she *smokes pot in Brenda's old room*! In general, Val's story arcs have her wildly vacillating between desperation to fit in with The Gang and perfectly reasonable disdain for their self-regard; she and Kelly take a nearly instant dislike to each other, which remains their default positions until Val's departure from the series. Between her eviction from the Bel Age Hotel over an unpaid bill; arrests for drug, solicitation, and bookmaking charges; a fake pregnancy intended to extort her married boyfriend; and what is eventually revealed to be her murder of her father after enduring years of sexual abuse at his hands, Val is probably the most compromised character, legally and morally. Great boobs and excellent hair, though!

ALEX DIAZ

It's an ongoing source of bafflement to your coauthors how seriously student government is taken at the fictional CU, but when it comes to Latinos Unidos agitator Alex Diaz (F.J. Rio), we have no problem with it—because Diaz's primary objective seems to be harassing Brandon. He starts strong, using a hit piece Josh Richland wrote for the *Condor* about Brandon, D'Shawn, and Randall/Lucinda but never published (because he couldn't prove the allegations therein) to try to blackmail Josh and Brandon into dropping out of the presidential race. D'Shawn interrupting a student senate meeting—and Diaz's defamation of both him and Brandon—to set the record straight throws a wrench in that plan. Josh and Brandon's victory isn't part of Diaz's plan either, so he mounts a challenge to the legitimacy of Brandon's presidency after Josh's demise, although unfortunately for us all, this too fails. But the third time's the charm: when the California state legislature implements a tuition hike and Brandon is caught out for not warning undergrads it might happen, Diaz runs against him on a "transparency" platform and wins in a landslide . . . as do we all when the stupefyingly dull student-government arc is finally put in the rearview.

GRIFFIN STONE

Steve's fraternity brother Griffin (Casper Van Dien) seems like a perfect match for Donna . . . to his and Donna's moms, who set them up on a blind date. Griffin gets dumped in favor of Ray Pruit after Griffin presumes flying Donna to Catalina in his prop plane is going to get him laid; Griffin's reaction is predictably classist, and classless. But he really shows his one-percenter ass when his and Steve's rave in an abandoned house ends in a near-fatal confla-gration: on the night of the fire, as a soot-smudged Steve sobs in the front yard, Griffin sidles away like it's got nothing to do with him, even though the house is owned by his father. It comes out later that Griffin's idea of "having permission to use the house" was actually Griffin stealing the key, but in the legal action taken against him and Steve, they *both* get com-munity service and a two-year ban on organizing parties. A pretty light punishment under the circs, but Steve is outraged at the "injustice," and runs Griffin out of KEG for trying to throw him under the bus.

RAY PRUIT

Blue-collar songster Ray Pruit—"with one 'T,' because that's all [his] mama could afford"—(Jamie Walters) hangs around an awfully long time given what a bad fit he is with Donna from the start. Ray meets Donna while he's working on a CU construction site and she's doing a dumb *Men Are from Mars*–ish video project, and he's immediately defensive about their differences in background; he remains at least that pissy through-out their relationship's myriad ups and downs. And we do mean myr-iad, and it's mostly downs: sexually frustrated by Donna, Ray lets himself be seduced by Valerie, but stays with Donna partly at the urging of his mother, LuAnn (Caroline McWilliams), who wants him to keep his ass on that gravy train. *Donna's* mother, Felice, tries to pay Ray to go away (and to this day we can't decide if that's evil or a power move). He becomes steadily more abusive toward Donna, culminating in that notorious shove down the stairs in the fifth-season finale. When expensive jewelry starts going missing in the sixth-season premiere, everyone's all too ready to believe Ray's the culprit (he's not). And while the DVDs have generally cut out Ray's musical performances due to rights issues, live viewers at the time had to suffer through them on a near-weekly basis. We feel for the late McWilliams, who has to serve an entire menu of trashy character tropes as LuAnn—she's a sloppy drunk, she's a gold-digger, her accent is soggy corn-pone, and she's one of those cigarette smokers who dresses up her off-brand menthol 120s in a little coin purse. We also can't help feeling for Walters, who left show business entirely because playing the man who physically abused the sainted Donna functionally ruined his career.

ALISON LASH

Alison (Sara Melson) attends Steve and Griffin's ill-fated rave with her girl-friend, Dana (Kristine Mejia). Alison and Kelly end up trapped in a bathroom by the fire, vainly screaming their heads off for help. (We will note here, not for the last time, that there is a window *right above their heads*.) Alison receives far worse burns than Kelly, and must undergo rehab and multiple skin grafts; the combined trauma may prompt her breakup with Dana and subsequent fix-ation on Kelly as a romantic possibility. Kelly doesn't like Alison that way, but a candlelit dinner with her, and Kelly's recent choosing of herself over Dylan and Brandon, causes much borderline-offensive gossip among the rest of the gang re: Kelly's sexual orientation. Ali-son, however, accepts Kelly's decision and isn't seen again.

J. JAY "JONESY" JONES

After Suzanne and Kevin defraud Dylan, Christine puts Dylan in touch with Jonesy (Wings Hauser), a former FBI agent who now does sketchier work. For a fee of half of whatever he can recover, Jonesy pledges to go after Kevin and Suzanne on Dylan's behalf, and pretty quickly finds them—living under assumed names, though still with Erica, who presumably could dime them out or at the very least *phone Dylan*. Anyway, Jonesy's cockamamie plan ends up requiring Val to honeytrap Kevin while Jonesy breaks into his online bank account, somehow. (This is 1995; the internet was still a mystery to most of us.) After Jonesy has restored Dylan's half of his fortune, Val then goes after Jonesy for some of *his* end, in con-sideration of her part subbing in for Jonesy's original femme fatale. One might think such a man of the world would not be so helpless in the face of a 19-year-old woman's wiles, but Val is *just that hot*.

PETER TUCKER

When Andrea's at the laundromat with Hannah one evening, Peter (James C. Victor) assumes she's Hannah's nanny and starts hitting on her from underneath an immaculately constructed '90s floof of auburn hair. (Which Victor came by honestly; his uncle was a hairstylist. Specifically, he was Sarah's mother's hairstylist.) He's not deterred when he learns Andrea's married; he is too! Because both Peter and Andrea probably got married too young—or, really, because Gabrielle Carteris was no longer pregnant and they had to find *something* for Andrea to do—they enter into an affair. Andrea is guilty and torn, but Peter's sweet D convinces her she has no choice but to leave Jesse and begin a new life with Peter . . . only to be spotted by Dylan at the no-tell motel they're using to bone, then functionally dumped when it turns out Peter has no intention of divorcing the wife who put him through med school.

PATRICK FINLEY

Following the hideous (barely noticeable) neck burn that entirely derails her (barely nascent) modeling career, Kelly falls under the sway of a charismatic psychology prof named Patrick Finley (Alan Toy) who's lining up recruits for an ill-defined program called The New Evolution. As a second-year psychology student herself, Kelly should be wise to the techniques employed by a would-be cult leader, right? Wrong! She is entirely taken in by jargon like "extern" and "negator," takes a job as his research assistant, and busily starts isolating herself from her loved ones. (Jackie's not concerned, we learn; she did est in the '70s, because of course she did.) Kelly's pulling the hardest away from Brandon, who—in his desperation—turns to Dylan to help him try to get her out. Posing as a rich and gullible mark, Dylan lets Finley know he will readily donate to build New Evolution facilities if Finley can convince Kelly to take him back; though it had seemed as though Finley was working on seducing her himself, he likes money even more. Dylan narcs on him, and Kelly breezily walks out of Finley's lair and back into her old life. Therapy? Why would she bother getting any of *that*?!

GARRETT SLAN

When a rapist starts preying on the women of CU, the first and most obvious suspect is Lenny Zeminski (Tracy Fraim): as a dorm resident, he has cause to be on campus at all hours; he wears the same boots as the assailant; and he did time in a military brig for sexual assault after his tour in Operation Desert Storm. The mob has turned on him and is in the middle of driving him off-campus when the viewer learns that he's innocent . . . uh, this time. The real perp is Garrett Slan (David Bowe), who stalks Donna, lurks in her apartment, and probably would have raped her. Fortunately, David comes over to apologize for an earlier fight with Donna, and she alerts him that something unusual is going on by repeatedly calling him "Dave." Garrett goes away for his crimes, but returns two seasons later, just in time for Donna to realize someone's stalking her *again*. Spoiler: Slan's still a creep, but he stalks her only the once.

CHARLIE ROLLINS

A fellow patient at Dylan's post-intervention rehab, Charlie (Jeffrey King) earns our esteem initially by getting in Dylan's face about Dylan wearing a Rolling Stones hat to group (which makes Charlie want to get high) and Dylan's standoffish attitude (which makes everyone want to slap him upside his head). Realizing that he's projecting his own shit onto Dylan—or that the hat is part of a larger product-placement effort for one of the world's most famous musical acts, sigh—Charlie relents, and after finishing the program, the two collaborate on a noir screenplay in the office of the Palm Wind Motel, where Charlie's the manager. As if encouraging Dylan's periodic writing affectation wasn't bad enough, Charlie doubles down by putting Dylan together with a hypnotherapist, which is how we end up with that inane "Dylan's past life in the Old West" episode. Worse, the investor he finds to back their project, Tom Rose, may have been involved in Jack McKay's "death"—and almost effects *Dylan's* death, after which we unsurprisingly have no further contact with Charlie.

DR. MOLLY CAMPBELL

Dr. Molly (Jane Daly) is the facilitator of Dylan's hypnotic journey back to a previous life, in which he was a bank robber reformed by the love of a good woman (played in his dream by Kelly, obviously . . . *eye roll*) and then murdered by the vengeful son of one of his victims. Dr. Molly is also respon-

sible, therefore, for the "Dylan and Kelly = soulmates" idea the writers then return to like dogs to vomit, only selectively remembering his *marriage* and two long-term relationships with Brenda. Damn you, Dr. Molly.

SHEILA SILVER

David's mother Sheila (Caroline Lagerfelt) is an offscreen presence for more than half of the series run: we hear that she's fragile in some unspecified way, and that she suffered in the divorce from Mel. David and Donna have to do some detective work to track her down when he belatedly goes to visit her in Portland, Oregon, because she has bipolar disorder and lost her job and home after going off her meds. Mel and David join forces to help bring her back to Los Angeles and sort out her treatment, after which she is presented mostly as a cautionary tale for what could happen to David if he doesn't take good care of his mental health.

ELLE

Horned up at a KEG event in Palm Springs, Steve keeps seeing a statuesque, bewitching woman around town, eventually managing to learn her name is Elle (Monika Schnarre). After a date, Steve is rounding the bases when suddenly he has a silicone "chicken cutlet" in his hand, because Elle is a trans woman. This storyline was cruel in 1995 and is utterly indefensible today! The next season, Steve runs into Elle again at a Rodeo Drive boutique and overcompensates performing his straightness by getting too grabby with Clare. Elle then happens to be the Chancellor's date for a journalism award banquet. A horrified Steve tries to tell Clare about Elle's gender identity, which is not his information to impart, but Clare doesn't believe him anyway. Steve then approaches Elle directly about not pursuing the Chancellor, which we're supposed to think is romantic because it involves him declaring his love for Clare, which Clare overhears because he says it in the ladies' room. Elle is defiant about her right to start a romantic relationship with the Chancellor, but ultimately decides to let him go, and we're relieved the show never tried again to portray what life in the 1990s was like for American trans persons.

Goings

JOSH RICHLAND

After a "brutal" campaign (per the show; in reality, nobody cares) against *eleven* other tickets, Josh and Brandon prevail as president and veep of CU's student government! But Josh doesn't live long enough to learn of his triumph; nervously awaiting the election's outcome at the Peach Pit (where else), Josh decides to take a drive to self-soothe . . . and his car is T-boned by a garbage truck just yards from the Pit parking lot. Brandon is left to rule alone, and Jason Priestley to conflate "grieving" and "trying to pass a poo made of throwing stars."

ANDREA & JESSE

The show's producers did what they could to make the struggles of a teen mom and her barely older husband compelling for their audience of teen and young twentysomethings. But once Andrea's affair with Peter had run its course, there wasn't really anywhere else to go—so toward the end of Season 5, the Vasquezes move to New Haven, where Jesse is going to teach law (lol) and Andrea is going to complete her education and become a medical doctor. Over the years, Andrea pops back for Steve's 21st birthday party; for their high school class's five-year reunion (where we find out she and Jesse are splitting up); and for Donna and David's series finale wedding.

JIM & CINDY

At the end of Season 5, Jim suspects he's about to get canned from his job. Instead, it's the other thing: he gets a huge promotion to the office in Hong Kong. Over the years that follow, the two are seen together again only once—for Brandon's scuttled wedding in the Season 8 finale—though they appear separately on a few random occasions. Even more improbable than that they would both skip their only son's college graduation is the idea that they would keep their large Beverly Hills house after relocating overseas and let their son's idiot friend continue living there after said idiot son had moved out himself.

"How cool can she be? She's from Buffalo."

Enter Val

Everyone is reconvening for their sophomore year at CU, mostly having spent the summer apart, and since social media hasn't been invented yet, they actually have news to tell one another! In person!

Andrea's baby, Hannah, is finally home from the hospital. After David subbed for one of the members of his backing band in the Season 4 finale, producer/sometime R&B artist Babyface invited David to tour with him in Japan, then changed his mind, whereupon Ariel lost interest in David, but not before giving him crabs. Donna fell out with Kelly when the latter—in an EXTREME out-of-character move—sided with David after his cheating, saying she understood the kind of "pressure" he was under . . . from Donna's celibacy? Shut up, Kelly: Donna is right to bug out of the apartment, though wrong to flee from the beach to Houston, in the *summer*, punishing only herself (especially her hair) with that oppressive humidity. Don't worry, though: Donna's back in town, and the blondes make up with the help of the angelic stylists who handle their roots.

But what of the big stories that closed out Season 4? Well, Dylan really did put every last cent of his money into that joint account Kevin cleaned out, and to hear him tell it, the police aren't pursuing the con artists who defrauded him. Brandon and Kelly are still fucking even though he now has a goatee; Brandon's parents and Andrea all know, but they've kept it quiet from everyone else, which is why it's awkward when Steve comes back from Hawaii convinced that Kelly is his soulmate. Cindy is sprucing up Brenda's room before heading out to the airport, and though the writing plays coy, for a while, as to whom the Walshes are picking up there, we finally learn that Brenda is staying in London "for the year" (*sob*). During her absence, her room will be occupied by Valerie Malone, an old family friend from Buffalo. Brandon tries to soften the blow of telling Steve about his dating Kelly by offering to introduce him to Valerie, and while Steve is dubious that anyone from Buffalo could meet his high personal standards of babe-hood, the fact that she's played by *Saved by the Bell* alumna Tiffani Thiessen obliterates his objections. Steve immediately starts trying to impress her—at basketball in the Walsh driveway; out at a hot new club (where Donna spots David with some other broad and is somehow overcome with feelings for him)—and is about to kiss her when Brandon accidentally cock-blocks him. What Steve doesn't yet know is why Val is there—and no, it's not *just* to replace Brenda with another brunette: Val's father recently died by suicide. And what *no one* knows, except the viewer, is that after an intense childhood crush, she's still horny for Brandon—yes, even with the goatee!!!

Getting ready for bed that night, Valerie is effusive about getting to live with the Walshes, forever her model of a perfect family. But as soon as she's alone on Brenda's old window seat, she calls her friend Ginger back in Buffalo (so . . . at, like, 5 A.M. Ginger's time) and reveals how she really feels. She thinks Brandon and his friends are a bunch of "avocado heads"! They "must be the straightest human units on the planet"! They went to a club and didn't even *try* to get served— whereas Valerie, throughout this conversation, is *rolling a joint*!!! She hopes Jim and Cindy won't try to act like her parents, but if they do, she knows what to do: "I'll just put on a happy face and dance." Oh, *Valerie*. Nothing could make us happy to see Brenda off, but your brand-new strain of bad girl energy is almost getting us there.

"And on a school night, no less!"

Dylan Is Bankrupt and Donna Is a Debutante

SEASON 5 | EPISODE 2
UNDER THE INFLUENCE

The school year's about to get underway for real, and with it the latest Brandon-fluffing season plot, as Brandon's editorialist nemesis, Josh Richland (Joshua Beckett), resurfaces to invite Brandon to be his running mate for CU student-body president.

The writing attempts to put this snoozefest on par with a national presidential run with references to "brutal" campaigning and rival-ticket scandals, but nobody has ever cared about university student government, and we will not be starting now.

Nobody really cares about Andrea's daycare ambivalence, either, especially when the childcare provided by the California system in this universe *is free*, but Jesse—who basically pressured Andrea into going ahead with the pregnancy and their marriage, let's not forget—is a judgy asshat about leaving Hannah with nonfamily caregivers. Why? Because, when he and Andrea visit the facility to check it out, another baby is crying. Andrea reflects a mere fraction of our annoyance when she snaps that, you know, babies cry, and unless Jesse expects her to stay home with the kid, they don't have a ton of options. That *is* probably what Jesse expects . . . and he comes close to getting his wish when a passing comment by a daycare employee about how fast kids grow up has Andrea reconsidering the stay-at-home-mom lane.

Maybe Andrea and Jesse should pay Dylan to babysit, because he could really use the money. On the other hand, he's downward-spiraling after the Scamily relieved him of his entire fortune, he's not *admitting* that the Scamily relieved him of his entire fortune, and if he's dumb enough to have signed over his *whole* bank balance without holding anything back to live on but a paltry savings bond, he's too dumb to take care of a child. He's also dumb enough to think reuniting with Kelly will fix his life. The reunion that *would* go a long way toward righting Dylan's financial ship—one with Jim Walsh—is apparently off the table: when Dylan sees Jim and Cindy eating at the Peach Pit, he informs them that they're no longer welcome there. Nat briefly suspends giving away food to pick a fight with his business partner, during which he lets it slip to Dylan that Kelly "went to" Brandon, a development Brandon intended to apprise Dylan of, only to get sidetracked by judging Dylan for falling off the wagon instead. Uh oh—time for Dylan to ruin a formal function with his hypocritical resentments!

We're not exactly complaining: the charity benefit the rest of The Gang is attending is mostly a backdrop for a tiresome subplot in which Donna plans to move to Houston for a semester to learn heritage curtseys like the Texas Dip (but mostly to get away from David, which, if we had a nickel, etc.). She, her overprocessed Roman-centurion-helmet hairstyle, and her confusing cleavage have just demonstrated this feat of acro-bore-tics when an already-drunk Dylan stomps into the party, swilling wine straight from the bottle and (he thinks) bad-assily slinging his boots up on the table to get his grievance on about "[his] best friend and [his] best girl" getting together behind his back. Booze evidently killed the brain cell that recalled he did the exact same shit to Brenda with Kelly—without doing Brenda the courtesy of breaking up with her first—but everyone's too scandalized by his making a scene to point that out.

Okay, not everyone. Val is openly turned on by Dylan's scruffy rudeness, quizzing a reticent (yet somehow still snotty) Brandon about the deal with "Brenda's Dylan," and Kelly feels guilty enough about the "Brelly" situation that she tries to apologize to Dylan the next day, only to find him doing body shots with a floozy who's wearing Kelly's terry robe, gasp! And Felice is more concerned that Donna made a "spectacle" of herself by dancing with D'Shawn than by any association with Dylan's antics, so we guess we can add "racist" to the list of Felice's noncharms—and "blind" to boot, because D'Shawn in a tuxedo (and Cress Williams's delightful chemistry with Tori Spelling) is the only "benefit" anyone derived from the occasion. Donna herself accepts Dylan's apology, and the parallels between their odd-man-out romantic situations prompt Donna to realize that everyone's reservations about her bolting for Houston have some merit. She decides to go to registration after all.

Also at registration? Clare Arnold, who, thanks to AP credits, is now a sophomore like The Gang. Dun dun dunnn?

"Brandon and I are going down swinging."

Rest in Power, Josh

All over town, people are getting comfortable in their new digs! Clare pushes through Kelly's suspicion that Clare still has hot pants for Brandon to get David's old room at the beach apartment. (Here's hoping Donna and Kelly had the boy stench professionally cleaned.)

Val has put her interest in Brandon on hold to start sniffing around Dylan: having found his framed and autographed (?) photo in a box of Brenda's stuff, and gotten intel from Brandon that he's spending his nights shooting pool, she easily picks Dylan out at the one pool hall in Los Angeles. Jim's having told Val in no uncertain terms to stay away from him seems to have only made him more enticing—well, that and the fact that both Jim and Brandon think Dylan's still rich, and told Val that too. Her first flirty round of nine-ball ends with her winning both the game and Dylan's interest, and leaving Dylan wanting more. When she finds him again the next night, she goes home with him, but still refuses to tell him who she is. It's not until she makes him drive her home for curfew that he figures out she's the Walshes' new houseguest. He's not thrilled to have been targeted and snarled back up with the Walshes, but whatever she did sex-wise was so impressive (we assume)—even to this famed swordsman—that he surely won't be able to leave those epic boobs alone for long.

Somehow, our A-story is Brandon and Josh's campaign for president and VP of CU's student government. The show does its best to give the impression that the whole campus is consumed with the election even though no one has ever cared about student government except the candidates, *maybe* their friends, and a handful of extremely committed nerds, but we aren't even six minutes in before we learn that (1) there are *12* tickets in the race, and (2) Josh and Brandon failed to secure the endorsement of the *Condor*, CU's student newspaper, which *Josh edited for two years*. Somehow this doesn't induce Josh to drop out—nor does Brandon's constant whining about the taxing requirements of the campaign, like asking people to vote for him or wearing a pleasant expression—so Alex Diaz (F.J. Rio), campaign manager for the Latinos Unidos ticket the paper *did* endorse, resorts to dirty tricks: he has a draft of a muckraking profile on Brandon that Josh drafted during the Task Force era (we can't miss it if it *never goes away*), accusing Brandon of having taken one of D'Shawn's exams for him to maintain his athletic eligibility, and Alex will release it unless Josh and Brandon drop out. At the time, Josh didn't run with the story because he couldn't prove it was true, so why he went ahead and wrote an evidence-free version that Alex thinks will persuade anyone is a mystery.

Whatever: even though Brandon, stepping in for an absent Josh, just wowed the attendees at a Meet the Candidates event by making an eloquent (read: empty) plea for "listening," he's ready to quit; though he knows *he* didn't help D'Shawn cheat, he fears that someone less upstanding than he is might have, and that if the story goes public, D'Shawn could lose his scholarship and potential career. Ultimately, D'Shawn himself storms the student senate meeting where Alex is slandering both him and Brandon to declare that he's done all his own schoolwork, because Brandon forced him to; once again, the show squanders an opportunity to explore what Alex accurately calls "academic apartheid" in favor of using D'Shawn to prop up Brandon's virtue. (Of course, it also lets D'Shawn say, "For those of you who don't think I have the God-given intelligence to go to school here, I just have to say that no matter what you think your political agenda is, you're nothing but a racist," and since that includes Brandon, we'll take it as a very sly burn.)

After the election, everyone gathers at the Peach Pit to wait for the results— which Steve and Kelly are helping to tabulate, so the swamp's not entirely drained yet. Josh needs distraction and goes out for a drive; Brandon declines to join him, so only the top half of the ticket gets T-boned by a garbage truck and burned to a crisp. "We finished counting the votes," Kelly tells Brandon as he watches first responders cart off Josh's corpse. "You won." Here's hoping student government doesn't require anything more intense than planning a dance or two from President Dante Hicks over here.

"This better be good, better be entertaining, or I'm leaving."

Kelly Becomes a Model, and Mackenzie Phillips Intervenes on Dylan

SEASON 5 | EPISODE 9
INTERVENTION

Kelly receives a once-in-a-lifetime modeling-gig offer from *Seventeen* magazine, despite being (1) of average height; (2) not nearly waifish enough by the standards of the time; (3) saddled with a scraggly shag that was contemporary for the mid-'90s, but is wretchedly unflattering; and (4) a bitch about it.

We're probably supposed to think this last issue is due to trauma from her child-modeling career (which we'd never heard about prior to this season) or her eating disorder (which the show seldom remembers, not that we mind), but Kelly's giving us "sulky," not "torn." Yeah, Jackie's acting kind of embarrassing about it, but it's not the draft, Gigi Hadidn't. Just decline the offer and get on with your life.

Elsewhere in the "should have given it a hard pass" department, Donna's new boyfriend, Ray Pruit (Jamie Walters), is getting hectored by *two* moms, starting with his own, LuAnn (Caroline McWilliams). LuAnn is ten pounds of cartoonish TV indicators for "trashy" in a five-pound sack: she smokes at the breakfast table; her honeysuckle accent has always relied on the kindness of strangers; and she has vicarious financial aspirations for Ray's budding relationship with Donna. *Donna's* mom is, typically, disappointed to learn that Donna traded down from grabby Griffin (Casper Van Dien!) to grubby Ray. Felice's reaction to learning that Ray lives in down-market Reseda is akin to a vampire hissing at sunlight, and she's as rude as you'd expect when Ray turns out not to care for aspic, a ridiculous classist test given that even richies think aspic is vile. Ray isn't cowed by Felice, telling her he doesn't come from much and he's sorry if that's not good enough for her (he isn't); Dr. Martin seems to like him. Then again, Dr. Martin also seems to think it's funny that a sex-tape mix-up subplot means he accidentally sees David and Clare Doing It, so what does he know.

What we *all* know is how badly The Gang's and senior Walshes' intervention on Dylan is going to go. Cindy gets things off to a promising start by mom-guilting Dylan into coming to the Casa to talk; Dylan agrees, but does a bump first, and neither changes out of his gross T-shirt nor combs his Greasy Quiff of Addict

Despair. He might have cleaned up if he'd known famous sober personage Mackenzie Phillips ("Ellen" here) were running the intervention, but Ellen's unable to control Brandon's unhelpfully snotty attitude, nor to prevent him from undercutting his assumed superiority by using laughably antiquated phrases like "geezed up on coke." Dylan is predictably unreceptive to Brandon's braying, but nobody else gets much traction either—not Nat for clocking Dylan for stealing from the Peach Pit After Dark; not Andrea, who refers to Dylan's "passionate intellect" (lol); certainly not Kelly, who acts like this too is an annoyance that's making her late for something else. Somehow it's Steve raging at Dylan for taking Valerie away before Steve could get it in (we're paraphrasing) that tips the scales, which is a strange choice, because the show has never entirely convinced us that Steve and Dylan even like each other, much less have the kind of friendship that would steer Dylan out of a tailspin, *but* after an obnoxious and weird speech claiming The Gang likes it better when Dylan's "sick" because it makes them feel better about their own lives, Dylan agrees to go to treatment.

It takes all of a day for Dylan's roommate to annoy him with twelve-steppery, so Dylan signs himself out over his counselor's objections and grabs a ride back to his house with Val, who happened to show up just then with some baked goods. That's not the kind of "baked" Dylan's about, though; Val sticks it out for a while, but when Dylan gets super-wasted (you can tell because he's misbuttoned his shirt) and beeps his dealer (oh, '90s), Valerie's out. Dylan gets himself to the pool hall somehow, but his cash-flow problems have now extended to his addiction. His dealer (Jon Gries, always a pro) won't front him any more cocaine, but he *is* . . . running a special on heroin? We're pretty sure the Columbia House model is not the standard when it comes to narcotics, but just go with it . . . to a turnout in the hills, where a disoriented Dylan wakes up the next morning and takes forever to prep his morning pick-me-up. He's just starting to feel the high when a cop car rolls by and forces a paranoid Dylan to peel out, but Dylan's in no shape to drive—and although the ensuing crash through a fence and down a steep hillside creates little suspense, with Dylan's Porsche going eight miles an hour tops, the soundtrack teams up with Luke Perry's drama-mask faces to let us know Dylan! Could! Be! Dead!

"We're gonna die in here."

Brandon and Emily Reunite While Kelly Almost Dies at the Hottest Party of the Year

SEASON 5 | EPISODE 13
UP IN FLAMES

Kelly's not just modeling for *Seventeen*; she's scored the cover! Maybe that's why she feels comfortable not just answering the phone at Casa Walsh like she lives there, but accepting a collect call from Europe that isn't for her. It's for Brandon, and it's Emily Valentine, calling to report that a Parisian stylist assaulted her with a mushroom bob and Manic Pixie Dream Bangs . . .

Actually, she's got a four-hour layover in L.A. on her way to a conference in La Jolla. Is Brandon around? He is, he says with his usual excessive heartiness, but Kelly's not happy that Brandon's meeting the great love of his life at the airport, and that's *before* she finds out the extent of his and Emily's reconnection at Thanksgiving the previous year, to wit: they boned. Kelly's within her rights to be unsettled by this information, particularly since it only happened a year ago (and since the Santa Anas, root of all ills, are blowing again), but Brandon blares at her to "stop the bombing" while standing in a pitched-forward way that suggests he's about to punch her. Later, Brandon can't sleep and goes out to the beach apartment's Deck of Contemplation to brood about the emotional infidelity he's considering committing.

What's good for the gander is good for Kelly, we guess, because she visits Dylan in rehab and baby-voices about her *Seventeen* triumph (lol) while flirtily holding Dylan's hand. Dylan takes that opportunity to share that all his problems started when he "lost" Kelly—and that's not totally off-base, in the sense that he pushed her away for good when she wasn't all in on the Scamily, but it's also the origin of years of tiresome soulmate fooferaw with these two. Meanwhile: Emily's thrilled to see Brandon at LAX, and lets an "I love you" slip out, which in turn leads to recriminations from Brandon—she didn't call; she didn't write; Brandon had no choice but to hop on Lucinda a few weeks later (okay, he doesn't say that, but we're happy to)—and the revelation that Emily's actually in town for a week, an interval she left open to see how things were between them. "Things" are awkward, but when Brandon escorts Emily to the door of her hotel room, it's not so awkward that he won't unhinge his jaw and glom onto her *whole face*.

That's an only slightly worse time than rave prep, which sees Valerie trying to suck (back) up to Steve by helping out with the setup at the abandoned house he and Griffin selected for this already-dated-in-1994 event. As David and Clare struggle with posting the party announcement to the correct internet bulletin board (hee), Donna tries to get Ray a gig. At a rave. With his acoustic guitar and breathy vocals. Ray does eventually land a spot in one of the "mood rooms" (hee!) in exchange for use of his truck, and anyway, Steve is too busy arguing with Griffin about cost overruns and catering (yes, really—don't *you* associate a rave with tacos?) to pay much attention to the light fixture that shorts out right next to Val. So it's probably nothing to worry about, right?

As couples start filing in—lady couples, drawn by David's accidental posting on a women-seeking-women forum—fuses continue to blow, and when the caterer points out that they're overloading the circuits, Griffin is a bitch about it. Still, everything's fine for a while; Steve even makes out with Val. But as Kelly decides the rave is dumb and gets in line for a last pee before catching a cab, the fuse box starts sparking again. Kelly and Alison (Sara Melson), her new friend from the bathroom line, head for a secret bathroom Kelly heard about, but stop to lounge in a screening room the rest of the party has somehow not discovered and overrun with spilled "smart drinks"—and to note, surely for no reason at all except our edification, that the room is "completely soundproof."

Cue the chaos upstairs when Muntz (Ryan Thomas Brown) goes to check the fuse box and is chased off by a wall of fire. An exit stampede ensues; in a nice moment for future EMT Jamie Walters, Ray wades back into the inferno to clear the second floor, spotting a postcoital Val and Steve while he's up there. (Griffin is decidedly less humanitarian, slinking away from the scene as soon as he can.) Alison's girlfriend tells Steve that Alison and Kelly are still inside the house, and Steve silent-film over-cries while the soundproof-deathtrapped Kelly also gets hysterical. Alison reassures Kelly that her girlfriend will make sure they're rescued, and tries to keep Kelly busy with wet towels, but it's difficult to invest in the so-called tension of the scene when they've chosen to hunker down in a bathroom WITH A WINDOW DIRECTLY ABOVE THEM. Alison and Kelly say an Our Father! Flames rise up the door! They hear voices just outside! The voices may be yelling, "Y'all, go out the window THAT IS RIGHT THERE!" but Alison's and Kelly's screams for help drown them out! If these two boneheads die, it will be of stupidity and careless production design!

"Well, Kevin makes my skin crawl, but I want to do this for you."

Val, Dylan, and Jonesy Steal Dylan's Money Back from His Scamily

Kelly's been having a hard time processing the trauma from the frat-party fire—not just her *unsightly disfigurement* (read: barely visible neck scar), but her complicated feelings about her disaster buddy, Alison—which is why Brandon should be glad she's getting useful advice from charismatic psychology professor Patrick Finley (Alan Toy). And he is glad!

He even joins her in her outrage when CU dares to deny Finley tenure, heading straight to Dean Whitmore (Gregg Daniel) to advocate for Finley, who had some of the most rapturous student reviews in the Task Force report! WHAT HIGHER AUTHORITY COULD THERE BE?! It takes very little pushing for Dean Whitmore to tell Brandon the issue is that several parents of Finley's students made allegations about inappropriate behavior at a retreat last year, and while anyone who's been to college would naturally assume that meant Finley molested some coeds, it's actually about his "messianic" teaching style and fears that he's using his CU courses to recruit acolytes. Still, Brandon keeps an open mind and, in a private audience with Finley, suggests that he address his critics directly. (Justly) paranoid, Finley assumes Brandon's referring not to his failure to publish but to the complaints, and accuses him of having had his mind poisoned by Dean Whitmore. Then Finley tattles to Kelly, who tars Brandon with the harshest slur a Finley follower can use: *extern*.

We barely have time to wonder if this golden couple could be torn apart by a cult leader, because we have to go to Mexico. Jack's former fiancée Christine has connected Dylan with J. Jay "Jonesy" Jones (Wings Hauser), an ex–FBI agent now working as a mercenary; Jonesy's located the Scamily, and he's willing to help Dylan get his money back in exchange for half of all funds recovered. Dylan drops everything to participate in the caper, only to find out when he gets to Punta Brava that Carrie-Anne, the foxy lady who was instrumental to Jonesy's plan, has fled; having just rudely blown off the foxiest lady *he* knows on his way out his front door, Dylan then has to call Valerie and see if she has a few days to femme fatale. Jonesy is dubious about using an amateur until he sees Valerie braless in a slip dress, whereupon his concerns melt away! Here's the gig: with Val acting as his wife, Jonesy will contrive an accidental meeting with Suzanne and Kevin; pose as an obviously shady taxidermist to get Kevin, now working as a smuggler, to propose a business deal; then Val will get horny Kevin alone and ask dumb questions about his finances to make him impress her (he's "on the cutting edge of cyber-finance," of course); finally, Jonesy will empty his account . . . somehow? (Dylan refers to his "eight million," though whether that's the full amount or just his half is unclear; as ever, the dimensions of Dylan's fortune are unknown and unknowable.)

Jonesy's plan goes off with such ease that of *course* Dylan has to complicate it when they're literally about to pack up for the airport: he won't depart Mexico without Erica. Jonesy leaves her extraction to Dylan to screw up on his own, which he quickly does: he slips in the gate after Kevin's just driven out and beckons Erica to come with him when her nanny's out of the room, but then Suzanne calls home to order Erica to take a shower before dinner (. . . she's old enough to menstruate but not to schedule her own bathing?), and is still on speaker when Erica moronically addresses Dylan by name. By this time, Kevin and Suzanne have figured out that Val is in league with Dylan, and there is truly no way this ends without them both getting turned into marlin chum if not for Jonesy heroically returning after all, *federales* in tow. Suzanne, Kevin, and all their household staff are frog-marched out; apparently it didn't occur to Suzanne to tell anyone in authority about the minor child on the premises, and Dylan seems only belatedly to remember to go find Erica's room and tell her that although she heard gunshots (and possibly heard swordplay, because yes, Kevin—a collector of "piratical material"—comes at Dylan with a fucking *cutlass*), he is alive and she is safe. *For now.*

A Very Special *90210* Book

Dylan and Brandon Deprogram Kelly

SEASON 5 | EPISODE 21
STORMY WEATHER

Reasonable people can disagree about whether the element missing from *Beverly Hills, 90210* prior to Season 5 was Amanda Woodward–style scheming, but surely we are all united in feeling that Val applying that kind of energy to blackmail-boning the likes of Ray is a waste of TV's best boobies.

What does she hope to gain? Isn't her ultimate goal for the gang to accept her? If so, how would it serve this mission for her to try to break up Ray and Donna? If not, what does she gain—more sex *with Ray*? It really says everything you need to know about this storyline that, simultaneously, Andrea has been fooling around with Peter (James C. Victor), a doctor who treated Hannah for pneumonia, and Andrea is a *lot* better at infidelity. Than Val!!!

The main thrust of "Stormy Weather" involves Kelly, who's fallen so far into The New Evolution, Prof. Finley's cult, that Brandon has enlisted Dylan to try to pull her out. The first phase finds Dylan spouting the pop-psych language of self-discovery to defend Kelly's beliefs to Donna and Clare so that Kelly thinks he's on her side. The second is a private meeting among Dylan, Kelly, and Finley, where Dylan also lightly shades Iris's New Age interests, allowing Finley to diagnose his likely resentment at having grown up with a parent who's spent her life "chasing rainbows"; when Dylan steps outside and Kelly tells Finley who Dylan's father was, Finley's (financial) interest is further piqued. Kelly makes Dylan her plus-one at the next day's "milledding," a coinage that really has nothing to do with the millennium and everything to do with wedding a wealthy older benefactor to a much younger female New Evolutionist; Kelly tells Dylan that the groom will be donating the lavish estate on which the ceremony has taken place so that Finley's organization can sell it and use the proceeds to buy a property in Oregon, which Finley plans to use as a "Learning Center." Then Kelly, giddy with her new enlightenment, passionately kisses Dylan—which Dylan later reports to Brandon in a debrief that evening; between Dylan's new perspective on Finley (that his followers seem happy and he's "not a bad guy") and Dylan's willingness to suck

CONTINUED ON PAGE 176

Outrageous Fortune:
DYLAN'S TRUST FUND

It's not your imagination: *Beverly Hills, 90210* really does make it impossible to deduce the exact size of Dylan McKay's trust fund. And it starts dissembling on that point immediately; in Dylan's first "real" episode, "The Green Room," he's pretending he's *not* rich so as not to damage his poet cred. While Dylan himself doesn't bother much with that fiction going forward, it's the smart play for the show, since as of this writing, nobody has found a way to make a risk-averse Treasury-forward portfolio good television.

But it's also frustrating, if you *are* a viewer who wonders, as we have many times, (1) how much filthy lucre this finance scion has; and more to the point, (2) how it is that he never runs out of it, given the myriad poor decisions, emotion-driven bad investments, and battles with drugs and alcohol that must have depleted it by now. Also, Dylan doesn't seem to disdain work or anything, but it's not like he ever has a *job* job. What does he put on his tax return as his field of employment—"Brooder"?

FOLLOWING A NONFORENSIC REVIEW OF
YOUNG MCKAY'S FINANCES, HERE'S WHAT WE KNOW:

. . . Not much. For most of the first three seasons, we know he has a trust fund; we know father figure Jim Walsh manages it (when Dylan will let him); and we know he has enough money to buy and maintain a '61 Porsche and a bungalow in Beverly Hills, though Dylan's ownership status of his house is unclear. It's worth noting how low-key Dylan is about the money: he re-wears outfits (sadly, one of them is that goddamn Baja top), and his primary hobby, surfing, isn't super-expensive after equipment investments are made.

We don't hear a number until the back half of Season 3, though, when the source of all these millions, Jack McKay, has gotten paroled and is maneuvering to get his hands *back* on Dylan's money. Dylan's mother, Iris, stashed her entire divorce settlement in an irrevocable trust for her son, and neither she nor Jim Walsh is wild about opening it early for Dylan, who will do just about anything to create a bond with his long-absent father, but they cave—and, in doing so, give us a number: $10 million.

Jack dies (for all intents and purposes) shortly thereafter, and Dylan is in sole charge of that money, with Jim as his advisor. Jim gives us our next clue as to Dylan's fortune a season later when he's sighing over Dylan's impulsive investment in the Peach Pit; we don't get an *amount*, but the *nature* of the resources is telling, as Jim says that "he'll always have millions." Interesting! But . . . confusing! Is the trust throwing off *that* much interest? If so, wouldn't he have to pay taxes on those gains? Or does it function like an automatic pet feeder, dropping another million of "kibble" into Dylan's bowl periodically? (There's still a tax implication!) (We are fun at parties!)

What we *can* infer from Jim's comment is that the show doesn't want us to worry our pretty little heads about the math; either Dylan has money, or he doesn't. And when he doesn't, he *really* doesn't, which is the next time we get a specific figure—after Dylan fatefully decides to fund Kevin's lab himself. Jim, fed up, fires Dylan as a client, freeing the Scamily to fleece Dylan without pesky expert Jim pointing out that moving a huge whack of money into another account all at once isn't how "investing" works; as of early in Season 5, that leaves Dylan with "nothing" except a paltry savings bond. He's somehow still got enough scratch to buy a table at the benefit he then ruins by yelling at Brandon and Kelly, and to buy booze and blow . . . so maybe they make savings bonds bigger in Beverly Hills, because where we're from, that'd cover two entrées and an Uber. Dylan's also able to afford rehab, and after *that*, he contracts Jonesy and Val to steal his money *back* from the Scamily. As Jonesy is draining Kevin's "cyber" account, he refers gleefully to "eight million," and this raises another set of questions: Did Kevin spend two mil of the ten on his dumb pirate collectibles? Hush money for the locals? Forged documents? Or is eight million just Jonesy's cut, meaning there's $16 million in play, and Kevin . . . we don't know, flipped some Microsoft stock or something?

Spoiler: There is no answer to these questions. Nor do we ever find out why Dylan needed an investor for his noir film project with Charlie when he probably has a million lying around that would cover that nut. We don't know how much he spent on travel during the period between his bride's murder and his Thanksgiving return three seasons later, or what his balance sheet looked like after several years in London (*not* a cheap city to live in), presumably supporting starving actress Brenda—and, eventually, his half-sister, Erica, after *she's* sent to London. When he returns, Dylan's living in a hotel suite again; he's paying for *Gina* to live in a hotel part of that time, and occasionally filling her room with long-stemmed roses; he's paying Matt to defend him on various drug-related charges; he's investing in the Money— er, Peach Pit again; he's giving money to a community center . . . how is the money just replenishing itself?

Is Dylan Midas? Is Dylan *Madoff*?! **IS HE D.B. COOPER?!?!**
We'll never know.

face with Kelly (maybe as part of the mission . . . and maybe not), Brandon doubts which side Dylan's actually on. Brandon has another angle to work, however, and goes to the Chancellor to demand the details of the lawsuits CU settled with Finley's disgruntled ex-students; the Chancellor finally gets sick of Brandon bugging him and decides to abandon his privacy concerns and look the other way as Brandon rifles through his files while the Chancellor's out.

From here, the plot *really* starts barreling toward its conclusion, almost as though the writers had a love triangle to reestablish while there were still enough episodes to go before the finale for it to be credible! Dylan tells Finley he will donate *all* the money for the Learning Center if Finley convinces Kelly to sleep with him. Given Kelly's current state of suggestibility, this would be the *easiest* payday of Finley's grifting career, because she goes straight to Dylan's to put the moves on him and simply refuses to believe Dylan demanded that Finley talk her into it. Also on the premises are Brandon and Greg (Stan Cahill), Finley's first teaching assistant, whom Brandon's tracked down from the information in his lawsuit. Kelly initially dismisses Greg as a "negator," but then he shows her a photo of himself at *his* milledding to a silver-haired tobacco heiress who funded The New Evolution for its first year, and the attempted-suicide scars on his wrists. It's not clear whether Kelly was more convinced by the physical self-harm or what we're supposed to think is the extremely icky marriage between a twentysome-thing male grad student and a perfectly attractive sexagenarian woman. Either way, Kelly confronts Finley about pimping her out to Dylan; he doesn't deny it, but also lets her just leave, so maybe he's not as good at cult-leading as he thinks. The triumphant score is pretty sure Kelly is going to be just fine now forever and, outside, Brandon is pretty sure they're going to pick back up as bf/gf without any lingering issues to work through. But Dylan is also present and declines to get a lift home with the seemingly happy couple. Away from Kelly, Brandon urges Dylan to join them, but Dylan refuses: "You want to cut her in half? . . . I'm trying to do the honorable thing here, man; it ain't my style, so just let me do it, all right?" Which guy will Kelly pick now that her brain is done being cult-broken?! Prepare to spend the rest of the season not finding out!!!

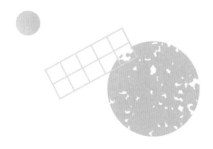

A Very Special *90210* Book

"This is going to be more memorable than I could ever imagine."

CU's Campus Rapist Targets Donna

> **SEASON 5 | EPISODE 23**
> LOVE HURTS

Dylan has been hanging out at the no-tell motel where his old rehab buddy Charlie (Jeffrey King) works—which, given the few demands made by its horny guests, is the perfect place for Charlie to noodle on his screenplay.

Dylan—having spent a whole episode this season wandering through his own subconscious while comatose—is intrigued by Charlie's concept of a hard-boiled noir that takes a turn when its protagonist starts dreaming about his past lives. He agrees to collaborate with Charlie, but soon he's distracted by an awkward matter in his own *current* life: from the reception desk, he spots Andrea on her way to commit adultery with Peter. Dylan privately tells her he knows, so he's there to talk about it if she wants, and he doesn't judge her (lucky for her; he's probably the only one of her friends who wouldn't). But getting busted, plus one more dumb fight with Jesse, convinces Andrea to tell Peter it's time for them to leave their spouses and commit to each other! Whoops: Peter might have bitched about his wife, but she put him through med school, and since he's not making big doctor bucks yet, he couldn't leave her even if he wanted to—which, by the way, he doesn't. After Peter's probably broken several traffic laws speeding away from Andrea's tragic misapprehensions, she runs out into the parking lot sobbing, and Dylan comes out to comfort her without calling her a dumbass cliché, as we probably would have done.

While Andrea's sex crime is merely embarrassing, all of CU is on edge following the rape of a student named Melody. Lenny (Tracy Fraim), a dorm friend of David's, is brought in for questioning, and though he wears the same kind of boots as the rapist and is way too into Captain Beefheart on *vinyl* to be respectable, it turns out he's not the culprit . . . this time. He tells David a vague story about going out wilding with some army buddies, while stationed at Fort Bragg after the war, and having awakened in a prison cell the next day, charged with rape; he served two years in a federal brig, and is a registered sex offender (who . . . is permitted to live in a coed college dorm?). David has no follow-up questions—as far as he's concerned, whatever Lenny may or may not have done is canceled out by his appearance on the Dean's List last year!—but before long, Lenny's record has leaked and he's getting hounded by screaming students. David dissuades him from leaving CU by promising to use his pull with President Brandon (and pathetic as it is when Brandon tries to use his fake title to be a big man, David trying to be a big man once removed is much sadder); David also gets approval to profile him for CUTV, as an ex-con success story, if Donna or Clare will help him. It's a hard pass from Clare, who didn't like Lenny even before he was a suspected rapist; Donna also refuses, then screams at David for having participated in getting Ray's band fired from the Peach Pit After Dark. (This made room for the *Flaming Lips* to play there, not that their performance was cleared for the DVDs.) David screams back that Donna's "a self-involved bitch," which isn't accurate, nor is it an effective insult when spat from under David's current shitstache.

". . . Wait, isn't there still a rapist at large?" In fact, yes! Lenny has just told Brandon he knows who it is when Donna comes home to find all the lights out in the apartment, courtesy of this balding dude named Garrett Slan (David Bowe), who'd generally made his job at the student union snack bar his hunting grounds, but who more recently stole a piece of junk mail out of Donna's unattended bag at the club and then broke into her apartment and cut the power. He's about to assault her (and her telling him "Please, I've never done this before," thus conflating sex and rape, is a framing that wouldn't fly in a writer's room today) when David lets himself in to apologize for their fight earlier. Donna screams through the door to "Dave" to leave her alone. We hear the outer door open and close, but Donna's ruse works: "Dave" comes back in with a baseball bat. Donna grabs a nearby knickknack and goes ham clubbing Slan with it; David takes his time before getting between them, and honestly, who can blame him.

Turns out Slan and Lenny were incarcerated together; Lenny was too scared to tell the cops what he knew about Slan's more recent crimes when he was called in for questioning himself, but sure, Bran will help Lenny take his dubious ethics to another school in the CU system: "The guy deserves a break." (He does?) David congratulates Donna for her cleverness in alerting him to the situation, and indeed, we are all impressed by her strong instincts to protect herself from harm. No need to worry about Donna's safety, *that's* for sure!!!

"Blame it on the watermelon."

The *Real World* One

Andrea is so guilty about *l'affaire* Peter that she's taking 20 minutes to dry a single dish. She wants to talk to Jesse, but out on his run he found a metaphor for their relationship in the form of a broken chair that they can restore for Hannah; when he asks what she wants to talk about, Andrea does that maddening only-on-TV thing and takes two minutes short of forever to whisper an unconvincing "Nothing that can't wait."

The DIY activity turns out to be fun, though, and inspired by their improved communication (and canoodling), Andrea and her also-only-on-TV Kmart-looking peignoir are inspired to confess that she's seeing a therapist about their marriage. The audience has not seen any such therapy, but assumes she's working up to admitting that she was Doing It with Peter, so it's a legit twist when it's *Jesse* who admits that *he* stepped out by boning a fellow law clerk on a trip to Kansas City.

At another ill-starred hotel, Valerie is enjoying the suite life (. . . sorry)—too much, as various dry-cleaning charges and ugly-shoe purchases have maxed out her tab. When her nonverbal offer to settle it in trade (*cough*) is declined by the hotel manager, she has to move back to Casa Walsh, a turn of events Jim is skeptical about, especially when he smells another visit from Val's friend Mary Jane. Val's also moving back in *on* Dylan, whom she runs into while he's performatively writing with Charlie at the Peach Pit, instead of in the peace and quiet of Charlie's motel. Dylan says he wants to keep it platonic with Valerie, and generally speaks to her as though she gave him an STI, but somehow she still wants to swing a leg over that snotty stick insect, and he doesn't take too much convincing.

How'd David and Clare convince the rest of The Gang to participate in their roommates-verité project for communications class? It's not important; suffice it to say that their original subject, Tuck (Joey Slotnick!), flakes on them hours before filming starts. But oh no, Clare already submitted a lengthy proposal "with character sketches"! That's how we end up watching a semi-scripted catastrophe featuring Brandon as "the Tuck," wearing a leather aviator cap and goggles with a Hawaiian shirt and practically daring the actual *Real World* Season 3's Puck Rainey to sue; Donna in an Amish nightie with a "British" accent that gives Brenda's Frahnche a run for its pounds sterling; a *Revenge of the Nerds* getup on

David that's actually a huge improvement over his usual XXXXXL gear; and Kelly getting wasted on vodka-soaked watermelon.

Said watermelon prompts a barrage of the uncomfortable revelations the writers needed to put in play with the season's end approaching, starting with Kelly's drunk overreaction to the news that Jackie is taking Mel back. Mel cheated! He lied! He "totally humiliated" Jackie! Of course, she's really talking about her suspicions regarding Brandon's absence on "fire night," and after raging that men make her sick (literally; she then rushes off to barf), she *in vino veritas*es to Brandon that she suspects he had sex with Emily Valentine while Kelly was trapped in a burning house. He's able to deny it, technically, but the moist monologue he then delivers about himself and Kelly spending their lives together is for naught: Kelly's already passed out. (We so get it.) Clare, meanwhile, is already spoiling for a fight with David thanks to his jeopardizing her grade with his poor project planning. (We so get this, too, and have these people learned nothing from Brenda and Dylan's awkward postbreakup lab partnership?! Don't work on school shit with your SOs!) When Clare sees David on the monitor comforting Donna with a hug, she accuses him of still having feelings for Donna, then makes sure David sees her making out with Steve "in character" later on. (Steve is crestfallen that Celeste has gotten engaged, but *Little* Steve is all about Clare's attentions, which Steve has to put a pillow over his lap to hide.) David admits he still loves Donna— a confession Felice would be happy to hear, since she's currently working an anyone-but-Ray angle with her dumb child—and snots that Clare still wants to Do It with Brandon.

After some more vodka-tinged pronouncements about rebounds and "overlap time," David and Clare have to edit their crapisode, and are soon arguing again—this time about whether to use the in-character footage or the "real" stuff. Things escalate when each finds tape of the other frenching third parties, and when David snits that maybe they should "just end this," Clare is more than happy to vacate her room in David's two-bedroom vest . . . for now.

Dylan's Past-Life Regression to the Old West

It's not the worst of the Zip's memorably misbegotten "concept" episodes, but Dylan's hypnosis trip back to a past life in the Old West only avoids that designation because the conceit doesn't take up the entire runtime.

Not that that's a good thing, necessarily, although watching David and Clare, recently apprised by accident of Ray's fling with Valerie, let both of *them* know that *they* know is passably entertaining, thanks to Kathleen Robertson's array of skillful stinkfaces. If only she'd applied them to Brandon's reelection campaign, which opens with most of The Gang plus the senior Walshes crashing a student senate meeting to celebrate the end of Brandon's first year of meritorious blah blah someone actually *ordered a custom cake* for this. The senate also unanimously issues a proclamation calling Brandon an "effective leader and dedicated advocate" (FOH), prompting El Braysidente to announce that he's running again. All the political talk makes Valerie horny for Brandon . . . or maybe she's just looking for any excuse to scheme against Kelly, and Kelly's upcoming trip to New York City for modeling go-sees (lol) is just the opening Valerie's been looking for to sow seeds of discord between Kelly and Brandon, *and* between Kelly and Dylan. Kelly, it will not shock you to learn, is a bitch about it.

But the real bitch in this plotline is the California legislature, which votes to raise undergrad tuition by 15 percent. Brandon knew the tuition hike could happen but didn't say anything, opening the door for good ol' Alex Diaz to run against him on a transparency platform, and win by a landslide. This is a nonsensical outcome, but it's one we endorse, because it screws over the golden boy . . .

. . . kind of like Kelly's doing in two different timelines. When Val brings a picnic basket over to Dylan's bungalow, she's box-blocked by Charlie, who informs her that Dylan's in a closed session with hypnotherapist Dr. Molly (Jane Daly). Charlie fails to protect *us* from Dylan's past-life adventures, alas, so to Sepialand we go, coming upon the "legendary" Billy McCoy (Dylan, of course) robbing a stagecoach that contains a cowering Kelly. Later, there's a bank robbery, during which Billy delegates most of the actual robbing to henchmen while sitting in a chair; and a shoot-out in a saloon, although we don't see that, possibly because the production splashed out on period-accurate spurs and ASPCA equine monitors, leaving themselves no money for squibs and other gunfight FX (or for a decent wig for Jennie Garth, who's wearing a pile of melted-looking Barbie hair with an Easter basket glued to it). Ye Olde Kelly's parodically bad magnolia acksint believes Billy is capable of meaningful change, though, and after a (deadly boring-sounding, tbh) summer of picnics and Bible study by a pond, Dylan falls in love with Ye Olde Kelly. He's reformed!

While present-day McKay is leaving a gazillion phone messages for Kelly at her New York hotel, past-life McCoy is enjoying good Christian family life, complete with ye olde rug rats and a droopy gray mustache lifted from a *Road House* costume. But of course there's that One Last Job his old fellow thieves ask him to pull, with the noble aim of saving from the hangman's noose a saloon singer Billy used to bang. Billy gets away with that caper, and packs the rescued Dixie (Michele Maika, doing alllll the acting) off to "Frisco" and a new life, only to get shot in the back by the vengeful son of a guy Billy's gang offed during a heist.

Too bad the kid couldn't have clipped Billy *before* Dylan's time travel dropped this soulmate turd in the punchbowl of the show, but here we fucking go with this. Kelly begs off the sad nonvictory party for Brandon at the Peach Pit (where else) because she's tired from her trip, but not too tired to answer the door to an agitated Dylan. Dylan's got a lot on his mind, and the feelings of his alleged best friend aren't on the list, because he and Kelly start making out, even though they hate each other.

Kelly Chooses Kelly

Andrea and Jesse have recommitted to one another just in time to move to New Haven so that Jesse can teach at Yale (lol) and Andrea can study at what had been her dream school all along.

The farewells are a multiday affair; while we hate to agree with Ray on anything at this point in the series, "How many times do you plan on saying goodbye to her?" is actually a fair question. Because we know Andrea pops back in from time to time and Jesse and Hannah can both go screw, *we'll* just give her a breezy "see ya!"

Why do we hate to agree with Ray? Because while he's always been moody and jealous, a recent trip to Portland found him shoving Donna against a wall during a fight. Now, having quit touring with his band at her request, he's complaining about her not spending enough time with him and trying to isolate her from her friends (in part because Ray's afraid Clare and David are going to dime him out to Donna for having slept with Val). Carefully, Donna tells Kelly that sometimes Ray hurts her feelings and puts her down—in other words, that he emotionally abuses her—but that she loves him; Kelly replies, "If you love him, then I guess you should probably follow your heart?" because she is the best student ever to pass through CU's *psychology department.*

To be slightly fair to Kelly: she's got her own shit going on. Dylan is convinced that he and Kelly should get back together, and tries to woo her with a first-class trip around the world. Kelly reminds him that she's still dating Brandon (and one might note that Dylan could have been confused given that she's still making out with Dylan on the reg), but she promises to think about it. The itinerary's on her desk when Val comes by to pick up some notes; it's careless of Kelly to make it so easy for Val to fuck her over.

Meanwhile, Jim finds out the reason he's been excluded from meetings at work lately is that higher-ups were getting ready to offer him a big promotion and raise . . . to move to Hong Kong. This allows Val to comment to Brandon about people getting the "travel bug" and segue smoothly to her intel about Dylan's trip. Instead of asking his supposed girlfriend about it, Brandon stomps over to confront *Dylan*, but since Dylan now believes he and Kelly are "connected in a way that [Brandon will] never understand," he DGAF and leaves Brandon to stomp back out, impotently . . .

. . . but then Brandon surprises Kelly the next day with a new pair of roller-blades (lolol), in one of which he's hidden an engagement ring: "It's no trip around the world, but I think we could take quite a journey together." Kelly astutely figures out that he's heard about Dylan's offer and is dismayed that Brandon felt he had to respond with this big and preposterous gesture; she won't say yes, but she doesn't say no, either.

Andrea and Donna both lobby Kelly to accept the proposal; Val tells Brandon she hopes Kelly leaves with Dylan because Val thinks Brandon deserves better. But if you're reading this, you probably already know how the love triangle resolves itself: Kelly tells both Brandon and Dylan, "I've made my choice, and I choose me."

We've critiqued Kelly's airy manner in addressing the guys (in the extremely unromantic location of the Peach Pit *parking lot*), and the fact that she delivers her answer to both of them at once. And there are some who will complain that choosing neither is a cop-out and a betrayal of the compact between viewer and show. But you know what? One guy who wasn't even *dating* Kelly came at her with a trip he'd spent thousands of dollars on without asking her first. And when the *other* guy heard about it, he tried to lock Kelly down with a marriage proposal after dating her on and off for one *very* rocky year. When Kelly finally is ready to tell them what she'd decided to do after each of them had been pressuring her for days, they both act annoyed that she is even trying to *talk* to them. In this moment, neither of them deserves to be dating Kelly, or *anyone else*, because they're *both* controlling turds! Kelly will mostly be wrong, about nearly everything, from here on out. But on this one, *Kelly is right*.

Ray Pushes Donna's 185-Pound Stunt Double, Bruce, Down Some Stairs

> **SEASON 5 | EPISODES 31–32**
> PS I LOVE YOU: PARTS 1 AND 2

The fifth-season finale is best known for two things, and one is antediluvian enough in its portrayal of Elle, a trans woman played by B-list cis supermodel Monika Schnarre—and Steve's "hilariously" horrified reaction to finding out she is a trans woman—that we won't dignify it further. Far less offensive, though interminable, is Dylan and Charlie's road trip to Tom Rose's house to raise financing for their movie.

Tom (*Law & Order* victim's dad James Handy) is a mobster who's keen to invest, if Dylan and Charlie can find a part for Tom's moll; he's also familiar with *Jack* McKay's work in the white-collar-scam trade. Dylan calls Christine Pettit (offscreen, boo) to see what she knows about what *Tom* knows about Jack's murder, and almost gets murdered himself as a result when Tom delivers the most baroque mind-your-own-bidness threat we've ever seen: he lures Dylan onto a funicular during a location scout, duct-tapes his mouth closed (Tom for president!), and dangles him over a gulch. Dylan evades death, but may wish he hadn't when he quits the project to take a bus back home . . . and runs into Brandon at the depot.

Brandon is also fleeing Palm Springs after a weekend designed to help him forget his troubles (Jim and Cindy moving to Hong Kong; his presidential defeat; Kelly choosing herself) only created more of them. (Not least the terrible *Midnight Cowboy* reboot he's about to embark on with Dylan.) Talked into joining the rest of The Gangsters at the KEG/Alpha Dumb Baby convention, Brandon gets so drunk on whatever Muntz has in his booze-gun contraption that Steve's Dad, Rush Sanders (Jed Allan), ejects him from a KEG dinner; hears from David and Clare that Kelly is having candlelit dinners with fellow fire survivor Alison back in L.A., and draws the same incorrect conclusion they did; gets arrested driving Val's car when one of her joints falls out of the sun visor during a traffic stop; and has a depressing (and final) confrontation with Kelly about her not understanding that they can't just go back to dating after she turned down his marriage proposal. Kelly has a point when she complains that Brandon's and Dylan's big gestures were more about competing with each other than they were about her, but if that was her rationale for choosing herself, why isn't she still, you know, choosing herself? Or Alison, who probably has lingering-trauma reasons for declaring that she's in love with Kelly, but is perfectly cute and brays a lot less than either of the boys? You're off the Brandon hook, lady; run!

Possibly it's because Kelly, a terrible psych major (and close friend), is clueless about what's really going on with Donna and Ray. Donna has agreed to take Ray back despite his escalating abusive behavior, if he'll come to the convention with her and cheerlead while she preps for her big speech at the Alpha reunion. If that's a test, Ray sets about failing it with a quickness, getting pissy with the valet at the hotel and siding with Felice about Donna's "inappropriate" attire. Ray then proceeds to tick every item on the abusive-partner list. He orders Donna out of the pool when he doesn't like how she's horsing around with Steve and Brandon. He upbraids her when she has to cut a horseback ride short to meet convention commitments, and blames her for his bad mood because Donna "made him" hang out with her friends. It's also "Donna's fault" that, when she tells him she's got no more time for his insecure and controlling bullshit, he gets so angry that he tussles with her on a set of outside stairs; trying to wrench away from him, she falls.

As obvious as it unfortunately is that it's Tori Spelling's 45-year-old male stunt double who takes the actual tumble, Spelling herself does a creditable job with Donna's fear and resentment in the aftermath of the incident—which is witnessed by Valerie, and immediately spun by Ray as an accident. Ray, Felice, and Kelly retrieve Donna after she's given a sprain diagnosis and shoulder sling, and Ray's attentive hovering prevents Donna from telling her mother and best friend what really happened . . . but if Kelly weren't so busy being a bitch about Valerie, she might notice that Donna can't meet Ray's eyes and takes a very long time to (weakly) back Ray's version of events. Even Felice thinks Ray's supportive "nursing" means he might have what it takes to "fit in" after all, and while he might have won over Felice at last, all he's getting from Donna is wounded glaring. Instead, when Val tells Donna she has Donna's back, Donna unloads on Valerie: "You're not my friend. You're not anybody's friend."

That's not entirely true; when Val wends her way back to the Zip, she finds that Casa Walsh has been sold—but Brandon has forgiven her for the wacky-tobacky incident, thanks to their long history as friends, which, he proclaims, is all they should be. But watching old home videos has the golden boy feeling nostalgic, and apparently horny, because we end Season 5 with Brandon succumbing to Valerie's woo and treating her to his signature sex move: gnawing most of his make-out partner's face.

SEASON *Six*

Comings

COLIN ROBBINS

Kelly chooses herself at the end of the fifth season—then comes back for Season 6 with a New York "artist" boyfriend, Colin (Jason Wiles). Kelly never quite has his full attention, thanks to his sugar-mama relationship with his art dealer, Claudia (Mary Crosby); and his nose-candy relationship with his *drug* dealer. After "helping" Kelly get addicted to cocaine, then getting dumped after Kelly goes to rehab, Colin takes up with Valerie, who'd been crushing on him for years after crossing paths with him on a teen tour of Europe in their earlier days. She's repaid when Colin jumps the bail Valerie put up the collateral for, but he's apprehended when Steve and Brandon blunder into the same dive bar he and his shitstache are hiding out in. Colin's packed off to jail, and we never see him again . . . but the craptastic mural he inflicted on the Peach Pit After Dark will be seared onto our retinas forever.

GINGER LAMONICA

The show's sixth season opens with a visit from Ginger (Elisa Donovan), Val's brassy Buffalo friend. Around the same time, people's valuables start disappearing! Val waits until a party for Kelly's birthday (which, since Season 3, has moved from spring to fall) to accuse Ginger of theft, and sure enough, it's a fair cop. Then Val drives Ginger to the airport, and we find out Val cooked up the whole thing so that Val could ingratiate herself to The Gang. It doesn't work for long, of course, and Ginger just returns, later in the season, to threaten Val with exposure if Val doesn't pay her off again, some more. By then, Val is broke, which is fine with Ginger: she'll accept a night with David in trade. Desperate, Val begs him to come (heh) through for her to preserve her position, such as it is; he agrees, but dumps Val right afterward, and apparently Ginger never returns.

TONY MARCHETTE

Dylan thinks gangster Anthony Marchette (Stanley Kamel) had his father Jack blown up, per intel from Jack's cellmate, so Dylan sets his hat for revenge, scheming to get closer to Marchette's kid, whom Dylan mistakenly believes is a son named Tony. Marchette's kid is actually a daughter named *Toni*, of course, and she's watched closely by bodyguard and Dutch uncle Bruno (Cliff Weissman). Dylan does manage to infiltrate Toni's heart, however, and despite the obvious loyalty conflicts, Dylan and Toni marry . . . but only hours later, a hit Marchette Sr. has ordered on Dylan goes (even further) awry when the hitters mistakenly kill Toni instead. Riven with guilt and grief, Marchette Sr. later dies by suicide, but not before moving Toni's grave to a secret location to screw Dylan over one last time.

s & Goings

TONI MARCHETTE

Obsessively protected by her father, Tony, Antonia Marchette (Rebecca "the Noxzema girl" Gayheart) is a CU student when she meets Dylan. His ulterior motives in befriending/ courting her give her some pause, but she's quick to forgive him and to take his side when her father's alleged role in *Dylan*'s father's death comes to light. Granted, her judgment may be affected by the fact that her only friendship is apparently with her bodyguard, Bruno (The Gang is obliged to step up to throw her a last-minute bachelorette party), but Toni is generally a sweet soul and kind to stray animals.

SUSAN KEATS

Season 6 finds Brandon committing to CU's student newspaper, the *Condor*, just in time for it to welcome a new editor-in-chief: Susan Keats (Emma Caulfield). The model is clearly snappy banter in the style of *The Front Page*, and sometimes the producers and stars almost get there! Though Susan can tell Brandon is an egomaniac, and kind of a male chauvinist pig, the two become a couple, and decide to spend the summer before their senior year of college road-tripping together; Brandon even turns down a prestigious internship at a grown-up newspaper to do it. Then, behind his back, Susan takes a job as a youth advisor on "Campaign '96" (no presidential candidate specified). Brandon screams his disappointment into her face and dumps her the next day.

JOE BRADLEY

Donna's relationship with wholesome Joe (Cameron Bancroft) seems almost preordained: he's the CU quarterback, she's a member of the Rose Court; he's waiting until marriage to have sex, so is Donna. But their pairing gets off to a rocky start when he has to defend Donna physically from Ray, who's not trying to hear it's over, and who then sues Joe for breaking his arm. The subsequent legal proceeding makes a mockery of both justice and journalism, but rids us of Ray. Alas, Joe's troubles have just begun. After a(n inadvertently hilarious) collapse during a skydiving outing, Joe discovers he has a heart problem. (Yes, he's a Division I QB; no, we don't know why this condition wasn't corrected when he was in Pop Warner.) Joe's ticker gets fixed, but his NFL dreams get dashed, and he opts to return to his hometown of Beaver Falls, PA (hee), to coach high school football. The marriage proposal he hopes will induce Donna to join him there fails to do so, and he leaves town forever.

JONATHAN CASTEN

Brandon is threatened in his relationship with Susan when Jonathan Casten (Carl T. Evans) comes through town.

Now a glamorous freelance writer racking up magazine covers, Jonathan was formerly the editor of the *Condor*, Susan's mentor, and her ex. Brandon is perturbed by the bond the two of them have—and rightly so, since Jonathan apparently regrets breaking up with Susan. He tries to break up Susan and Brandon for several episodes before giving up and leaving town again.

RYAN & AUSTIN SANDERS

The fact that *Steve* calls his half-brothers Austin (Travis Wester) and Ryan (Tori's brother, Randy Spelling, future IRL life coach—you heard us) "flying monkey boys" should tell you what you're dealing with here, and Rush's inconsistent parenting is probably the common denominator. Austin and Ryan open their tenure on the show by sneaking into the PPAD to try to get drunk, then vandalizing Steve's car. They're next seen at a party at the Walsh house that culminates in Ryan going to the hospital with alcohol poisoning. Future appearances include a Peeping Tom "caper" we're supposed to think is funny and romantic competition for Kelly's half-sister, Joy (we'll get to her), but at some point, either Travis Wester left the business or the budget only had room for a Spelling, because by the end of the series, only Amherst College pre-med student (lllllllol) Ryan remained to butt heads with Steve over his academic future (and possibly to set up a spinoff that never happened).

JOAN DIAMOND

This is a lot of baloney to try to justify Joe E. Tata's berth in the opening credits. When Steve organizes a Roger Corman film festival, Nat is reminded of both the part he played in a roller derby film back in his acting days, and his cute old girlfriend Joan (Julie Parrish), with whom he broke up under parental pressure because he was Catholic and she was Jewish. Steve schemes to reunite Nat and Joan, and it works—maybe too well, as Joan gets unexpectedly pregnant. Joan can, one would think, be forgiven for not being terribly conscientious about contraception given that Parrish was 55 years old at the time of her first appearance on the show, but fine. Joan and Nat go on to marry and she safely delivers a baby, Frankie.

BILL TAYLOR

Is it weird to talk about a "canonical" Bill Taylor when the character's primary attribute is his tendency *not* to show up for things? Probably, but there *are* two Bill Taylors. There's the one with no lines from The Gang's high school graduation who looks like the Monopoly guy; and then there's the one we all remember: John Reilly, aka *General Hospital*'s Sean Donely. Bill says he's coming to town, then flakes on plans with Kelly, numerous times during the series. The most notorious instances include when Kelly skips the dance with Shaw, only to get stood up at the Peach Pit; and when Bill says he's moving to L.A., then stands Kelly up with the realtor, leaving her an apologetic check, which she uses to snort cocaine. And when he *is* around, there's always drama—the college-graduation party he throws Kelly to pre-apologize for having to go to jail *that very night*; the affair with Valerie's mother that ends with Bill runaway-grooming the sitch mere minutes after both daughters made their peace with the match; the list goes on. It's telling that Bill's last appearance in the series—though not the last time he screws up!—is at a wedding that doesn't happen.

DANNY FIVE

When Colin decides Kelly's doing too much coke, Kelly goes around him to his dealer, Danny Five (Gordon Currie). Whether it's all the Colombian marching powder she's doing; the reddish-brown dye job and manky goatee Currie's sporting; or fighting off a fellow dealer who expects payment in sexual favors, Kelly's too distracted to notice that Currie also played Cousin Bobby, the Walshes' relative with a disability with whom Kelly had a contested flirtation in Season 2.

TARA MARKS

While in rehab for cocaine abuse, Kelly rooms with a runaway named Tara Marks (Paige Moss). (BMW driver Kelly is in treatment in the same facility as a penniless teenager with no means of support? Seems unlikely, but okay!) Kelly is kind to Tara and offers to let her stay at the beach apartment once she's discharged from the hospital, despite the bad vibes Donna and Clare feel radiating off Tara. Donna's and Clare's instincts are very sound, as Tara becomes obsessed with Kelly: she interferes with Kelly's attempts to date a cute doctor, gives herself a hair

makeover to resemble Kelly, and hits on Brandon to see what it's like to be with the kind of guys Kelly dates. The hair incident is what finally convinces Kelly to ask Tara to leave, but Tara's not ready to say goodbye, forcing Kelly at gunpoint to drive them to a cliff by the beach, where Tara intends to kill them both with carbon monoxide poisoning. Kelly tricks Tara into giving up her gun and shoots out the windshield; in the hospital, Tara is reunited with her apparently loving mother—all thanks to St. Kelly, of course.

PRINCE CARL

Okay, so . . . Clare knows a Prince? His name is Carl (Nick Kiriazis), and while we're told he's the heir to a throne somewhere in Europe (unclear), his accent lets us know he was raised in New Jersey. While Clare remembers him as an annoying brat who always skated on the consequences of his mischief due to his title, he's grown into a real smooth smoothie who does an end run around Clare by ingratiating himself to Steve for a few episodes. By the time Steve has agreed to let Carl throw him a 21st-birthday party on the *Queen Mary*, Prince Carl has no compunction about telling Steve he's going to try to get Clare to break up with Steve for him, and Steve just lets it happen without telling Clare what's going on? Carl seems to think he and Clare are destined because their mothers were friends. Clare does not agree, and Carl returns to the Duchy of Passaic or wherever the hell he came from.

Goings

DYLAN MCKAY

Shattered by the accidental assassination of his brand-new wife, Toni, Dylan decides not to revive his vendetta against her father—even though, to be fair, Tony Marchette's attempt to murder Dylan himself is the kind of escalation of hostilities few would fault Dylan for answering with violence. Instead, Dylan loads Toni's rescue cat, Trouble, into a precarious box on the back of his motorcycle (do not do this, dear reader!) and departs Los Angeles. Before long, we hear he has ended up in Europe, to live with Brenda, occasionally sending telegrams to mark special occasions. When Erica resurfaces in Los Angeles, in Season 8, as a teen sex worker—rescued by the spectacular reporting of Brandon Walsh in the *Beverly Beat*, of course—an offscreen Dylan sends for her to come live with him overseas. Does this mean Dylan and Brenda find lasting happiness together in Europe, the continent from which no one ever returns? Maybe . . . maybe not!

"To hell with these people! To hell with you."

Val and Ginger Run the Good-Con/Bad-Con on The Gang

SEASON 6 | EPISODE 2
BUFFALO GALS

A gangster told Dylan that *another* gangster, Tony Marchette (Stanley Kamel), killed Dylan's father.

Does Dylan bother to verify that information instead of just taking at his word a criminal who's well motivated to shift suspicion off himself? Does he reach out to Jonesy, Christine, or another "industry professional" to help him investigate/bring Marchette to justice? No and no. He enlists *Brandon's* help to research Marchette and his movements (including "a GIF file from the internet," hee), and stakes out Marchette in a convertible, *with the top down*, "disguised" in a windbreaker straight out of a "beachcomb your way to a lucrative retirement!" ad. Dylan continues sucking at covert-itude by tailing Marchette and his entourage into a small elevator, where he openly glares at Marchette the entire time; and on to Marchette's office, where he lets one of Marchette's goons get a niiiiice long look at him—*and* drops the print-out of Marchette's picture he'd brought along, which the goon has to hand back to him, so Brandon's condescending warnings that Dylan be careful aren't totally off-base.

Brandon's got enough on his plate without worrying about Minuscule Poirot: Casa Walsh fell out of escrow, basically in the middle of a KEG rave (yes, another one) Steve threw (no, he never learns) that leaves the place trashed. Fortunately, a montage of cleanup and furniture rearrangement comes along to reset the house, though it fails to explain who exactly is going to be covering the mortgage. Brandon's probably hoping to reset his relationship with Kelly when he shows up at the beach apartment with birthday flowers . . . only to run into Kelly's new love interest, "New York" "artist" Colin (Jason Wiles), coming out of her room. "So much for 'I choose me,'" Brandon grumbles, and we would resent having to agree with him, but we're too busy using graphing calculators to figure out how Kelly turned 18 in an episode that aired in *March* of 1993, and is now turning 21 in September of 1995.

Yes, Kelly's turning 21, not 71, so it's baffling that she also "chooses" to celebrate reaching drinking age with a Dave Koz concert. (*Colin's* not even going! Alas, it's so he can finish his gift for Kelly, a garish reimagining of the Sistine Chapel with a birthday cake.) But Kelly's choice of concert isn't as mystifying as the lengths Val will go to get The Gang and its bitchy queen to make her one of them. Val's friend Ginger (Elisa *"Clueless"* Donovan) is visiting from Buffalo, and while her arrival corresponds pretty much precisely with valuables starting to go missing—a ring at a party on the Martins' boat; cash from a cookie jar (. . . literally) in the Casa kitchen; Steve's vulgar Cartier watch—the ring is found in Ray's coat pocket, so everyone's happy to assume *Ray* stole it. Ray somehow spent the summer in Donna's good graces, working on the Martin yacht and, you know, not facing charges for assaulting his girlfriend. Donna is, in fact, now willing to sleep with Ray, albeit when she's so drunk that he can't justify proceeding. But Ray's as uninterested as ever in diplomacy, and bolts town to clear his head, which only makes him look guiltier to Donna's friends (well, to Steve) even though the thefts continue while Ray's away. When he returns, he's reluctant to attend Kelly's birthday party, with good reason (Kelly spends much of it seated between the unchosens, Dylan and Brandon, surveying them with a slappable look of satisfaction; also, Dave Koz), but Donna orders him to accompany her or lose her number. His attendance, and the resulting near-scuffle with Steve, make for a much more effective reveal when Valerie outs *Ginger* as the thief, opening the (nifty!) false-bottomed hairspray can in Ginger's bag to reveal the remaining missing loot. Words are exchanged! Ginger stomps off! Val is hallowed with The Gang's approval and gratitude for selling out *that* friend for these "friends"!

. . . Except the whole thing's a con! Val flew Ginger out, and paid her, for just this purpose: to let Val demonstrate her loyalty to The Gang at Ginger's "expense." Ginger doesn't see why Val so desperately wants in with these dingleberries; we'd love to tell her that the show's conception of Valerie as a needy schemer ever gets more consistent, but we can't.

"'Soulmates.' Right."

Dylan and Toni Get Engaged; Susan and Brandon Deliver a Baby in an Elevator

SEASON 6 | EPISODE 9
EARTHQUAKE WEATHER

This episode features shake-ups literal and figurative—yes, there's an earthquake, but there's also Donna's ongoing struggle to get Ray out of her system.

She's finally ankled him after finding out he slept with Valerie (among other sins), but because she's a saint, and a dumb baby, when Ray appears to ask if she'll go to his new therapist with him, Donna doesn't feel she can say no. Neither Clare nor Donna's latest boyfriend prospect, CU quarterback Joe Bradley (Cameron Bancroft), thinks this is anything but a ploy by Ray . . . and even if his efforts to address his violent tendencies are sincere, his taste in therapists is terrible. Dr. Unethical shares Ray's family history with Donna, then warns Donna in private that she's "risking a potentially dangerous situation" by spending time with Ray. Why the hell did she suggest Ray reach out to Donna, then?! Anyway, when Donna's compassion for Ray doesn't extend to taking him back, he doubles down on the pumpkin-smashing of a previous episode by breaking the beach apartment's glass front door with a crowbar. Donna does leverage the story to jerk tears during a Rose Court interview, but yet another secret is uncovered when, looking at photos of past Rose Court hopefuls, Donna spots what's clearly Felice in the 1969 snapshot—belying Felice's vocal disapproval of Donna's participation. Felice swears Donna's mistaken, but she's shook.

Elsewhere, Brandon and his new love interest, CU newspaper editrix-in-chief Susan Keats (Emma Caulfield), have finally made it official after weeks of fourth-rate Hepburn/Tracy–ing. They're at a college-newspaper conference and enjoying the amenities of the hotel . . . including a rooftop pool, but when the elevator doors open and the car contains a pregnant woman, Brandon and Susan walk right in, because they don't know they're on TV. Sure enough, an earthquake hits, the elevator gets stuck, their fellow passenger's water breaks, and Brandon and Susan have to deliver the child while waiting for the power to come back on. Very long story short, it's a boy, and Mom names it Brandon (ugh).

We bet the newest Brandon is less of a baby than Kelly is about Dylan preparing to marry someone else. That's right: Dylan has cozied up to Tony Marchette's daughter, Toni (Rebecca Gayheart), in order to get closer to, then avenge himself upon, her father. But Dylan has legit fallen in love with her after knowing her for all of 12 minutes, possibly because she's the Noxzema Girl? And while they're shopping for the Hawaiian real estate that will let them escape the Montague/Crapulet drama that is their familial entanglements, Dylan ups the ante by proposing. Toni accepts; Toni's bodyguard/de facto uncle Bruno (Cliff Weissman) is shocked, but happy for them.

Kelly is . . . one of those things. She's already gotten snotty with David about his romantic relationship with Valerie, and when The Gang is thrown together by post-earthquake disarray at the Peach Pit, she marks another square on her hateful bingo card, snapping at Dylan that he didn't consider *her* feelings when he announced his engagement. She also gets snarky about the past-life-soulmates trip he laid on her last year, which is fair. Dylan tartly reminds Kelly that he "asked [her] first," remember? But she chose herself. That's also extremely fair, so Kelly has to back down, and whispers that she'd love to hate Toni but Toni seems really sweet.

Toni *is* sweet, but she still shouldn't wear a cropped halter top when she and Dylan visit Tony Sr. to share their big news. Of course, that's hardly Tony Sr.'s biggest issue with these nuptials. But Tony Sr. grits out a blessing through his evident revulsion, even bestowing upon Toni the Bible her late mother carried down the aisle. Maybe there's a détente on the horizon! . . . Nah. The door has scarcely closed on Dylan and Toni when Tony Sr. turns to his henchman-in-chief and says he wants Dylan dead.

Dylan Marries Toni, but "As Long as We Both Shall Live" Is Not Actually Very Long

SEASON 6 | EPISODE 10

ONE WEDDING AND A FUNERAL

The time has come for Dylan to go through a time-honored rite of passage: marrying the daughter of the man who killed his dad.

Sadly for Toni, the show busted its budget paying the actors playing her dad, his henchmen, his seasonal hired goons, and Toni herself, so instead of supplying her with any friends of her own, it forces her to spend the run-up to the wedding with the female Gangsters, smoking cigars (because: mid-'90s) and watching some half-assed exotic male dancing. Meanwhile, Dylan's male friends "kidnap" him to the Walsh house for a sedate bachelor party (one whiskey shot for everyone but Dylan, who gets iced tea; then there's poker) that also happens to disrupt Tony's plans to have said seasonal goons stage a break-in at Dylan's house in which Dylan himself would have been killed. Thus foiled, Tony decides to de-escalate on the day of the wedding by finding Toni—already gowned—at the beach apartment and begging her not to marry Dylan. Toni knew his blessing for their engagement wasn't sincere, and tells him he's created his own hell and will have to live in it, before flouncing off in a puff of hair he'll never see again! (Spoiler!)

Bruno comes through as Toni's substitute father, walking her up the aisle to the private beachside ceremony where only Bruno, Brandon, and a string quartet bear witness as Antonia Elizabeth weds Dylan Michael, promising, "I'm going to be with you for the rest of your life." . . . In a sense?

Officially, Dylan and Toni are planning to leave Los Angeles after the wedding to get away from their dads' bullshit, though it seems likely that Dylan's friends' intrusiveness also informed their decision: someone went over to Dylan's house after the reception to create a fire hazard, lighting the fireplace and a shitload of candles in the unattended house. The next afternoon, Steve and Nat show up in fucking tuxedos with a surprise room service tray of brunch. You think maybe the happy couple had plans for the first day of their marriage other than you nitwits watching them eat lox?

Tony tries one more time to make peace, and since Toni believes that her father is "trying," Dylan agrees to go meet him that evening. Bruno is pleased that things seem to be working out, and suggests to a fellow henchman that maybe Tony's going to offer his new son-in-law a job! The henchman who's actually in the know snorts, "If he makes it out alive, maybe he'll give him a job." Bruno figures out what's actually in the offing (as it were) and tries to warn Dylan, but Toni's taken the phone off the hook. It's raining, and Trouble the cat is missing, and Toni won't leave town without her, so she decides she will go see her father while Dylan locates the cat. Bruno tracks down Brandon at the Peach Pit to tell him what's going on. Brandon races over to Dylan's to intercept him, but Toni's already gone, and Dylan and Brandon are seconds too late to stop Tony's assassin from shooting Toni through the windshield and speeding off. When Dylan drags her out of the driver's seat, she has but a tiny trickle of blood in the corner of her mouth after getting shot in the face. Rest in peace, Noxzema Girl.

Afterward, Dylan doesn't dispute that he was the intended target, but won't talk to the cops, since it won't bring Toni back. After the funeral, a shattered Tony hands Dylan his gun and orders Dylan to end his torment by killing him, but Dylan refuses: "My father is gone. Your daughter is gone. We're even now." Dylan goes home to pack his dumb duffel bag, hug Toni's wedding gown, wrestle a just-returned Trouble into a cat carrier, and strap it to the back of his motorcycle. Brandon appears just in time for a manly goodbye hand clasp before Dylan closes this melodramatic chapter and heads off to three seasons' worth of extremely offscreen adventures with Brenda.

Accepting the Things We Cannot Change:
SUBSTANCE ABUSE AND RECOVERY IN THE ZIP

Look, neither of us is an expert in drugs or alcohol, drug or alcohol *abuse*, or recovery. Well, one of us could give you two grafs standing on her head about rye whiskey, but enough about Sarah. The point is, we may not know everything there is to know about mood-altering substances or getting sober . . . but we know more than the *Beverly Hills, 90210* writers seem to. For a show that relies so heavily on booze, powder, pills, and Alcoholics Anonymous for both character beats and sweeps-based dramatics, Bev Niners seem almost comically estranged from the realities of use, abuse, and sobriety.

In the show's defense, sometimes it does get it right: Kelly's rough-road makeup when she's jonesing for cocaine, and the guilt gifts she buys to distract her friends from her altered state and flakiness, for example. One of the few things that doesn't annoy us about the notorious drunk-at-prom sequence is Tori Spelling's deft work as a champagne-drunk teen who hasn't eaten all day, and Matt's desert acid trip is mostly goofy, but Daniel Cosgrove sells it.

The exceptions don't disprove the rule, though. Of the many depictions of controlled substances and their abuse/the aftermath that would prompt even an Amish toddler to mutter, "Mmm, yeah, not how that works," here are our nine egregious "favorites":

1. A bunch of high school boys wait around for Steve to make Mucho Mah-velous Mango Margaritas instead of just doing shots, which work faster.

2. Brandon, having gotten a DUI and a trip to the drunk tank thanks to get-ting behind the wheel after a few MMMMs, loses his license for only three weeks as the result of an offscreen hearing.

3. At a rave where "U4EA" and other stimulants are the drug coin of the realm, *heroin* addicts sit in the corner looking chilly and sad instead of just staying home.

4. David—who's been using meth by dissolving it in orange juice—tries to write a check to pay for his re-up, and when this doesn't work, he asks for a line of credit like he's in a frontier dry-goods store.

5. A writer thought putting the phrase "geezed up on coke" in Brandon's mouth during an intervention would convince Dylan to go to treatment, versus inducing everyone watching to get "geezed up" on laughing hysterically.

6. Dick's (Dan Gauthier) downward spiral proceeds directly from pot to heroin, and a suspiciously prompt fatal overdose.

7. Physician Dr. Martin fails to spot, when deployed by Donna, the *ne plus ultra* of obvious drug-seeking behavior, "I spilled the pills down the sink."

8. Characters who have attended rehab for other substances—Kelly, David—can still consume alcohol, and do so without comment.

9. Dylan is positioned in the first season as a regular attendee of Alcoholics Anony-mous meetings, and struggles with his sobriety periodically during his first stint on the show, but if he's sober, he's sober; at his sixth-season bachelor party, he does "shots" of iced tea. Dylan's *second* stint on the show features him drinking cham-pagne not five minutes into his return, and while he's obliged to go back to treatment for narcotics, he continues to drink, and no one calls *him* out on it either.

Some of this magical non-realism is born, of course, from the writers' not wishing to glamorize or encourage drinking and recreational drugs, especially when The Gang was still in high school. After that? When it comes to substance-abuse realism, we "just say no."

"The holidays are over, and so are we."

Kelly Snorts Coke with Her Dad's Check

SEASON 6 | EPISODE 17
FADE IN, FADE OUT

The not-as-clever-as-it-thinks episode title is probably referring to the rare Nat storyline nobody asked for: Steve's throwing a Roger Corman film festival at the Peach Pit for class credit.

That's how The Gang discovers that Nat was an actor in a past life, under another name. (The movie, *Unholy Rollers*, is real; Joe E. Tata really was in it, and the real Roger Corman nicely settled whatever bet he lost by appearing in this episode.) Nat's not keen to revisit those days, because he got his heart broken by a costar, Joan (Julie Parrish), who shows up at the film fest hoping to reconnect with Nat now that she's a divorced grandma.

But the title could also refer to Joe's bum-ticker-itis, which is discovered by chance when he goes to the CU infirmary about his swollen ankle. Referred to Donna's dad for a consult, Joe doesn't like what Dr. Martin has to say and gets a more favorable second opinion so that he can continue to play football. This storyline will play out for what will seem like forever, and it's all the more molasses-y when you remember that Joe's supposedly a Division I quarterback who would have had such a problem caught and corrected in junior high.

Elsewhere, we have to sit through a tiresome jealousy plot when Susan's ex, Jonathan Casten (Carl T. Evans), embarks on his previously announced campaign to get Susan back. Brandon is right to feel threatened: Jonathan is about a foot taller than the golden boy *and* living the dream freelance-journo-wise (not that any outlet would send a 23-year-old to interview Elton John, as Jonathan's doing in this episode). To protect his territory, Brandon is snotty to Jonathan on the phone, then enlists Valerie to help him scheme up a way not to pass along Jonathan's messages to Susan. It works, for now, but it's really tough to root for anyone in the situation except Susan, who needs to ditch both of these wads.

Ditto Kelly's daddy issues, honestly. *General Hospital*'s Sean Donely, John Reilly, takes over as Bill Taylor, who's back in town and making noises about staying permanently. Jackie tries to manage Kelly's optimism, and based on the times the audience *alone* has seen Bill blow Kelly off, she's right that Kelly should be wary. But Kelly is determined to believe, meeting Bill's plane at a private airstrip and acting . . . kind of flirty with him? Episode director Jason Priestley should have asked Reilly and Jennie Garth to dial back the weird sugar-baby chemistry that's happening in their scenes, but on the other hand, the writing is at times unexpectedly insightful on the ways a grown child might rationalize an indifferent parent. Before living down to his reputation, Bill sticks around long enough to get Kelly's hopes up with a house hunt, and to counsel her on her relationship with Colin, which is taking on water thanks to Colin's intransigence on the cocaine issue. (We mean he won't stop doing it, despite having promised to quit after the holidays.) It's not clear which of them Kelly's really talking about when she tells Bill that Colin's broken one too many promises; what *is* clear is that Colin has just blown a rail when Bill and Kelly show up at his loft to meet and be a bitch to him, respectively. Bill's almost amused by Colin's, uh, heightened state, but Kelly is furious that Colin replaced the coke Val took from him with more, and tells him they're through.

Colin's just as angry with Val when he finds out she gave that coke to Kelly, and that Kelly kept it and seethed instead of talking to him about it. IRL, someone in this chain of melodramatics would have just chucked the stuff, but this way, Kelly can still have it on hand when Bill stands her up yet again, missing a lease-signing appointment and checking out of his hotel without telling her. After a vain dash to the airport, Kelly comes home to find flowers and an apology check, and while we generally endorse throwing money at problems, Kelly's response probably isn't what Bill had in mind. After staring at herself in The Vanity Mirror of Self-Pity for a very long time, she yanks open a drawer, takes out the vial of coke, and stares at *that* for another half an hour as the soundtrack *Friday the 13th*s its concern. Finally, she taps out a line, rolls up the check, and, with a teary "Thanks, Dad," snorts her next sweeps-period obstacle.

Susan's Up for a Journalism Award for Telling "Nancy's" Abortion Story

SEASON 6 | EPISODE 19
NANCY'S CHOICE

If Kelly thought she was handling her coke habit, she finds out otherwise in an embarrassing way: one of her profs has noticed Kelly missing classes, and warns her to get her shit together in time for an upcoming exam.

David and Donna have also separately taken notice of Kelly's decline, while Val is trying to steer Colin toward sobriety by arranging a meeting for him with an art collector. Kelly declares her intention to quit coke, and gets Colin to throw out his stash . . . but when the collector is most drawn to the work Colin did while high, Colin is convinced that coke is the key to his "creativity" (our air quotes, not his, of course), and the $10,000 he nets from selling two paintings permits him to restock his pharmacy. By the end of the episode, Kelly quits quitting and gets face-deep in Colin's fresh supply.

Susan might welcome a Valium to get through the stress of *her* story: she's up for a journalism prize recognizing a piece she wrote about the decision by a pseudonymous college student, "Nancy," to terminate a pregnancy. Brandon is super-psyched about Susan's achievement until he finds out Jonathan, as Susan's former editor, has also been invited to the banquet; then Brandon's a pissy bitch about it, accusing Susan of still being in love with Jonathan as though *she* contacted the award committee and ordered them to make sure Jonathan was there to loom over Brandon. Susan tries to explain that Jonathan actually didn't want her to write Nancy's story: he's anti-choice and thought she infringed on Nancy's privacy, whereas Susan—who admits that she did have to "talk her into" letting Susan write it—feels it helped Nancy heal. Brandon has no empathy for what Susan suffered when her mentor disapproved of her, and continues pouting about the banquet so performatively that when he shows up *dressed for the event* to the *Peach Pit*, Nat is forced into ordering Brandon to go support his girlfriend and quit being a jackass already—in almost those words!

Arriving at the banquet, Brandon sees that Steve and Clare are already seated with the Chancellor and Elle, the trans woman Steve met in the Season 5 finale and who has happened to show up at the event, where she has immediately attracted the Chancellor. (Steve invades the ladies' restroom to forbid Elle from dating the lovelorn Chancellor, but Elle's interest succeeds in boosting his romantic confidence, and the less said about this transphobic mess of incorrect pronouns and improbably predatory behavior, the better.) Susan wins the award, and while we may not approve of Jonathan's politics, we must applaud *his* choice to show Brandon up by standing for Susan, as boorish Brandon fails to, when she goes to the stage. Afterward, Brandon urges Susan to tell Nancy about the prize, which Susan admits won't be hard: she's Nancy, and Jonathan fathered the fetus. Brandon responds as expected, asking, "How'd that happen?" but then blows our minds *by taking it back*: "You know what? I don't have the right to ask you that question. You don't owe me an explanation." HOLY SHIT, GROWTH *IS* POSSIBLE! Susan answers anyway: her sister had just been killed, and both she and Jonathan were drunk when they had unprotected sex; when they learned of her pregnancy, he proposed marriage. Susan's decision to terminate the pregnancy over Jonathan's objections broke them up. Then *Jonathan* comes out to say, "I didn't think that I could forgive you, but I was wrong." It's unclear what Jonathan feels he was wrong about, but Susan seems relieved, and since Brandon also assures her that knowing she had an abortion before she met him doesn't change his opinion of her, Nancy made the right Choice after all.

"We'll get a little light-headed, and then we'll fall asleep, friends forever."

Tara Tries, but Fails, to Kill Kelly

SEASON 6 | EPISODE 28
THE BIG HURT

Considering what the A-plot is, it's *wild* how much other business the producers cram into this episode. Clare used to be friends with a literal prince?

Supposedly, Carl is the scion of some royal European line, but whenever Nick Kiriazis (who plays him) opens his mouth, the viewer can only surmise that he's in line to inherit the throne of Old Metuchen. Anyway, the ballad of Clare and Carl (Carl is into Clare; royal starfucker Steve is oblivious) is just one of the many plotlines getting established now so that they can pay off in the finale. See also: Donna finding her loyalties divided between razzle-dazzle David and dependable old Joe. Donna and David are making music videos together, which so far just means he shoots her badly dancing in pleather hot pants on a burned-out car near Powerman 5000, a band; Joe is scandalized by Donna's sexy performance, but never wants to keep her from having her own life. (Commendable, but: having sat through Donna's awkward gyrations and push-up bras in *two* episodes by this point, we feel Joe could stand to be as vicariously embarrassed by her antics as we are.)

In the A-plot is attempted murder, a relatable issue most college juniors face. After her casual coke habit spiraled out of control, Kelly entered in-patient rehab, and was assigned to a room with a runaway named Tara (Paige Moss). After they were both discharged, Tara went to live with Kelly in the beach apartment and proceeded to engage in shady behavior, including sabotaging Kelly's budding romance with a doctor, keying Val's car, hiding a loaded gun among her few possessions, and getting her hair dyed and styled to look exactly like Kelly's. Not until Tara tries to bite Kelly's lewk does Kelly start to see what all her friends have been trying to tell her—that Tara is seriously unwell and unstable—and orders her to find other accommodations, which is where we pick back up with Kelly and her wee twin, Tara, in "The Big Hurt."

After fatally overfeeding Kelly's fish, apparently out of pure spite and not with any larger strategic plan, Tara posts up in the *Condor* darkroom to hit on Brandon; rebuffed, she babbles, "I just wanted to see what it would be like to be Kelly." On what Kelly and Tara agreed will absolutely be Tara's last day (slowest eviction ever), Tara goes for a walk on the beach, carelessly leaving her suitcase unattended for Kelly to rifle through. Upon her return, Tara learns that Kelly, having found letters from Tara's parents, contacted them to tell them where Tara is. Was Tara ever going to go to the halfway house, as promised, before Kelly went snooping? We'll never know, because when she finds out about this betrayal, she puts a new plan in motion: she orders Kelly, at gunpoint, to drive them down to an oceanside overlook. Kelly tries to flee on foot; Tara knocks her out with the butt of her gun and, while Kelly is unconscious, ties her wrists to the steering wheel and rigs up a hose to pump carbon monoxide into the car. Kelly wakes up to learn that Tara's done the research and determined this murder-suicide method to be the most "gentle": "This isn't going to hurt." Kelly eventually figures out that she should play along, and convinces Tara to let her face her future with her hands free. Tara unties her, and Kelly has the sense not just to grab the gun but also to shoot a couple of holes in the windshield and empty the rest of the ammo into the sky while Tara sobs, "Friends don't lie! Friends don't lie." Of course, *we* know Kelly was never Tara's friend: she was in this to soak up Tara's adulation and, once Tara is sedated, on suicide watch, and in a locked ward, Tara's mother's gratitude: "Kelly, we know she would have died if it wasn't for you. Bless you." Between this show's two blonde angels, it's impossible to predict which of them will actually get canonized first!

It's Steve's 21st Birthday, but Colin Isn't Invited, and Neither Is Susan's Career

SEASON 6 | EPISODES 31–32
YOU SAY IT'S YOUR BIRTHDAY: PARTS 1 AND 2

Steve is turning 21, so he's celebrating with a huge party on the *Queen Mary*, headlined by the Goo Goo Dolls, instead of getting a pony keg with his non-fake ID like any other frat guy in America.

In Steve's defense, this very extra blowout isn't his idea—it's Prince Carl's, and while Carl can afford it, what he's going to want in return is probably too high a metaphorical price for Steve. Carl has romantic designs on Clare; their moms were besties, so he's able to leverage having known Clare forever, her mom's-death issues, and Steve's unquestioning admiration for him. This isn't the only time the show uses Clare's orphan grief to gin up tension in her relationship with Steve, but it's the most painfully prolonged instance. Long story *somewhat* shorter: Carl uses the party to manipulate Steve into giving Carl "permission" to take a shot with Clare. Steve says nothing to Clare about this, which is dumb, and when she finds out Steve "let" Carl try to win her, she's incensed at Steve. But as usual, she can't stay mad at him. Clare asserts that Steve is *her* prince, the actual prince cedes the field, and we never find out exactly which county in New Jersey was his fiefdom.

As with most Steve/Clare aggro plots, it's much ado about nothing, but Prince Carl's grandest possible gesture gets the whole gang in one place to wrap up various season storylines . . . or plant seeds for next season. Donna spends much of the episode dodging Erik (Michael Woolson), the thirsty music manager. Joe has just gone back to Beaver Falls (hee) to coach high school football, and Donna declined to join him, so she can't use a boyfriend as an excuse, but she's still obligated to parry Erik's fairly aggressive Pepe Le Pew–ing to protect her and David's career, and it's grossly played for laughs. What's worse, Erik's true purpose is to push Donna and David back together. Again.

Also back together: Nat and Joan, although Joan isn't feeling very well, *hmmm*! Surely she's not *pregnant*, right? Because the woman is a grandmother, and also viewers don't tune in for middle-agers' birth control fails? (More than once, anyway. Jackie Taylor was one thing but enough already.) If only *that* development had taken place offscreen instead of Dylan and Brenda's reunion in the UK, but we find out about "Brylan II" secondhand when a letter Dylan sends for Steve's birthday is return-addressed from Brenda's London flat. Dylan seems to have moved on from his wife's death kiiiiind of quickly, but we still love those two together, whether we actually see it or not. Bonus: it's bound to annoy Kelly.

And speaking of women choosing themselves over Brandon, it's time for the show to character-assassinate Susan. The *Condor* power couple is planning to spend the summer on an Americana road trip; Brandon even turned down a job at the *Boston Globe* to Route 66 it with Susan. He shouldn't have, if he's serious about a journalism career (and we'll note that Susan neither asked nor expected him to turn it down), but he doesn't regret the decision, *until* a fax arrives offering Susan a job at Campaign '96. (Whose campaign, we never find out. "Politics for America!") Susan swears she's not considering it, but because she's not willing to bet her future on a college relationship, she ends up accepting the offer. Brandon feels betrayed, and proves Susan made the right call when he shoves his face *inches* from hers and screams at her for taking the job. We're meant to take Brandon's side and dismiss Susan as a hypocrite, but our issue with her behavior here isn't that she put Campaign '96 ahead of Brandon; it's that she's *apologizing* to him for thinking strategically about her professional prospects, and almost begging him to come with her to Washington. "The man behind the woman" isn't a position Brandon's ever going to want (despite his short stature making it a frequent given), so Susan's dismissed with a bratty cheek-kiss. Bye, lady. Hope the Campaign Campaign worked out!

Brandon's next stop is a peeler bar in Port Long Beach somewhere, where he, a sulking Steve, and Pauly Shore (?) are drowning their sorrows . . . just down the bar from Colin, who's jumped bail and is lying low (well, as much as he can with that hilarious "mustache") until he can buy his way onto a freighter out of town. And he's not just hiding from the cops. Valerie, who used the club as collateral for Colin's bond, has called in the Jonesy cavalry to help get her and Nat's money back. Jonesy sends a moonlighting FBI guy (Jon Hensley) who's both cute and a good investigator, but somehow it's Brandon and Steve—fresh off a barroom brawl that saw Brandon get punched *really hard* in the face, not for nothing—who end up spotting Colin by chance, chasing him into a shipyard, and delivering him to the cops. Colin says he's sorry and is hauled off to do his time, and after he completes the And We Never Saw Them Again trifecta, Val is free to make out with Agent Ballen. If only the pillow talk included Val snitching on Kelly for having previously aided and abetted Colin's escape . . .

Comings

KENNY BANNERMAN

A former colleague of Jim Walsh's, Kenny (Joey Gian) tries to straighten out the Peach Pit After Dark's finances. Apparently this is a pre-punishment for Kenny's entering into an affair with Valerie, then stringing her along with promises to leave his wife. His *actual* punishment for that is Valerie faking a pregnancy, then blackmailing him to keep it quiet. When Brandon finds out what Val's up to and dads all over her about it, she grudgingly returns the hush money, and while Kenny may never leave his wife, he does leave the show.

MARK REESE

After his stint at the paper ended in heartache, Brandon is recruited by Mark Reese (Dalton James) to run (?) the nightly news broadcast at CU's TV station. It quickly starts to seem, however, that Mark has befriended Brandon only to get close to Kelly, and while she doesn't appear to be that interested in him at first, he wears her down over time. In the course of their relationship, there are two main points of contention: that Kelly keeps delaying sex with Mark; and that she acts like she's still in love with Brandon. The latter issue isn't helped when both are up for the same graduate scholarship and Brandon gets

it, despite Mark's superior connections. Mark is so disgusted that he abandons his house for his roommate David to live in alone, and is never seen again.

JIMMY GOLD

Kelly meets retired magician Jimmy (Michael Stoyanov) when she is assigned to volunteer at a hospice for people living with AIDS. After Alison, Jimmy is the second out gay character to get a multiepisode arc, and Stoyanov does lovely, understated work that's all the more impressive given what tense-necked, mannered choices Jennie Garth gives him to play off. Kelly bravely survives the experience of getting Jimmy's blood on her hands and, if he is to be believed, makes his last days on earth a little happier than they might have been otherwise.

TRACY GAYLIAN

Hired as CUTV's news anchor in large part due to the way her legs look under the desk, Tracy (Jill Novick) is a CU junior and former farmgirl who becomes Brandon's latest brunette girlfriend. The two make it unscathed through a hostage situation at the station. They are, however, not so lucky when she goes into one of his dresser drawers, finds the wedding ring he had used to propose to Kelly in Season 5, and wrongly assumes it's for herself. Tracy loses all her dignity in the

s & Goings

midst of the crisis, but when we see her again in the Season 8 premiere, she's vacationing with her much-hotter new man and much-prettier new hair, so she comes out ahead in the end.

CLIFF YEAGER

Donna risks her life trying to save a fawn from raging wildfires, and thus requires rescue herself. The first responder is firefighter Cliff (Greg Vaughan), who is hotter than any other guy Donna ever dates. However, he leaves town for a while to work on an oil rig, during which time stupid Donna reunites with David. Cliff won't give up on Donna as long as she isn't actually married, but she sticks on David (for now), and Cliff takes off again—this time for a job at Disney World.

DICK HARRISON

It's not terribly realistic that a character ostensibly born in the mid-'70s would have a midcentury name like "Dick," but we're always happy to make Dick jokes, and anyway, let's not speak ill of the dead. Dick (Dan Gauthier) presents himself as a rival to Steve for Clare's affections when Clare tires of Steve's unmotivated frattishness; he defeats Steve in a rowing showdown (uh huh) for Clare's heart, but Steve's newfound focus wins Clare back over, and Dick and Steve end up becoming friends.

Dick seems poised to enter (hee) The Gang, until Dick's occasional pot-smoking downward-spirals him—in a matter of days, by the way—into heroin, then a fatal overdose.

TOM MILLER

Fresh off a gig on the Alaskan pipeline (sure), Tom (Kane Picoy) stops in Los Angeles to reconnect with his high school girlfriend, Valerie. She's never mentioned Tom before, and he's got about as much charisma as unsalted peanuts, but Tom's an important piece in the exposition puzzle about what really went down with Valerie and her father. Tom told Valerie that he'd go to the cops about the abuse if Valerie didn't; the ensuing confrontation between Valerie and her father ended in Valerie murdering him. Tom backs Valerie's version of events as she tries to force her mother to face the truth about her late husband's proclivities and demise. He's also yet another pawn in the Kelly/Val power struggle, but after the writers realize he's kind of boring and have Kelly break things off with him as a favor to Valerie, Tom leaves.

JOY TAYLOR

Kelly isn't the only kid Bill Taylor flakes on; Kelly's got a half-sister, Joy (Ruth Livier), whose existence Bill and Jackie Taylor have hidden from Kelly her entire life. Kelly is unsurprisingly (and understandably) a bitch about this development, but softens toward Joy, and the two of them bond over shared tales of absentee Bill. Joy returns for the big grad blowout Bill throws for Kelly, at which she makes eyes at Ryan Sanders . . . which might explain why she declined to return thereafter.

EVAN POTTER

Donna pitches Brandon a fashion-based weather report for CUTV—what could be more useful in Los Angeles than a forecast that tells you how to dress for a four-degree swing in temperature? But the gig gets a lot less fun when she discovers that, just as she did in Season 5, she's got a stalker. Garrett Slan's recent release from prison makes him the obvious suspect, but it seems he's a little *too* obvious: the real culprit is Evan (J. Trevor Edmond), a crew guy on the broadcast. When Donna figures out he's the perp, Evan takes the whole studio hostage and tries to force Donna, at gunpoint, to confess her love openly, and not just in the code he thinks she's been using to send him messages during her weather reports. Her gambit for getting him to lose track of his gun involves her attacking his face with one of her classic overly tongue-intensive kisses, but it gets the job done, and Evan is apprehended.

CHLOE DAVIS

An aspiring musical artist who comes through the club, Chloe (Natalia Cigliuti) attracts David's attention, and he offers to produce a demo with her. However, Chloe is more interested in sex with David, and triggers all of Donna's concerns about his fidelity given that David has a history with horny women in the music industry. Donna needn't worry; Chloe doesn't last long.

ABBY MALONE

After a couple of seasons of increasingly dark hinting as to what really led to Valerie's father's "suicide," Valerie's mother, Abby (Michelle Phillips, formerly of the Mamas & the Papas), shows up to ask Val to sign paperwork for a second mortgage on the family homestead. Given that this is where her husband (1) molested at least one of their children and then (2) died by suicide, you'd think Abby would be raring to get out of there, but she denies knowing the former took place . . . and it turns out the latter isn't exactly what happened either. Abby is extremely— and screechily—resistant to hearing the truth, but does accept Valerie's version of her husband's demise while swearing she knew nothing about it. That story changes later in the series, when Abby claims she did know but hoped her husband would get help; that doesn't come out until after Abby's been left at the altar by Bill Taylor, then gotten married to a much younger man, only to suffer a vengeance box-block by Valerie. (Did we mention shit gets rull soapy at the end here?)

CELIA MARTIN

All of a sudden, toward the end of Season 7, Donna suddenly has extended family—specifically, her paternal grandmother, Celia (June Lockhart). When Donna brings David with her on a visit to Celia's house, we get the backstory on her marriage, which Tori Spelling and Brian Austin Green perform as Celia and John Sr.: they met during World War II at a USO event. Before he was sent overseas, they married, and she became pregnant with Donna's father. Then John Sr. was killed in action, and Celia never remarried. Celia plants the seed (heh) for Donna to question whether remaining a virgin until marriage is the right choice for her, or if she should enthusiastically accept all the love the universe makes available to her while she's still alive to enjoy it— so when Donna does sleep with David in the Season 7 finale, he has Celia to thank.

ROB ANDREWS

We just noticed this: so many of Jason Lewis's standout TV roles have him playing an actor, and that's what he's doing here as Rob Andrews, Indiana carpenter-turned-thespian and Valerie love interest. Rob's utterly forgettable arc involves Valerie scheming with his manager to convince him to do a particular movie; hiring Valerie as his manager; and getting disgusted with the entire business we call show after a single bad review—not even of his acting; of the movie!—and moving back to Indiana. What a baby.

DERRICK DRISCOLL

There's not much Valerie won't do to get under Kelly's skin—including trying to sign on as an investment client of Kelly's father. Because Val's not using the correct side of her brain to make this decision, she's a perfect mark for Derrick Driscoll (Corin "Parker Lewis" Nemec!), who's posing as one of Bill's associates as part of a big-store con. Driscoll folds the tents as soon as he gets Val's nest egg, leaving her screwed penniless for the second season finale in a row . . . though for what it's worth, if she *had* invested directly with Bill, the outcome probably wouldn't have been much different.

Goings

CLARE & CHANCELLOR ARNOLD

Clare takes a while to come around on the idea of her father dating Steve's mother (while Clare and Steve themselves are still dating), partly out of fear that Samantha will replace her in her father's affections. Then Samantha and the Chancellor break up due to Samantha's hectic schedule and frequent travel, and Clare gets all pissy about that. In the season finale, the Chancellor bids farewell to CU for a job in France; and in the moments after their college graduation, Clare tells Steve she's going with her father, to look after him. She invites Steve to come with them, probably not really expecting that he will, and (1) he doesn't, but also (2) he fucks Val that night, so: add Clare to the very long list of people whose lives improved after leaving The Gang and, probably as a result, never felt the need to return, even for a visit.

"All this blood. It's infected."

Kelly Might Have Caught Salad-Borne AIDS

> **SEASON 7 | EPISODE 4**
> DISAPPEARING ACT

At this point, the show has settled into a groove that's soapier than ever; three-quarters of this episode's storylines are either undoing shit that came before (like David, washing out as a solo independent music video producer and pouting back to CU) or setting up shit to pay off later:

Val is having an affair with Kenny Bannerman (Joey Gian), a financial advisor who is *definitely* getting ready to leave his wife *any day now*; and Brandon, somehow CUTV's news director despite his complete lack of broadcast qualifications, is currently casting the equally inexperienced Tracy Gaylian (Jill Novick) as his new anchorwoman now, and his next love interest later. (Brandon and his deputy, Dalton James's Mark Reese, try to calm Tracy's pre-record nerves by taking her out for a few drinks, and a scene in which two male college seniors get a younger female student they barely know *so drunk* that she passes out on the bar is a lot less hilarious now than it was probably intended to be back in 1996.)

Meanwhile, Kelly—recommitting to her studies after her cocaine-streaked junior year—is volunteering at an AIDS hospice, where she's made friends with Jimmy Gold (Michael Stoyanov, aka Blossom Russo's brother Anthony!), a close-up magician who, in this episode, is preparing to come out of semi-retirement for one last show. Perusing Jimmy's photo album, Kelly identifies Gordon, Jimmy's late partner, and comments that he "has a kind face." "Like an open invitation," says Jimmy. Maybe producers put more care into defining Jimmy as a character than is usual for anyone in a three-episode arc, or Stoyanov imbued his performance with a casual grace that this show's daytime-soap-vet guest stars didn't bother to bring to their roles, or both; Jimmy just feels more three-dimensional than what we are accustomed to seeing even from the opening-credits cast—which by the way now includes Joe E. Tata, so . . . one could also argue that *he's* bringing the average down.

Anyway, the humanity Stoyanov gives Jimmy is even more impressive given the absolute dogshit he's forced to play in this outing: chopping vegetables for a salad, Jimmy cuts himself, and when Kelly brings him paper towels, she gets his blood all over her hands. As she tries not to barf from panic, Jimmy confirms that she didn't have any cuts or even a ripped cuticle, and therefore, she's going to be fine: "You can't get AIDS this way." By 1996, everyone watching *should* have known that, but a refresher is never a bad idea. What *is* bad is the show's portrayal of everything that surrounds this accident. Kelly never got any basic safety training? This hospice doesn't employ an actual nurse? A college senior who came of age post-AIDS and has had multiple sexual partners has neither been tested herself, nor ever asked any of the dudes she's slept with whether they have been tested? She tells Jimmy—whose death is imminent— "I can't believe there's an incurable disease that kills lovers"? If she does test positive, she's prepared to *move out of her apartment*?!

But, of course, Kelly's melodramatic nightmare about coming down with "AIDS rash" doesn't come true: she does not have HIV and therefore can stop dodging Jimmy and go to his cabaret, where he slays—charming even a reflexively homophobic Steve, and using his own compromised health as a setup by getting overcome by a coughing fit and then "coughing up" the frog in his throat. Afterward, Kelly the clod says that while she was waiting for her test results she was terrified of being left alone—says this *to Jimmy*, who was *not* as lucky as she with *his* test results and *has* been left alone, not least *by Kelly herself*. (Seriously: just a few hours of training, Friendship House, damn.) Kelly remembers to tell Jimmy she's sorry she abandoned him and that she'll never do it again, which may be true if only because she won't have the chance: "It's a matter of days," he says. Kelly snuggles in close to take a photo of the two of them, because her ordeal has taught her not only to take more care with her own safer-sex practices but also that you can't get AIDS from touching an HIV-positive forehead, either.

"She's not a hostage. She's my girlfriend. We're in love."

Donna's Stalker Reveals Himself and Takes Some Hostages

We understand that Fox was determined to get as much work as possible out of this show's exhausted producers, and we empathize: scripted primetime-drama episode numbers should not *start* with a 3. Even so, it's kind of shocking how many past plotlines are revived to converge in "We Interrupt This Program."

First of all: Donna's got a stalker again. Having started doing insipid weather reports on CUTV's news show, she's attracted notice from someone unhealthily interested in her. After crossing paths with Garrett Slan in the previous episode, she reasonably assumes that he's the culprit, given that he *already stalked her* two seasons ago. After she secures a restraining order against Slan, causing him to leave town, Donna assumes she's done getting stalked and can safely return to TV. One crew guy, Rusty (Brian Donovan), has just accused Brandon of having dimed him out to the cops and is leaving for the last time when Donna returns; he levels some fair but hostile criticism of her segments before another crew guy, Evan (J. Trevor Edmond), defends her . . . then stands way too close as he picks out a lipstick for her to wear and starts talking about the gifts he's sent her, ranging from roses to a dead rat; he also admits he tried to run her over. (An unbalanced youth with violent plans for a quasi-love object? Let's call this Retread Plotline #2, Tara all over again.) Donna figures out that *Evan* is her stalker (this time) and tells Brandon, whereupon Evan reveals his gun, takes everyone in the studio hostage, and orders Brandon to put him on the air live. Kelly is watching in the student union when their show comes on and calls David, but gets his machine because he's helping produce a demo for aspiring singer-songwriter Chloe (Natalia Cigliuti)—and that would be Retread Plotline #3: a boyfriend isn't around when his girlfriend's facing death, much as Brandon wasn't around for Kelly when she was trapped (under a window) at Steve's flaming rave.

If you've ever seen a hostage situation depicted before, you know how the storyline marches through the expected signposts—sly 911 call; A/C shut off so that a delivery of cold drinks can also admit the SWAT team; gunman's wild demands for escape conveyance. What Evan actually wants from Donna is hard to determine: he thinks she's been sending him love messages through her weather reports; he thinks she loves him, and wants her to say so on the air; he also thinks she's a lying, manipulative bitch and repeatedly threatens her life. As the hours wear on and Donna gets increasingly hot and exhausted, she also yaws between strategies for saving herself. Basically, daring Evan to either kill or rape her doesn't startle him into letting her go, so Donna decides to play along with his delusions about her love for him: she's been planning to dump David, and she and Evan *should* go to South America! She wants to kiss him, but not while he's holding a gun on her! He duly puts the weapon down (see also: Tara just closing her eyes, after untying Kelly, with her gun in her lap; eyes on the prize, would-be murderers!), and Donna kisses him. Presumably the reason she jams her tongue far enough into his mouth to flick his uvula is that she's counting on Brandon—by this point, the only other hostage left—to get to it. Of course he doesn't, so Donna is forced to kiss Evan again, even *more* probingly, and while doing so kick the gun away herself. Evan dives for it, but Brandon leaps out of the control booth to tackle him, and Donna gets to the gun first and has Evan at gunpoint when SWAT bursts in (. . . again). "You said you wouldn't leave me," Evan gasps. "I lied," Donna replies. It's no "Go ahead, make my day," but since Dirty Harry never had to disarm an antagonist by *licking his larynx*, we'll let Donna have this W.

"You have to make up your mind—once and for all."

Brandon Chooses Tracy (for Now), and Valerie Tells Her Secret to Her Mother

SEASON 7 | EPISODE 20
WITH THIS RING

The aftermath of Valentine's Day is still unspooling for everyone— plus Ryan (Randy Spelling), to whom Steve is obliged to give The Talk about safer sex, but let's not dwell on that.

Let's also not dwell on the quad-wrangling among Donna, Cliff, David, and Chloe: Donna is dating Cliff on the side, to punish David for taking her for granted, or something? But she doesn't end things with David, despite observing that, "with

David, everything's just always difficult," which is extremely true. There's also the fact that Chloe has just made her big play for David by unzipping her top moments before Donna appears, which would give Donna a natural out.

This foolishness isn't interesting enough to merit a headline in Kelly's journal; that's reserved exclusively for her Brandon feels. (And possibly only happening so that Jennie Garth can hold the physical diary in front of her real-life pregnancy.) Kel's wearing a lot of black and brooding, but she might take heart if she knew Tracy and Brandon can barely get through a meeting about CUTV News's 100th broadcast without making it awkward for everyone *else* at CUTV News. See, Tracy found Kelly's refused engagement ring in Brandon's drawer, mistook it for one he intended to use to propose to Tracy, preemptively accepted, and derailed their relationship . . . and she and Brandon haven't discussed the incident since it happened a week ago. Why would they? But Tracy's ready to rumble now, unconvinced by Brandon's announcement that the ring is nothing Tracy needs to worry about. Why didn't Brandon tell Tracy about the ring before? Why doesn't he have anything else to say now? Maybe she should just leave so that he can control both sides of the conversation like he always does! . . . *Tracy* actually says that; it's not us editorializing, and we like that she's finally giving Brandon what-for, although she shouldn't waste her breath on Brandon. Her so-called boyfriend is far from contrite, acts like Tracy's being tiresomely unreasonable, and has to be told by *Kelly* that because Tracy's upset, he needs to go after her.

After another fight (and some hall-of-fame ugly crying from Jill Novick), Brandon finally realizes he should return the ring. Great news, right? Not so fast: for some goddamn reason, the jeweler is *also* played by Jason Priestley, with a risible "German" accent and seven pounds of old-age makeup. While Brandon and Heinie von Vatzefack discuss Brandon exchanging his past for his future, Kelly has also had a conversation with Tracy, and realizes *she* needs to tell Brandon how *she* still feels. That's how Kelly and Brandon end up on the sidewalk outside the jewelry store, standing two inches apart and agreeing that "they can't" and "it's too much." Agreed! Both of you, shut up! No such luck: Brandon returns to Tracy's room to give her shit for confronting Kelly, and then to give her a tacky bracelet he got in exchange for the diamond. It's a very for-Mom gift choice, especially after all this *Sturm und Drang* (. . . sorry), but Tracy is mollified. Elsewhere, Kelly takes a sad beach walk and fingers the ring, which *she* bought and is wearing on a chain around her neck.

But the sickening content is just getting started. With her mother, Abby (Michelle Phillips), about to return from San Francisco, Val is having black-and-white nightmares again, but in these, "Daddy" blames her for "making" him do terrible things. In her waking life, Val refuses to sign mortgage paperwork for the family home, but the bad dreams continue, prompting Tom (Kane Picoy) to tell Val she should have it out with Abby—now. In the middle of the night,

Val goes to Abby's hotel room and lays it out—and she does not mince words: "Rape, Mother. Incest, child abuse!" She gets a ringing slap for her trouble, but the next day, Abby comes to the club to try to mend things; she understands now why Valerie hated her all these years, but she swears she didn't know. "He told me *you* said I had to," Valerie says, a realistically monstrous detail in the portrait of Valerie's father that's more than a little surprising for this show. At last, Valerie unburdens herself: the molestation began when she was 11 and went on for years, and on the fatal night, Tom told Valerie that if she didn't (or couldn't) go to the police, he would. Valerie confronted "Daddy" and told him to leave or get help, or she'd tell the cops; her father shot himself that night, but the largest source of her guilt is that she was glad he was dead. It's rough stuff, but Tiffani Thiessen handles it ably.

And Valerie gets what she needs emotionally, to an extent. Abby will sell the house now that she knows what went on there, and gratifies Val by crying that, while she truly didn't know the abuse was going on, she should have. Valerie announces that she's going to put this part of her life behind her, completely, period, and we're not sure it works that way, but this is the means by which Tom gets written off the show forever. Sure enough, we never see him again. The ripples of this backstory, on the other hand . . .

"This is not cool; this is stupid!"

Dick Dies

SEASON 7 | EPISODE 21
STRAIGHT SHOOTER

Donna is still torn between boring, overly invested Cliff and bratty David.

Cliff takes an early lead thanks to Chloe partially disrobing in the previous episode, and to David dismissively apologizing for not being there for Donna with "the whole hostage thing." Treating your ostensible girlfriend's trauma like it's car trouble that inconvenienced *you* is grounds for dismissal where we're from, and while that may not be Felice's rationale, she's doing everything she can to steer Donna toward Cliff. Sadly, a half-assed note from David telling Donna he loves her is enough to get them back together (. . . for now), and Felice's shudder of disgust as they french speaks for us all.

But enough about the *Groundhog Day* of relationships on this show: It's time for the final turn of a Mach 2 downward spiral. Steve and Dick have permitted Brandon to get back on his basketball bullshit again, via the three-man hoops tourney their team, "the Marauders," is participating in. Their prospects look grim from the jump (so to speak) when Dick fires up a joint and immediately loses his shooting stroke—while also subjecting himself and the audience to a dad-ish lecture from Brandon. Dick and Steve accept Brandon's ultimatum about playing high, but that night, Dick gets sloppy drunk at the PPAD, and Brandon is a pill (. . . so to speak) about that too. He'll soon long for the moment when Dick was merely wasted, though, because Dick pulls Steve aside to say he's got something better than booze or pot: "China White!" Steve's not trying to hear about opiates . . . until Dick assures him that he can just snort it and not have to fuck with any needles. Intrigued, Steve tells Dick to save him a bump.

Steve will have to pick it up on the other side of the rainbow bridge, however, because the next time we see Dick, he's overdosing on the bathroom floor. Any gravity the scene might have had is dispelled like a fart in the wind by Dan Gauthier choosing to cross his eyes in his last moments; screechy acting choices by Ian Ziering as he beseeches Dick not to die; and the fact that Dick didn't just slide down a slippery slope from pot to heroin (a slope that does not exist, anyway): he was practically fired down it out of a cannon. Cliff's CPR can't forestall Dick's demise, and Val and David are left scrambling to keep scandalous photos from appearing in a listicle a scenester magazine is writing about the club . . . and themselves from appearing in court, after Steve tells authorities he thinks Dick bought the heroin at the After Dark.

Ziering is determined to get Emmy-reel footage out of this storyline by any means necessary, which is how we end up on the floor of Steve's room at Casa Walsh, watching a bleary Steve load a one-hitter. He deflects Brandon's judgment with an overwrought survivor's-guilt Mad Libs of clichés about nightmares and forks in the road. Then Steve and Brandon visit the crappish memorial to Dick that's sprung up outside the PPAD. Steve is outraged that the jetsam includes a "pot pipe," and smashes the bong, then delivers a PSA to the assembled on the dangers of controlled substances. Dick's Marauders jersey is spread out before the memorial's candles and bouquets, because nothing could pay higher tribute to "scholar-athlete" Richard Harrison than the polyester tank top of a weekend round robin.

The Gang Graduates College

Nothing could stop this dedicated group of young people from completing their studies, although cocaine, meth, fire, a cult, expulsion threats, a stalker, a *different* stalker, a date-rape accusation, a troubled runaway, and tape of a shaving-cream-covered penis did try. Now, it's time for the Class of '97 to graduate, but there's a bunch of drama they'll need to wade through first . . . and even more *after* the ceremony.

Val arrives at her second consecutive season finale having just had a smooth-talking white boy steal all her money; this time, the culprit is Derrick Driscoll (Corin Nemec), supposedly an associate of Kelly's father, Bill, but actually a con artist. Val's destitution is coming at an especially unfortunate time, since Kelly and Brandon have just reunited (ugh), and though Kelly is willing to move into the Walsh house, it's contingent on Brandon kicking Val out. Val, of course, overhears Kelly's bitchy ranting; she starts trying to guilt Brandon out of evicting her, and enlisting his friends to talk him out of it, but Brandon's interest in continuing to fuck Kelly wins out. Out of options, Val waits until everyone's at Nat's graduation party and leaves Brandon a clue-filled "goodbye" note, though he waits until *the next day* to go where David directs him: a spot on the Malibu bluffs overlooking the PCH where she and David, when he was experiencing depression, discussed jumping to their deaths. Brandon convinces Val to come with him to their graduation and promises she still has a home. It's not entirely clear how serious we're supposed to think Val was about dying by suicide: when Brandon tells her why Val is staying, Kelly (bitchily) assumes she faked it to manipulate Brandon, and Val herself is chirpy afterward. But the viewer also sees Val standing on the bluff the night before graduation; no one she knows is there to see her, so it wasn't for anyone else's benefit. Whatever: Val lives to make out with Steve at a huge Roaring '20s–themed post-grad blowout, if you can call that living.

"Wait, why is Steve making out with someone who isn't Clare?" Well, the Chancellor is leaving CU for a job in Paris. Clare blames Steve—she thinks her dad is leaving the country because Samantha broke his heart—and alternates her usual chill attitude with barbed remarks, so it's not a huge surprise when she announces that she's also going to move to Paris so that the Chancellor isn't alone. Wanly, she suggests that she and Steve could try long-distance, but Steve curtly tells her, "It's not meant to be," and "I'm sorry" is Clare's last line on the show. Kathleen Robertson has done fine as an actor, writer, and producer since this moment in her career, but she *and* Clare deserved a better send-off than that.

Speaking of deserving better: Donna, who decides that the night of her college graduation is the right time for her to have sex with David. She lights dining-room tapers, posts up in her bedroom in a *white* teddy (what else), and waits for David to get so bored alone in the living room that he comes in to see what she's doing. David's so long ago abandoned any thought of sleeping with Donna that he thinks the "surprise" she's been hyping all night is just the chance to *look* at her in her lingerie, but she tells him *this time* she definitely is going to do sex on him. "How did I get so lucky?" David asks. "You waited," Donna replies. Nikki, Ariel, Clare, Val, and Ginger would beg to differ, but sure.

Back to the Roaring '20s party: Kelly's ready to blow it off because she is being sour about every damn thing at the moment. (To be slightly fair: Jennie Garth is very noticeably pregnant at this point; of course she resents having to stand around on her swollen ankles shooting the *31st* and *32nd* episodes of this season.) Then Kelly's half-sister Joy (Ruth Livier) tells Kelly that Bill is the mysterious host, throwing the party as a graduation gift for Kelly, and Kelly consents to attend, seemingly to glare Bill in the face rather than just deny him the chance to make up for years of absentee parenting with a gesture this extra. Finally, she decides to believe Bill's desire to be in her life is sincere . . . just in time for him to get hauled off by federal marshals: he made a deal to host this dumb event, but he's about to get indicted on charges of fraud and embezzlement and will absolutely serve time, shrugging, "I'm guilty!" Kelly's so chastened by her father's selflessness that she decides she's okay being Val's housemate after all. How lucky everyone is that Princess Kelly is willing to relax her high personal standards and let them also shit in toilets blessed by her alabaster ass cheeks.

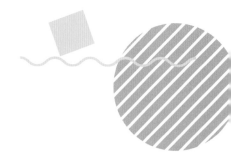

A Very Special *90210* Book

Comings

CARLY REYNOLDS

Single mom Carly (Hilary Swank!) meets Steve when he's giving some toughen-up-kid advice about soccer to Carly's red-haired moppet, Zach (Myles Jeffrey). She's not impressed, and ends up dumping a drink on his head the next time they meet, getting herself fired from her waitressing job . . . but Steve gets her a gig at the Peach Pit. Because Steve is basically a large child himself, he's able to bond strongly enough with Zach that Carly feels okay about dating, and getting serious with, Steve. A patrimony scare and various Zach-based disagreements about responsibility manage not to derail their relationship, but when Carly's father takes ill in Montana, she and Zach move back to Big Sky country to care for him, leaving her rented bungalow for various combinations of Gang roommates to cycle in and out of.

NOAH HUNTER

Someone—and we are sure we don't know who—thought that Dylan left a vacuum in the show's cast that should be filled by another brooding rich guy with an enthusiasm for aquatic diversions. Enter Noah (Vincent Young)! The Gang is on vacation in Hawaii when they happen to meet Noah, who initially presents himself as an itinerant deckhand for wealthy sailors. But a few episodes into his tenure, he reveals to Brandon that, actually,

he's the heir to Hunter Oil & Gas (or, as he seems to believe it's pronounced, "Hunner"). Brandon manages to keep this secret, which is inconvenient for Val, who is super-horny for Noah but has been reconfigured as a gold-digger for Season 8. What does Noah have to brood about, if he's so rich? He was engaged once, but his fiancée was killed in a car crash that, much later, we learn Noah caused by driving drunk, yet that does not stop him from driving drunk a *bunch*. Eventually Noah's financial secrets come out, permitting him to bail various other characters out of their dumb decisions the way Dylan did in his day. Unlike Dylan, he drifts into a relationship with Donna, who stands by him after he gets arrested for raping Val, and after he drives *so* drunk he thinks he may have struck and killed a child, but finally cuts him loose when she finds out he lied about having gone to Harvard. Very normal stuff.

DEVIN TAGGART

David's attempts to get into the music industry go through a variety of phases, one of which finds him trying to produce acts while also booking the stage at the club. David discovers a band called Cain Was Able, fronted by Devin (Phil Buckman, previously an under-five partygoer in the Cousin Bobby episode), and loves their sound, which is why it's too bad Devin is casually racist and anti-Semitic! Donna, who overhears Devin use the phrase "Jew me down" on the phone, has to prod David not to sell out his own community—or, failing that, not to promote the career of neo-Nazis. It takes a violent set at the club for David to realize Cain Was Able's fans probably aren't the kind he wants to cultivate.

TERRI SPAR

After Rush gives Steve and Brandon the free weekly paper that they re-christen the *Beverly Beat*, they hire Terri (Fatima Lowe) as "production manager" to do all the actual work while they're out loafing at the Peach Pit or "chasing stories." Terri suffers all she can before quitting offscreen, and frankly, who could blame her?

COOPER HARGROVE

Donna and Val briefly run a personal shopping business together that also evolves into event planning, a completely different skill set in which neither of them has any experience. No matter! One of their clients is Cooper Hargrove (Christopher Orr), who's presented as a Howard Hughes type, except young and hot. Because Val is under the misapprehension that Noah is broke but is still sexually attracted to him, she balances him out with Cooper for the perks. Eventually she double-books them for the same event and loses them both.

EMMA BENNETT

A relationships columnist trying (extremely hard) for *Sex and the City*–esque relevance, Emma (Angel Boris) joins the *Beat* team with two objectives in mind: a regular column and Brandon's dick. She gets both, but Brandon's guilt about sleeping with her gets in the way of the continued colleagues-with-benefits relationship Emma says she wants, and she ends up threatening him with a cassette tape (hee) that would prove to Kelly that they Did It. Finally, Emma resigns, and we thank her for her yeoman service in breaking Brandon and Kelly up, even though it doesn't last.

JANET SOSNA

Steve and Brandon replace Terri with the smart, sassy, wildly overqualified Janet (Lindsay Price). Though she tries to resist his charms, Janet starts dating Steve, who accidentally gets her pregnant sometime between the ninth and tenth seasons and convinces her to marry him. Janet also abets Steve in his decision to remake the *Beat* as a tabloid with partially or entirely fabricated stories—a development that leaves the two of them marooned in "comedy" plotlines thereafter.

JOSH HUNTER

The arrival in town of Noah's brother Josh (Michael Trucco) fleshes out Noah's back-story a little more: Josh is the product of their father's first marriage, and since Noah is their father's second wife's child, Josh always disdained him. Noah probably should have disdained Josh right back, since he's basically walking around with a full pharmacy in his luggage, and shows up just in time to re-up pillhead Donna's painkiller supply after she runs through the ones she's prescribed after a fender bender. Josh also roofies—or, as everyone on the show insists on saying, "roofs"—Val at the club, though a phone call distracts him from actually taking her somewhere to rape her. Noah takes her up to his office with him instead; a very problematic plotline about what constitutes rape when both parties are inebriated ensues, in court. Josh skates on any legal charges, but is exposed when the Rohypnol he claims to take as a sleep aid is discovered in his bag, and that's a wrap on Josh.

DR. GARY MONAHAN

The newest doctor at the free clinic where Kelly works, Dr. Monahan (George Del Hoyo) seems like a dream. Naturally, he's actually a nightmare—for Kelly, who's sexually harassed and assaulted by Monahan, but struggles to get anyone at the clinic's parent foundation to take her complaint seriously; and for viewers, who by this point in the series reflexively cringe when the show tries to take on Big Issues.

JASPER MCQUADE

Part of latter seasons' vain attempts to keep David in relevant storylines about his "music" "career," Jasper (Paul Popowich) is the lead singer of Jasper's Law, a band David joins as a keyboard player.

David nearly gets kicked out almost as quickly when bandmate Mark (Eddie Ebell) tries to blackmail David into keeping quiet about Mark's addict nonsense. Jasper takes David's side, only to see a sleazy record exec push to sign David and the band—without Jasper. A subsequent "David's Law" single gets David some attention; Jasper brings the shadiness of this to Brandon's attention, and it's so weird that Brandon elects not to do a journalism about how his friend screwed over a colleague!!

LENNY & LEAH

Leah (J. Robin Miller) comes into the clinic seeking treatment for injuries that clearly stem from some kind of domestic violence situation, and we feel even more deeply for Leah when St. Kelly goes overboard trying to help her. Leah stays with controlling husband Lenny (Christopher Daniel Barnes) in the end, because she finds out she's pregnant, but she and Lenny return in Season 9 to drive a wedge between Kelly and Matt (Daniel Cosgrove) before they've even started dating when Matt elects to represent Lenny. They're also Brandon's last big story, and just as conflict-of-interest-laden as all his other ones.

CELIA MARTIN

This season, we lose Donna's grandmother, who convinced Donna she didn't have to be married to fuck, and then died in hospital. RIP to a real one.

*"That's the good thing about amnesia: I have no idea who
I'm supposed to please so I just please myself!"*

Kelly Doesn't Realize How Lucky She Is Not to Remember Brandon

SEASON 8 | EPISODE 5
COMING HOME

"Why did this high school show continue past college graduation when four years of its characters' attending college was already pushing its luck? What could it even be *about* anymore?" You fool. You absolute child. Just look at this episode about Kelly trying to rebuild her relationship after experiencing amnesia as a result of getting shot in a drive-by in an airport parking lot, a place where such things routinely occur? FEEL STUPID YET?!

But seriously: what. It's not like we didn't all notice that the series had been sliding into prime-time soapery before this, but what screams "we are out of ideas" louder than "AMNESIA"?

As big a melodrama cliché as it is, the amnesia also doesn't draw anything new out of the performers who are primarily tasked with playing it. Real-life new mother Jennie Garth mostly seems logy, though it's funny that the behaviors still innate in Kelly—editing the living-room throw pillows; coldly staring at a stranger David's invited to crash at the beach apartment instead of pretending she doesn't mind if he stays—are consistent with what we've observed about her Being a Bitch About Everything in latter seasons; even her crush on Noah (Vincent Young) just feels like a half-assed retread of her attraction to Dylan, in that Noah is a half-assed retread of Dylan. Meanwhile, as the woman he loves recovers from trauma, Brandon makes sure she knows her inability to remember their relationship is *very annoying* to him. (Kelly has moved back into the beach apartment because it's the one place she can remember living, and only Donna has the sensitivity and consideration to tell her where her bedroom is.) Somehow, what locks in Kelly's memories of Brandon isn't *reading her journal*: it's seeing his face in print? See, Steve's father, Rush, has taken a pennysaver he owned and given it to Steve and Brandon to try to turn into a respectable free weekly; Brandon isn't exactly starting strong by putting a quarter-page photo of himself above his Editor's Letter (incorrectly identified as an "editorial") in the debut issue of what they've decided to call the *Beverly Beat*. And just to be clear: it's not Brandon's *writing* that strikes a chord with Kelly; it's beholding his intensely concerned eyebrows in black and white.

Fortunately for Brandon, Donna brings him something to be concerned about: sweatshops! It seems as though Donna earned a degree in fashion marketing without ever learning about unethical labor practices endemic in the apparel industry, and after turning down the wrong corridor after a job interview, she is shocked to learn that undocumented workers are being paid less than minimum wage for jobs without any legal protections! While she puts Brandon (*scoff*) on the case, her personal-shopping business partner, Val, is deciding whether she wants to pursue their millionaire client, Cooper Hargrove (Christopher Orr), or continue trying to get something going with Noah despite the fact that, as far as she knows, he's broke. He's not, but that isn't the only secret he's been keeping: after she stalks him to a scenic overlook, he breaks down crying (which, in Vincent Young's case, means "trying to cry, convincing no one") and tells her his tragic backstory: he had a girlfriend named Beth, but he "lost control" driving a car she was in, killing her. In the years (sigh) to come, we'll get a lot more detail on this tale, little of it consistent, but for now: sad, right? Val is moved . . . but she's also a gold-digger this season, and Noah's soulful bereavement/intractable constipation can't compete with Cooper Hargrove's aerospace millions and insouciant charcuterie.

"My money's ruining everything!"

Erica Gets Her Pimp Arrested

SEASON 8 | EPISODE 11
DEADLINE

In any given postcollege episode, it's challenging to figure out where the show is in the inept-ownership life cycle of the Peach Pit After Dark.

Midway through the eighth season, it's David's turn to get in way over his head: his relationship with Donna is pretty much on the rocks after he forged one of her checks to cover his PPAD bills, then doubled down on dumb "business" "decisions" by borrowing money from a loan shark. Because David's as lucky as he is twatty, though, a mystery benefactor has bailed him out of the usury situation. As David makes a big show of plugging in a space heater that will be important later, Valerie offers to investigate who covered David's debt. David thinks Val only wants to ally herself sexually with whomever has that kind of money, and because Season 8 is the Val, Notorious Gold-Digger stage of *Valerie's* character life cycle, the audience is supposed to agree with David instead of thinking it's a shitty, retrograde thing to say.

When that space heater starts a fire later in the episode, David falls out of the bungling-entrepreneur tree for real, hitting every branch on the way down: the fire didn't hurt anyone physically, but it trashed the PPAD office, which is where he was living after Donna (correctly) ejected him from the beach apartment for stealing from her, so now he has to live in his car. He can't make an insurance claim because his premiums were another bill he got behind on. And he's hoping his landlady, who's already looking for an excuse to leave his ass at the curb, won't find out about the fire, but she does, and she has fully had it with his late payments and code violations. The landlady's happy to take Noah's check, though, for it is he who rescued David from both her and the loan shark. Val's furious to learn that Noah's actually rich, because she dumped him when she thought he was "a bum," and David's even more ungracious, whining that Noah's taking everything from David: his club, his dignity, and his girl. At no time does it occur to David that committing felony theft against Donna means he functionally stole Donna from *himself*, but he brats at Noah that *Noah* can run the club, then. Noah mopes about his fortune's deleterious effects on relationships, although Donna doesn't seem to mind that he downplayed his wealth, and ending this iteration of her relationship with David gives new meaning to the term "angel investor."

If only Noah could underwrite a team of researchers to instruct the writers on how journalism, the Constitution, or custody of a minor child works! Instead, we get another underinformed Brandon, First-Amendment-Crusader plot. In previous episodes, Brandon and Kelly (who has regained her memory by now) rescued Dylan's half-sister Erica, who'd run away from Iris McKay's treehouse to become an underage sex worker in Los Angeles (and been recast—now Johna Stewart-Bowden is playing her, as a less simple-seeming 16 than previous actor Noley Thornton could probably have managed). Off the streets (and drugs), Erica's set to go live with Dylan in London, because it's a snap to transfer custody of a minor to a 23-year-old who's not a citizen of the country he's currently living in, when said minor is a disputed witness in a criminal case? Erica and Dylan do not speak to each other *directly* about this scheme at any time, by the way, but we can roll with that if it means Erica leaves again. First, though, Erica has to turn around and rescue *Brandon* from, well, himself. Brandon's searing *Beverly Beat* exposé (snort) on Erica's seamy life and times has run him afoul of the district attorney; when he refuses to reveal that his source for the high crimes and misdemeanors of Erica's pimp, Riggs (Vincent Irizarry), is Erica herself, the ADA has him arrested. Despite his customary supercilious attitude toward law enforcement, Brandon's somehow granted bail, and gives his blessing to Erica's plan: if she can get Riggs arrested on totally separate charges, the DA won't need Brandon to name Erica as a source.

You're right: that *doesn't* make any sense. Brandon and Kelly getting to sit in an unmarked police car and listen in while a wired-up Erica finds Riggs at a newsstand (?) and induces him to sell drugs to an undercover cop doesn't make any sense either. Why wouldn't LAPD just . . . send in an undercover cop and get Riggs on a straight buy-and-bust? Why is a minor child coming up with, then participating in, a setup this dangerous? No matter: Riggs is arrested; Brandon is vindicated; Erica is put on a transatlantic flight in a Hillary Clinton–esque red sheath dress and frock coat; and we never see her again.

"I didn't know how wrong this would feel."

Brandon Cheats on Kelly

"Santa Knows" is equal parts predictable *Beverly Hills, 90210* Christmas-episode elements—a child's faith in Santa is restored; a Poor Little Rich Boy learns to love the holidays thanks to St. Donna, even though a lifetime of antiseptic staff-organized Christmases threatened to stunt his capacity for yuletide wonder—and soapy wild cards designed to lure viewers back in the new year.

Or, perhaps, reassure said viewers that David *isn't* a complete self-absorbed waste of time? When he's not colluding with Valerie to make Donna and Noah jealous by pretending he and Val are getting it on, David's trying to help his new friend, Ben (Esteban Powell). Ben is living at the car wash where he works (and where David used to work, for about five minutes), because Ben's parents kicked him out when he told them he's gay. Ben bought them gifts anyway, and David accompanies him to his parents' house to witness Ben's mother lamely refuse said gifts on the grounds that Ben's father will only throw them away. She can't hide them? Or change the locks on her shitty husband instead of enabling his bigotry against their child?

Nobody points this out, but doing so wouldn't make the situation any less depressing for Ben, who lies to David that he's going to stay with an aunt and uncle, probably to escape David's aggressive and tone-deaf "help." David figures out that this aunt and uncle don't exist, though, and returns to Ben's sad lair to confront him. Ben cries badly and gives up the razor blade he was planning to end his pain with, and David, having suffered from depression and suicidal thoughts himself, is a supportive listener. . . . Ha, no: he's shouty and impatient, and seems offended that Ben still cares about his parents' opinion. Big of David to go back to the senior Bens' house, then, and use a smug guilt trip about how he saved Ben from hurting himself to broker a holiday peace among the Ben family (during which, for the record, Ben's parents never apologize). David's Christmas bore-acle accomplished, we never see Ben again; and the universe smiles on David by bringing him closer to Valerie via the Ben situation, so now they're not just *pretending* to make out!

Neither are Brandon and Emma (Angel Boris), the *Beat*'s new try-hard Faux-rie Bradshaw. It hasn't gone any further than kissing as of the episode's beginning, but Brandon is freaked out when he comes home to find Emma and Kelly giggling in the Casa Walsh kitchen. Kelly's very interested in the twists and turns of a serialized story Emma's writing about her "friend's" pursuit of a "committed guy," not realizing who friend and guy really are. *Emma's* very interested in nailing the golden boy, and lures him to her apartment claiming that he needs to pick up her column on disk (oh, the past) because her email isn't working. Brandon *could* just tell Emma to turn the damn thing in whenever—it's the holidays, and she's not fil-ing breaking news—but he wants her just as badly. A seemingly endless montage of Danielle Steel TV-movie sex ensues.

Later, Kelly fails to clock the sleigh of guilt gifts Brandon's piling up under the tree, the overapologizing he does for being late, or the shame brows he knits for 45 minutes during a hug. Granted, she's got *mishegas* of her own at work: her free clinic's new savior, Dr. Monahan (George Del Hoyo), is a sexual harasser, and nobody at the foundation that funds the clinic's work is trying to hear it when Kelly suggests he's a creep. Even after Dr. Monahan tries to kiss her at the Christmas party, Kelly can't get any support from the foundation functionary she confides in; she's told making an official complaint at her first job out of college will make *her* look bad.

Brandon's little better than Monahan, really, although we're meant to feel sorry for him as he stammeringly tells Emma that their fling was a one-and-done. We don't feel sorry for anyone in the situation, though: not Brandon, and not Emma, whose big talk about "no strings attached" was exactly that. She's quite stung at getting dismissed by Brandon; she got him a Christmas gift, after all! So it's a sort of poetic justice that, instead of refusing that too, Brandon takes it home with him . . . and when Kelly begs to break the house rule and open just one gift before Christmas morning, Brandon lets her choose the one in his bag, which is from Emma, instead of just telling Kelly it's not for her. Kelly's thrilled to find a men's watch in the box, and hugs him; over her shoulder, Brandon suppresses a series of dread vurps. But it's probably going to be fine!

"If Valerie wins, Noah's a rapist."

The Show Bungles Yet Another Rape Story

SEASON 8 | EPISODE 22
LAW AND DISORDER

One week ago, Val woke up naked on the couch in Noah's office at the club and surmised that he had "roofed" and raped her. (The word was "roofied," even then, so it's weird that EVERYONE in the episode sounds like they're talking about replacing shingles.) Now, Val is testifying about it in her $10 million civil suit—because of course we all know this is how fast the American legal system works!

Val has an uphill battle here, not only because the nature of the crime means she can't remember exactly what happened, but also because all her so-called friends (other than David, who's dating her again) doubt her story and are apparently eager to sell her out. (Which of them do we think told Noah's attorney about Val's failed fake-pregnancy/blackmail scheme, which happened before Noah came to town—Kelly or Steve? Sound off in the comments!) Only Brandon seems to understand that the DA's refusal to bring criminal charges doesn't necessarily exonerate Noah, nor does Val's choice to seek damages in a civil trial mean she's acting out of greed. This is not to say Brandon is supportive of Val; instead, his wishy-washiness about the case becomes just another point of contention in his very recently reconciled relationship with Kelly.

Also being a bitch? Donna, who's spent the last week developing a full-blown prescription drug addiction. Noah's visiting brother, Josh (Michael Trucco), got her hooked on uppers so that she could function at her fashion-design job without falling asleep from the heavy painkillers originally prescribed for a back injury; now he's cut her off. Donna also can't get a refill from an ethical pharmacist, so she lies to her father about having accidentally spilled down the sink the ones he already *un*ethically prescribed her; he gives her a few days' supply, saving her having to break into his clinic's drug cabinet and snatch them herself. Officially,

Donna needs her pills to function at work, but deadline pressure plus her fuzzy head drive her to steal spec designs off the desk of a coworker named Danielle (Nicole Cannon), who doesn't dime her out for . . . reasons?

Donna's drug problem has, if nothing else, benefited her by giving her a project that keeps her away from the trial. Noah's lawyer having successfully discredited Val with her friends' testimony about her various past arrests, things look bad for her as the trial starts to wrap up—until Josh takes the stand and tells a well-edited version of the events leading up to the rape. "Reluctantly," he admits that taking a four-minute phone call left plenty of time for Noah to have dosed Val's drink. The jury finds in Val's favor (not that we ever hear what they award her), but Donna isn't present for Noah to lean on because she's on his boat, rifling through Josh's luggage in search of drugs. Josh catches her in the act, and Noah arrives shortly thereafter to scold her, but Donna has a trump card: she's found Rohypnol, prescribed to Josh! Surely Noah wouldn't turn his back on his own flesh and blood, Josh babbles, but he's wrong. Noah takes the evidence to Val and promises to back her up if she wants to use it to press criminal charges against his brother. Everyone seems to think the fact that Noah was not the one prescribed the Rohypnol means he didn't dose her with it; we know he didn't, but he absolutely *did* have sex with Val when she was unable to consent, and (now) not even he is trying to claim otherwise. Never mind! As far as The Gang's concerned, Noah is innocent! Brandon and Kelly can stop fighting and resume boning! And don't spare one more second thinking about Josh: we neeeeever see him again.

"Well, I guess this is one big happy ending for you."

Actually, They . . . Don't

> **SEASON 8 | EPISODES 31–32**
> THE WEDDING: PARTS 1 AND 2

The only thing late-season *90210* likes better than a fillerriffic two-part season finale? Torturing Valerie far out of proportion to her so-called sins.

Various other members of The Gang make Brandon and Kelly's impending wedding into a referendum on *their* romantic situations—Steve's trying to woo a married woman away from her husband, in vain; Noah outs himself as a "marriage is a tool of The Man, maaaan" douche, even though he's been engaged. But Valerie's on the outside, as usual, and grappling with a life-and-death situation with only David for help. In fact, Val's current predicament is indirectly David's fault: he broke up with her because of work stress (classic David), so she went out, got lit, and had a one-night stand . . . but didn't use a condom, and found out the next morning that her trick, Johnny, is an IV drug user. Confiding this to David, Valerie is affectingly distraught, and it's too bad Tiffani Thiessen's genuine and poignant performance is wasted on fucking David, who gets aggro with Val to get tested, then acts put-upon that she's frightened and he has to keep pushing. You initiated the breakup, dude. You don't have to be here!

Val dodges learning the truth, good or bad, for a while, but when she runs into Johnny at the PPAD, he admits that he lied about being clean: he's HIV-positive. Val, even more terrified now, finally consents to get tested, though she refuses to go in for the results until after the wedding, and the season ends on her walking into an office to get the results, which we don't get to hear, because why else would we subject ourselves to Season 9 if not to find out Val's fate?! (We'll save you the trouble: she tests negative.)

Valerie's pitch-dark journey of self-loathing and contemplating her mortality *really* does not pair well tonally with the schmaltzy agita that attends the Zip's latest wedding. Maybe that's why Dylan and Brenda decide to blow it off? (But they offer to meet up with Brandon and Kelly on their honeymoon in Corsica, because honeymooning with your twin and her boyfriend, who used to fuck your wife, isn't weird at all. Talk about dark!) Or maybe they see from across the pond what the audience also figured out several episodes ago: the "Brelly" engagement is one of those "it's level up or break up" moves, and they chose wrong. Friends and relatives mouth bromides about pre-wedding jitters and "natural" anxiety, but between the arguments over the rings, the conversation with the minister that reveals Brandon and Kelly haven't had *any* meaningful discussions about kids or finances, and Brandon *the writer's* aversion to scripting his own vows (not to mention the C-minus draft he comes up with), it seems like someone should suggest they trust their instincts. Someone like Jackie would be the logical choice, but she's more invested in their going through with it than you'd think given that *her* biggest reminder of how spectacularly a marriage can fail, Bill, is there to cowalk Kelly down the aisle. Who is still inviting Bill anywhere, by the way? The guy *just* ditched Valerie's mother, Abby, at the altar—minutes after he got out of jail!

But it's not until Brandon and Kelly run into each other outside their respective dressing rooms at the church that common sense prevails. After an awkward exchange of tellingly anodyne and sad wedding gifts, bride and groom finish each other's sentences: they love each other; they don't want to get married. They walk down the aisle together and smugly announce their decision to the assembled, all of whom stay for yet another very basic Casa Walsh reception instead of grabbing their gifts and bolting, as we would. Before their first/last dance, Kelly and Brandon pleasantly agree to break all the way up instead of returning to the passionless limbo that got them here in the first place. Good thinking! No reason for a late-night wedding-cake snack to turn into a valedictory bone in the Season 9 premiere, no sirree!

Comings

DYLAN MCKAY

We still have so many questions about why Dylan is back in the Zip. I mean, we know why from a meta standpoint: the show needed a shot in the arm from a famous original Gangster with so many old-guard cast departing. Still: why is he initially salty about Brenda, with whom it was implied he was content-edly coupled offscreen (*as God intended*) for some years, and then why doesn't he mention her again? They shared custody of his half-sister, Erica, right? Why doesn't he mention Erica either? Why is his addiction to narcotics back, and then gone, but he's merrily drinking alcohol throughout as though one recovery has nothing to do with another? And seriously, what is the deal with his inheritance when yet another sentimental investment in the Peach Pit doesn't make a dent in it? We understand intellectually that he's come back to (1) stake his claim as Kelly's soulmate and (2) shore up the Nielsens, but would it have killed the ninth- and tenth-season writers to watch a couple of episodes of his original run?

DANIEL HUNTER

Bringing the great Ray Wise in to play father Daniel to Vincent Young's Noah really just raises more questions about how much thought went into the creation of Noah's character. For one thing,

how could a man with such crisp diction have sired such a mushmouthed son? For another, producers seem already to have forgotten that Noah is supposed to be from "back east," installing Daniel and his wife, Noah's mother Blythe (Leigh Taylor-Young), in a cavernous west side mansion. But there isn't time to dig into these questions: shortly after telling Noah that he's run the family business into the ground, Daniel fatally shoots himself in the head.

SOPHIE BURNS

A post–*Melrose Place* Laura Leighton comes to the show early in its ninth season for a six-episode arc as Sophie Burns, who first meets Steve by chance after pulling a short con on the 3rd Street Promenade and leaping into his very illegally parked car to make her getaway. Sophie scams her way into a spot on the Walsh couch by spinning an obviously false story to Steve: she's a college student whose move into her dorm room has been delayed due to . . . reasons. She also somehow scams her way into a student loan despite not being registered in any classes. What the viewer knows, but Steve doesn't, is that she's come to L.A. to become famous, and doesn't care how. What we *all* know, but the characters don't, is that she's just a bit early to take advantage of the reality TV boom; in a few years,

she could have been a VH1 mainstay. For a while, Sophie strings Steve along for room and board while actually boning David. The latter tries to get Sophie to choose a path into the entertainment industry and pay her dues . . . but then tells her she's too good for commercials and *also* too good for porn. In the end, all of that strikes Sophie as too much work: she meets a rich dude who makes her his sugar baby, removing her from the action and allowing Steve and David to be bros again.

CARL SCHMIDT

Valerie and Abby seemed to have reached an understanding about Val's father's crimes and death back in Season 7, but either the writers weren't satisfied with it, or they just forgot about it, because after Abby's aborted engagement to Bill Taylor, she next shows up with a new fiancé, Carl Schmidt (Bruce Thomas, whom the casting agents also forgot just played Joe's brother Hank a couple of years prior). For reasons that remain obscure but play more like self-destructive decision-making than revenge, Val bones Carl the night before his and Abby's wedding. Carl, now hypnotized by Val, leaves Abby to get an annulment, which prompts Valerie to confess to Abby that she slept with him, and Abby in turn to threaten to turn Valerie in to the police for the murder of

her father. Our kingdom for a continuity editor, truly.

MATT DURNING

Apparently, a degree from Hamilton's nonexistent law school entitles Matt (Daniel Cosgrove), whose office shares a plaza with Kelly and Donna's boutique, to practice in all kinds of specialties, since we see him handling divorces, wills, and every kind of legal scrape the members of The Gang variously get into. Conveniently, Matt arrives in Kelly's life just one episode before Brandon exits the show, so even though he instantly has far more chemistry with Donna, Matt and Kelly start dating, by which we mean start fighting, about whether she really wants to be with Matt or with Dylan, in every episode until the series finale.

GINA KINCAID

Donna's Olympic-skater cousin from the "bad side of town," Gina (Vanessa Marcil) doesn't cross paths with Valerie . . . which is really too bad, because Gina is a lot better at messing with The Gang guilt-free than Valerie ever managed to be. (Not that she's awesome at it. Her scheme to extort Mel Silver after seeing him at her and Noah's After Dark strip-club "start-up" goes about as well as you'd expect.) She also has unbelievably shiny hair, and uses it to ensorcel both David and Dylan, then ping-pong between them (and we don't blame her for preferring Dylan, but he's obviously still into Kelly, while refusing to stop messing with Gina's head). Gina also struggles with an eating disorder dating back to her training days, and with resentment of Donna dating back to her childhood . . . which is not everything it seemed to be at the time, because apparently Donna's father went nuts at a key party and impregnated his wife's sister and then everyone just pretended Gina wasn't his biological child.

LAUREN DURNING

Soap-opera problem alert: Matt has a secret wife! We're given to understand that Lauren (Cari Shayne) has been living in a mental institution since fairly early in her marriage to Matt, but now she's better? Also, Matt still considers himself Lauren's husband even though he moved across the country rather than remain near enough to her to visit; and even though he never told the woman he was dating that she wasn't the only one in the picture. Soon after arriving in L.A., Lauren is told she has to stop taking the experimental drug that has caused her incredible recovery because it might kill her, so Kelly and Dylan go to Mexico to acquire MacGuffinol without a prescription. Lauren finally decides the risks of taking the drug are too great, and returns to New York, divorcing Matt and leaving him to Kelly.

BOBBI KINCAID

Gina's mother, Bobbi (Karen Austin), is what Sarah's mother would call a real piece of work. In addition to being an abusive skating mom, Bobbi spent most of Gina's trust fund on herself, so mother and daughter threaten to sue Felice, the trustee of the fund, for not taking better care of Gina's money. (How Felice and Bobbi came out of the same family of origin is beyond us . . . but then, they do have similar taste in men?) A chastened Felice agrees to replenish the fund if the Kincaids drop the suit, and Gina and Bobbi toast to a successful scam—but it's unclear whether Bobbi merely pretended to be a selfish spendthrift to aid the con, or whether Gina leveraged her mother's natural shittiness into a payday for herself. It's probably the second thing, because when Gina finds out her biological father isn't the late Rick, whom she still idolizes, but rather Dr. Martin, Bobbi doesn't bother coming back from Colorado to help Gina sort through her feelings. Even Dr. Martin's death doesn't get Bobbi on a plane to grieve the biological father of her child, who is also her sister's husband. Classy.

BEN & MICHELLE SOSNA

Janet's parents, Ben (James Shigeta) and Michelle (Leslie Ishii), pop up whenever the show's producers think we need a reminder that Janet's too good for Steve, as though every scene Janet and Steve share doesn't do that automatically. They disapprove of Steve because he's not of Japanese ancestry, and try to fix Janet up with a guy from their community. They also disapprove of Steve for employing Janet at the *Beat* and wasting her potential. Then they disapprove of Steve and Janet for getting accidentally pregnant and marrying young. You know what? The Sosnas are right most of the time. Janet, you should listen to your parents.

PIA SWANSON

Pia (Josie DiVincenzo) is a high-powered publicist—allegedly, since she (1) agrees to take on Now Wear This as a client, and (2) thinks Kelly's shifting self-righteous ethics make her a solid hire for Pia's PR firm. But a Filofax that stuffed doesn't lie!

WAYNE MOSES

When Donna comes across beach volleyballer Wayne (Shawn Christian) outside the boutique, she's immediately attracted to him, but sublimates that into an offer to have him model for her men's line. But Donna's also feeling pressured to commit in her relationship with Noah, and when Wayne offers to bring her on his beach-volleyball tour (snerk), she can't resist the attraction of a lower-key lifestyle—or some non-Noah D—so she dumps Noah and fucks Wayne. But between Wayne's insensitivity about Kelly's PTSD and a weird performance from Shawn Christian in which he always seems seconds away from giggling, Wayne is soon given the boot.

JOE PATCH

After playing a tiny role in the Season 2 Halloween episode in which Kelly is almost date-raped, Cliff Dorfman returns for a series of episodes, starting with Kelly's rape, in an alley, by Dorfman's Joe Patch. Kelly is barely holding it together at the store when Joe comes by and they recognize each other. He has started moving toward her when Kelly retrieves from her purse a handgun that Dylan has illegally acquired for her, and shoots Joe dead. When Matt comes down to deal with the immediate aftermath, he has to tell Kelly he knew him: Joe was Matt's client, and might have been incarcerated on the night he assaulted her if not for Matt's work on his behalf. YIKES.

Goings

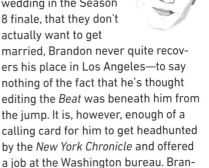

BRANDON WALSH

After he and Kelly mutually decide, minutes before their wedding in the Season 8 finale, that they don't actually want to get married, Brandon never quite recovers his place in Los Angeles—to say nothing of the fact that he's thought editing the *Beat* was beneath him from the jump. It is, however, enough of a calling card for him to get headhunted by the *New York Chronicle* and offered a job at the Washington bureau. Brandon makes some noises about turning down the job and staying in town with all the same people he's been hanging out with since high school, but given that the episode is called "Brandon Leaves," there isn't actually that much suspense about what he's going to do—and other than a couple of video messages in the series finale, he stays good and gone.

VALERIE MALONE
After yet another argle-bargle with Kelly, ostensibly about who's going to whose Thanksgiving dinner but really about Kelly (wrongly) blaming Valerie for the wedding that wasn't, Valerie finally, *finally* gets fed up with Queen Kelly's shit—and everyone else's— and decides to go back to Buffalo. Before she leaves, a détente of sorts is reached with Kelly after David, instead of just telling his stepsister to stop being such a C, puts Valerie's shit with her father on Front Street to guilt Kelly into backing down. But Valerie's still going, and the underwhelming reaction to her announcement from the so-called friends she broke her ass trying to win over for four-plus years should, we hope, tell her she made the right decision. (When she returns for the series finale, the writing starts right back in with the slut-shaming. Sigh.)

"A hundred, ninety-nine, ninety-eight, ninety-six, ninety-seven. I can count."

Noah Runs Afoul of the Law Just in Time for The Gang to Meet a Lawyer

SEASON 9 | EPISODE 4
DON'T ASK, DON'T TELL

Remember how Noah was rich, like Dylan? Well, now he's broke, like Dylan was for a while.

Noah's father, Daniel (Ray Wise), was so ashamed of having run his family's company into the ground that he died by suicide, so now Noah's also half an orphan! Like Dylan is! As far as Dylan or we know, anyway! Since *Noah* never met Dylan, all these commonalities probably wouldn't register, but then he isn't really dealing with *any* of his emotions: he's self-medicating with booze, including at his father's memorial service and . . . while driving. He gets pulled over, spectacularly fails the roadside sobriety test, and gets arrested.

Meanwhile, Noah's business partner, Val, has parental drama to deal with too. If she thought sleeping with her mother's fiancé on the eve of their wedding would just be a fun diversion, she was wrong: Carl (Bruce Thomas, hoping no one recognizes him from having played Joe's brother back in Season 6), is now obsessed with Val, and when she spurns him, he disappears from the episode, telling Abby offscreen that he intends to get their marriage annulled. Val tries to dodge Abby's increasingly frantic questions (maybe he left because you reek of desperation, Abby, damn), but finally admits that she boned Carl—and, since they're talking about husbands of Abby's with whom Val has had sexual contact, she reminds us all of Abby's greatest dereliction of maternal duty. Abby claims she tried to stop Val's father's abuse: "I failed!" "I didn't," Val replies. "Dad didn't commit suicide. I killed him." Now, nothing in Val's manner with Carl indicated that she was boning him out of revenge; certainly it would not be hard to believe that someone with Val's history of abuse might make regrettable and complicated sexual choices later in life, but that isn't actually in evidence on-screen. Eventually, Val firmly tells Abby she doesn't think it was a mistake to have murdered her father; Abby orders her to turn herself in for the crime, or Abby will.

Through all this, newly unemployed Kelly has been nagging Donna into blowing off deadlines and loafing around town with her, which is how they happen past a shopping plaza where a cute blond guy is reading the paper, but fails to notice them. Kelly, however, notices an empty storefront and announces that they're going to open a store to sell Donna's designs. Donna is timid enough to tell Kelly she can't do it, but also enough of a doormat to let Kelly ignore her worries, and one day later they're fixing up the place when that blond guy comes back to introduce himself to his new neighbors: he's Matt Durning, attorney-at-law (Daniel Cosgrove); he has an office upstairs; and he's on-site when Val calls to tell Donna about Noah's arrest. Noah is apparently still drunk in court and shrugs off Matt's attempts at lawyering, confidently entering a plea of "not gilldy" himself. (He later has trouble with "eulogy" which, based on the evidence, Vincent Young apparently thinks is pronounced "OH-logy," but no one on set cared enough to correct him.)

Noah—who we know has already *killed someone* in a car accident, for which he was presumably represented by the best attorneys Hunter Oil money could buy—is awed that Matt has a defense strategy. Thanks to a debatably faulty breathalyzer Matt discovered in his 3.5 hours as Noah's attorney, Matt gets Noah off with an extremely light fine, probation, and counseling for his alcoholism. Kelly is *less* impressed to learn that one of Matt's other clients is Lenny (Christopher Daniel "Prince Eric from *The Little Mermaid*" Barnes!), an abusive husband whose wife, Leah (J. Robin Miller), had been a patient at the clinic where Kelly used to work. Since Kelly is used to the men in her life doing whatever she wants, she's shocked when Matt tells her that lawyers and their clients aren't always best pals and that no, in fact, he's not going to drop a client just because a woman he's known for 36 hours is being a bitch about it.

"So what you're all saying is 'get the hell out of here,' right?"

Brandon . . . Leaves

Following her ahead-of-its-time attempt at a career as a cam girl (only the *very* determined could jerk it at 2000-era "live" refresh rates), grifter Sophie (Laura Leighton) has downshifted back to pursuing fame via show business.

She claims that her mysterious flyers—"Where's Sophie?" they ask, with her photo and phone number—earned her an audition for a commercial. However, when David accompanies her, the receptionist knows nothing about it, and Sophie has to do a short-con bribe to get in the door, not to mention endure a lecture from David about her cutting the line past all the people who actually have agents and take acting classes—you know, paying their dues, like David did by writing a jingle for a hemorrhoid cream ad so that he could work his way up to scoring movies? Oh wait, that's right: he flounced out on that opportunity because he thought he was too good for it, which is why he's now bothering club-goers by doing a live call-in show for college radio right where and when they would rather be dancing. Anyway: David turns on a dime at the shoot for Sophie's head shots, convincing her that it's good she failed to book the commercial because she's meant for bigger things. Thanks to the photographer's invitation, she and David end up at a sun-dappled midafternoon garden party for adult-film professionals—they just love high tea (?)—where David doesn't quite convince Sophie that her big break shouldn't be in porn. Finally, she leads David to a spot on Sunset where she's arranged the erection of a "Where's Sophie?" billboard. David's impressed by her refusal to follow the stodgy old rules of show business success; Sophie won't make out with him until he looks at her two-storey visage first.

Noah and Val, meanwhile, continue wrestling with their parental pain, with far different results: Noah refuses to confide in Donna about his grief over his father, preferring to continue getting drunk all the time (hey, his court-ordered AA meetings don't start until next week) and melodramatically breaking and burning shit in the mansion his mother's trying to sell. He also takes a few minutes to show Val the specific spots where his late father told him he "wasn't going to amount to anything," and while we know Noah didn't grow up in this house, we do grant that it's possible Daniel took time out from giving Noah his first tour, last month, to create new memories of Daniel's disapproval that Noah could chew on forever. Val gets off a lot easier, literally: Abby decides she's *not* going to turn Val in for her father's murder—and it's a good thing too, since Matt apparently had no interest in crafting a legal strategy for her and "advised" her to hope for a sympathetic jury. Hamilton Law would disavow him as a graduate, if it existed.

Brandon returns from his interview in triumph: the *New York Chronicle* has offered him a job in the Washington bureau. He's dismayed that Kelly barely registers a reaction to his news—other than to express shock that he got it—because all the stuff she got up to while he was gone is still ongoing: she's dividing her time between setting up the store she and Donna will be running and interfering in Leah's legal business. (Read: judging Leah for having gone back to Lenny, despite his abuse, when Leah found out she was pregnant.) Ginning up a story on custody battles for the *Beat*, using Lenny and Leah as its centerpiece (despite the fact that their case is still in progress?) allows Brandon to both (1) make Kelly notice him and (2) nose around Matt, obviously his new rival. Kelly, enforcing healthy boundaries for once, responds to Brandon's continual demands on her attention by reminding him that he was the one who wanted them to move on, so he should

5 REDEEMING BRANDON QUALITIES

By the time Brandon leaves the show, we can't wait to see the back of him. Positioned from the very beginning as *Beverly Hills, 90210*'s moral center, Brandon may have succeeded in that regard for younger viewers; we didn't find him nearly as grating back then. But for a "pretty liberal guy" the audience is meant to side with, boy is that self-righteous little gum-chomper an asshole sometimes.

Our free and frequent expression of this opinion on the *Again With This: Beverly Hills, 90210* podcast is how this sidebar came to be. Listener Jennifer challenged us to name five redeeming qualities about Brandon Walsh—and it took a village, but after much discussion and contemplation, we've come up with a list:

1 We've made much sport of the over-pomaded shelf that is Brandon's default hair"style," but he never subjected us to faddish men's-hair variations like the Caesar or the man-bun.

2 He is not unkind to animals, that we know of.

3 He is not an anti-vaxxer or an abolish-the-penny truther, that we know of.

4 Unlike his twin and most of his friends, he had jobs.

5 His reimagining of *The Real World: San Francisco*'s Puck in the "Unreal World" episode came from a place of such farty glee that we legit laughed, several times.

hurry up and let her do that. Instead, he goes to the store opening; stares at her through the glass like a creep (though, to be fair, what might actually be upsetting him is Kelly and Donna's choice to call their business Now Wear This); recites, to Steve, a completely apocryphal story about falling in the hall on his first day at West Beverly *as though we did not watch Brandon's first day at West Beverly in the series premiere*; and announces that he's not taking the *Chronicle* job after all. Evidently, he did not read the episode title, but the rest of the cast did, and gets him to the Peach Pit for an alleged *Beat* anniversary party that turns out to be Brandon's Bon Voyage intervention. There's some hugs, some nightswimming, a few manly tears, and a tribute on David's weeks-old radio show—which must flummox listeners who only vaguely know who *David* even is, never mind this high-school friend. And then Brandon, at long last, fulfills the promise of the episode title. Farewell, Minnesota! It's been . . . something.

"You don't look happy to see me."

Exit Val, Enter Gina, and Reenter Dylan

SEASON 9 | EPISODE 7
YOU SAY GOODBYE, I SAY HELLO

It's a busier Turkey Day than usual in the Zip, as Steve and Janet (Lindsay Price) negotiate their fuckbuddy relationship (Janet insists on "no emotions," just work stuff and Doing It; Steve wants more, but can't admit it yet), and David bones a listener to his asinine radio show, with disastrous results.

Denise (Christa Sauls) calls in to complain about her boyfriend and her parents during the segment between songs where David gives advice. Denise then later appears at the PPAD and comes into the booth to grind on David, but he doesn't connect her with the obvious schoolgirl of the same name he'd just spoken to. In his defense, the actress looks 30, but when David finds out by chance that Denise is very much *not* 30, and that her parents want to press charges, Matt has to explain to him that *a minor* cannot give meaningful consent and that this is serious.

It could be worse: David could be self-medicating after his father's suicide and driving while blackout drunk, as Noah's doing. Noah's latest wreck occurs when he passes out behind the wheel (while listening to David's show; coincidence?), and he finds himself with a crushed headlight and forehead bruise the next morning, but doesn't remember how he got them. He also can't say for sure that he *didn't* commit the hit-and-run a mile from the After Dark that put a kid in a coma. Noah's not concerned enough about his possible role in the kid's eventual demise to put the brakes on his drinking, and Donna's not concerned enough to break up with him, or to demand that he get some help—even though he's adding this tragedy to a list that includes raping Valerie and possibly killing his fiancée in a car crash. It turns out Noah *isn't* the hit-and-run driver, and he vows to quit boozing; Donna simpers happily; and that's the end of *that* problem!

But the most memorable aspect of the episode is its jam-packed arrivals/departures board. Valerie's finally realized she doesn't have to put up with The Gang's shit, and made arrangements to move back to Buffalo after yet another dustup with Kelly leads to dueling Thanksgiving dinners. That's Brandon's fault for asking them to pack up his things and ship them east, which is how Kelly finds a letter Valerie wrote advising Brandon not to marry Kelly, so Kelly blames Valerie for the demise of the wedding even though, as we saw, Kelly and Brandon made that decision very mutually. Stuck in the middle, David gets Kelly to back down by sharing every single aspect of Valerie's very private paternal trauma, including that Valerie killed her father. It works, barely. After Kelly grudgingly admits to her part in her and Valerie's enmity (and Valerie hurls a turkey out the back door of Casa Walsh), they agree that they're even, and at the dinner that's relocated to Casa Walsh's living room, Valerie announces that she's leaving town—that night. We're sad to see her go, but thrilled she can finally make some real friends who aren't bitches about everything.

It's really too bad Val barely crosses paths with Gina Kincaid (Vanessa Marcil), Donna's impossibly glossy-haired figure-skater cousin from "the wrong side of the tracks." One of Gina's first acts on the show is to get fired from the "Cabaret on Ice" show she's in, allegedly for her shitty attitude but possibly also so that she can devote herself full-time to fucking with her richie cousin. She wastes no time there, "babysitting" a drunk Noah with kamikaze shots and acting deeply sketchy about a relatively innocent photo-booth strip in which she's kissing Noah on the cheek (and he's visibly blacked out, again). Together, Gina, Valerie, and their respective shiny hair and flawless boobs could have really made life a schemey hell for Kelly—or solved crimes while looking hot, or both. As it is, the same cab that takes Valerie to the airport seems to have turned right around to deposit . . . Dylan McKay! He's standing at Casa Walsh's front door when Steve opens it to take the trash out, and it's kind of weird that Dylan doesn't ring the doorbell, but Luke Perry's verrrry reluctant line deliveries in his first scene might hint at why. Or Dylan was girding himself for the highly awkward reunion with Kelly that ensues. Everyone else is thrilled he's there, and peppers him with questions about how long he's staying (he doesn't know) and how Brenda is ("Why don't you call her and ask her?"); Dylan's focused on the fact that Kelly doesn't look happy to see him.

Kelly's got to be wondering, as we are, who has custody of Erica if Dylan's moved back to the States, but she finally moves in for an uncomfortable hug as Matt derps nearby. Then everyone drinks champagne to celebrate Dylan's return, including Dylan, who is supposedly in recovery.

Magical Thinking:
MENTAL ILLNESS ON THE SHOW

The show's treatment (so to speak) of mental illness is a lot like the show's treatment of substance abuse: once a breakdown has served its plotting purposes, the writers aren't interested (or qualified) to pursue it much further. We lit majors can't really speak to various mood disorders or chemical imbalances (mis-)used by *Beverly Hills, 90210* to create drama. We *do* suspect that there's a mystical facility to which troubled characters are dispatched by the writers, one that cures them of their various emotional and mental maladies—completely, and without real-world hassles like adjusting meds or ongoing talk therapy. It accepts every kind of insurance (jk! everyone is rich and pays out of pocket!); it allows for no nuance. **It's the Magical Thinking Hospital!**

PATIENTS INCLUDE:

ROGER AZARIAN, admitted after the pressure of his father's expectations led to suicidal ideation; during a visit from Brandon, he enjoyed the end of a Dodgers game and seemed well on his way to "all better."

EMILY VALENTINE, whose borderline personality disorder was marinated in group therapy, then passed off later as a temporary affliction, not considered serious enough that she couldn't live on her own in San Francisco or go to France to study marine biology.

LAURA KINGMAN, who may have sublimated possible trauma related to a sexual assault, which manifested later in obsessive behavior and suicidal thoughts.

KELLY TAYLOR, the lone sufferer of an eating disorder in history for whom the problem never resurfaces, not even when she embarks on a modeling career. (Gina Kincaid, whose adolescent bulimia persists into adulthood, must not have sought treatment at the MTH.)

TARA MARKS, whose delusions and stalking may not have been cured, but who did not merit a follow-up on the show after her parents admitted her to (this?) hospital.

DAVID SILVER, who long feared that his mother Sheila's bipolar disorder would settle itself upon him hereditarily. This did occur, but the writers didn't wish to entangle themselves in an arc involving ongoing treatment, so David's "version" of the illness was deemed mild enough not to require medication or regular visits to a therapist. Thanks, Dr. Candyman!

LAUREN DURNING (Cari Shayne), Matt's wife, who received in-patient treatment for schizophrenia until the writers needed to throw a wrench in Matt and Kelly's relationship; this plot twist occasioned the discovery of the correct medication for Lauren. Alas, MacGuffinol turns out to have possibly fatal long-term side effects, and Lauren returns to the MTH when her dramatic-obstacle duties are discharged.

When you want all the plot generated by a psychological problem, but none of the responsibility that comes with remembering it exists for your character, send them to the Magical Thinking Hospital—where every mental illness gets the same size Band-Aid, and it always works.

Kelly's Unfolding Rape Trauma Is Invisible to a Dickmatized Donna

We give the character of Kelly a lot of shit for what a tiresome, snotty busybody she has become in the later seasons of the show—by which we mean "since she started dating Brandon in the Season 4 finale." But for most of "Agony," in which Kelly has to go on with her life after being violently raped, in an alley, by a stranger, the writing evinces not just thoughtfulness but actual research about sexual assault, and Jennie Garth delivers a performance that's often devastating in its understatement.

Obviously, we can't know how Ian Ziering and Lindsay Price felt about being trapped in another "comedy" plotline—about Steve attracting an art critic's attention for a photo that, it turns out, was a fluke the camera snapped after Steve dropped it—but *we* are embarrassed for them.

"Agony" immediately situates the viewer in the aftermath of Kelly's rape, and how doing all the things she is "supposed" to do as a survivor is a secondary trauma all its own. Although it's probably supposed to be reassuring for her to hear that Sgt. Cohen (Carrie Dobro), the detective on her case, has handled "hundreds" of previous rapes, it's a horrifying number. That Nurse Schipper (Charmin Lee), who's currently treating Kelly, is one of Cohen's previous rape survivors only reminds us all how many people each of us know, in our real lives, who've been assaulted. Nurse Schipper seems regretful that, when Kelly asks whether Schipper's rapist was apprehended, Nurse Schipper must say he wasn't, but . . . that is also a depressingly common outcome. The requirement that Kelly relive the event by answering the detective's questions is nearly as invasive as the rape kit. The nurse gives Kelly a card with the hotline for RAINN (the Rape, Abuse & Incest National Network) and recites the phone number in her dialogue— then, as now, it's 800.656.HOPE—and for the show to do this advocacy for RAINN's excellent work is wise and laudable. But it's all very bad!

After her ordeal at the hospital, Kelly has no refuge at home: Donna is so wrapped up in her crush on beach volleyball pro Wayne (Shawn Christian) that she doesn't notice Kelly has come home in hospital-issue sweats, and has few follow-up questions about the lie Kelly provides about how she cut her lip. She subjects Kelly to more than one girly gab sesh about whether it's okay for Donna to have casual sex with Wayne—when she's not dodging Noah's pressure to move in with him—oblivious to what it might mean that Kelly is exclusively dressing in shapeless black and gray and conversing only monosyllabically.

Dylan, on the other hand, is aggressive, demanding to know why Kelly blew off an appointment to talk him out of using heroin again—get a sponsor, Jones!—and Kelly tells him the truth, enlisting him in supporting her while she goes through the futile exercise of looking at mug books. Maybe Matt could have helped, except (1) he's already dubious about her various conflicting stories about her recent past and suspects her of cheating on him with Dylan, and (2) unbeknownst to both of them, his current burglary client, Joe Patch (Cliff Dorfman), is Kelly's rapist, and Matt is busy (successfully) finding technicalities in the arrest to get those burglary charges dropped. Throughout all this, Gina keeps catching Dylan and Kelly together and misconstruing why they seem to be so intimate. Gina's preparations for an audition for a big figure-skating tour are affected by both her stress and her bulimia, and when she misses her slot because she vomited and fainted in the bathroom at the rink, David is there to administer first aid by roughly jostling her head around.

Eventually, Kelly confides in Donna, who puts off both the dudes in her life to tend to Kelly at home. A despairing Kelly tells her that, statistically, if a crime hasn't been solved within 48 hours, it won't be, and that, for her, it's been "116 . . . and a half." The pointed pause Garth leaves in that sentence, unfortunately, marks the end of the storyline's muted effectiveness. Then Dylan shows up with an item Kelly has requested: a loaded handgun. Great, whatever follows won't be melodramatic and preposterous at all.

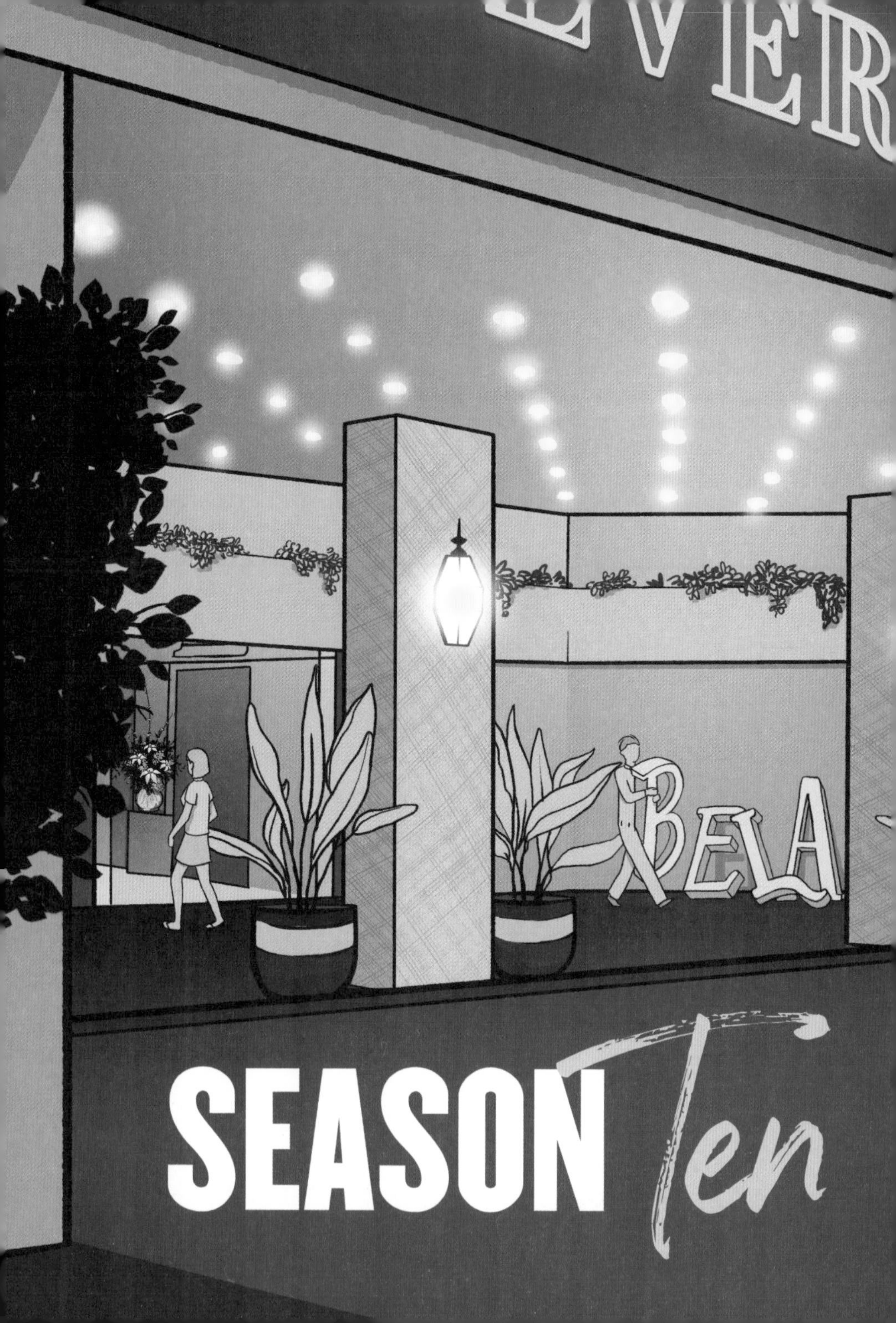
EVER
BELA
SEASON Ten